MOON GIRL AND DEVIL DINOSAUR

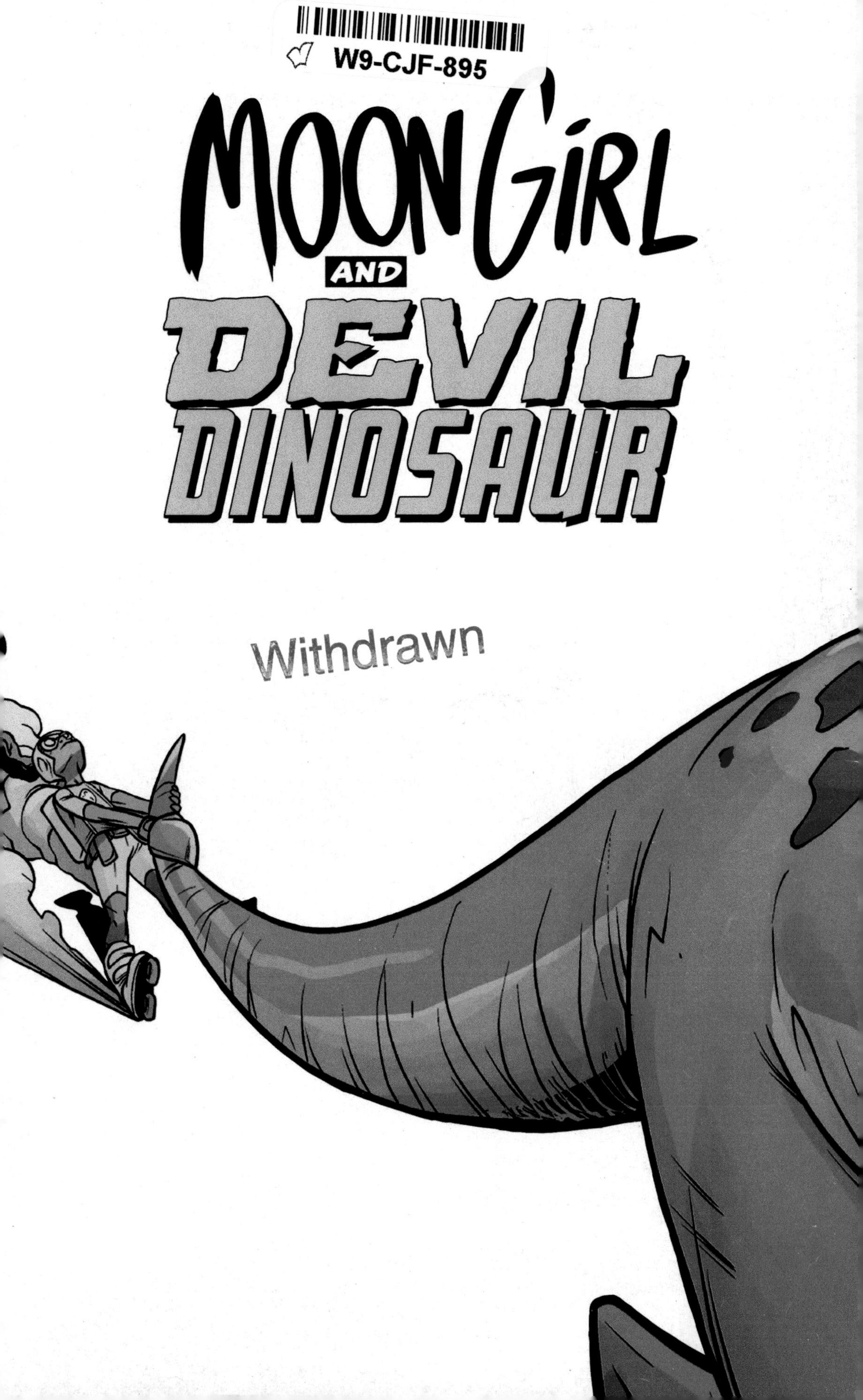

LUNELLA LAFAYETTE IS A NINE-YEAR-OLD PRODIGY LIVING WITH HER MOM AND DAD IN MANHATTAN'S LOWER EAST SIDE.

DEVIL DINOSAUR IS A BRIGHT RED, TIME-DISPLACED TYRANNOSAURUS REX.

THEY ARE SHUNNED AND IGNORED BY MOST BUT, FOR BETTER OR FOR WORSE, THEY HAVE EACH OTHER!

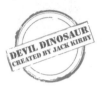

DEVIL DINOSAUR
CREATED BY JACK KIRBY

COLLECTION EDITOR: Jennifer Grünwald
ASSISTANT MANAGING EDITOR: Caitlin O'Connell
ASSOCIATE MANAGING EDITOR: Kateri Woody
EDITOR, SPECIAL PROJECTS: Mark D. Beazley
VP PRODUCTION & SPECIAL PROJECTS: Jeff Youngquist
SVP PRINT, SALES & MARKETING: David Gabriel
BOOK DESIGNER: Jay Bowen

EDITOR IN CHIEF: Axel Alonso
CHIEF CREATIVE OFFICER: Joe Quesada
PRESIDENT: Dan Buckley
EXECUTIVE PRODUCER: Alan Fine

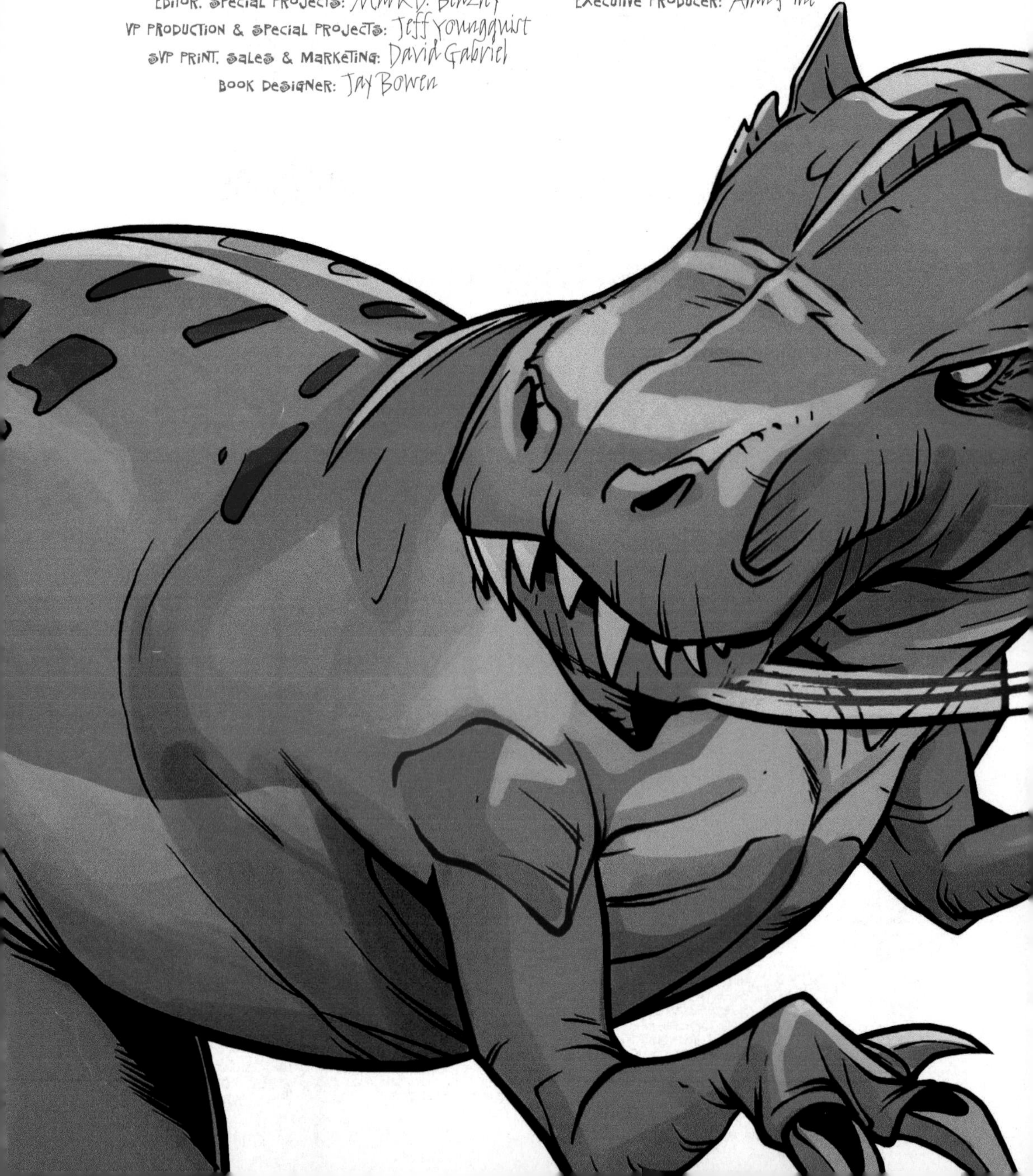

MOON GIRL

AND

DEVIL DINOSAUR

THE SMARTEST THERE IS!

Brandon Montclare & Amy Reeder
WRITERS

Natacha Bustos (#3 & #5-18)
& Ray-Anthony Height (#4)
ARTISTS

Tamra Bonvillain
COLOR ARTIST

VC's Travis Lanham
LETTERER

Leonard Kirk & Tamra Bonvillain
DREAM ART. #13

Amy Reeder
COVER ART

Chris Robinson
ASSISTANT EDITOR

Mark Paniccia
EDITOR

MOON GIRL AND DEVIL DINOSAUR VOL. 3: THE SMARTEST THERE IS. Contains material originally published in magazine form as MOON GIRL AND DEVIL DINOSAUR #13-18. First printing 2017. ISBN# 978-1-302-90534-7. Published by MARVEL WORLDWIDE, INC., a subsidiary of MARVEL ENTERTAINMENT, LLC. OFFICE OF PUBLICATION: 135 West 50th Street, New York, NY 10020. Copyright © 2017 MARVEL No similarity between any of the names, characters, persons, and/or institutions in this magazine with those of any living or dead person or institution is intended, and any such similarity which may exist is purely coincidental. **Printed in the U.S.A.** DAN BUCKLEY, President, Marvel Entertainment; JOE QUESADA, Chief Creative Officer; TOM BREVOORT, SVP of Publishing; DAVID BOGART, SVP of Business Affairs & Operations, Publishing & Partnership; C.B. CEBULSKI, VP of Brand Management & Development, Asia; DAVID GABRIEL, SVP of Sales & Marketing, Publishing; JEFF YOUNGQUIST, VP of Production & Special Projects; DAN CARR, Executive Director of Publishing Technology; ALEX MORALES, Director of Publishing Operations; SUSAN CRESPI, Production Manager; STAN LEE, Chairman Emeritus. For information regarding advertising in Marvel Comics or on Marvel.com, please contact Vit DeBellis, Integrated Sales Manager, at vdebellis@marvel.com. For Marvel subscription inquiries, please call 888-511-5480. **Manufactured between 5/5/2017 and 6/6/2017 by QUAD/GRAPHICS WASECA, WASECA, MN, USA.**

10 9 8 7 6 5 4 3 2 1

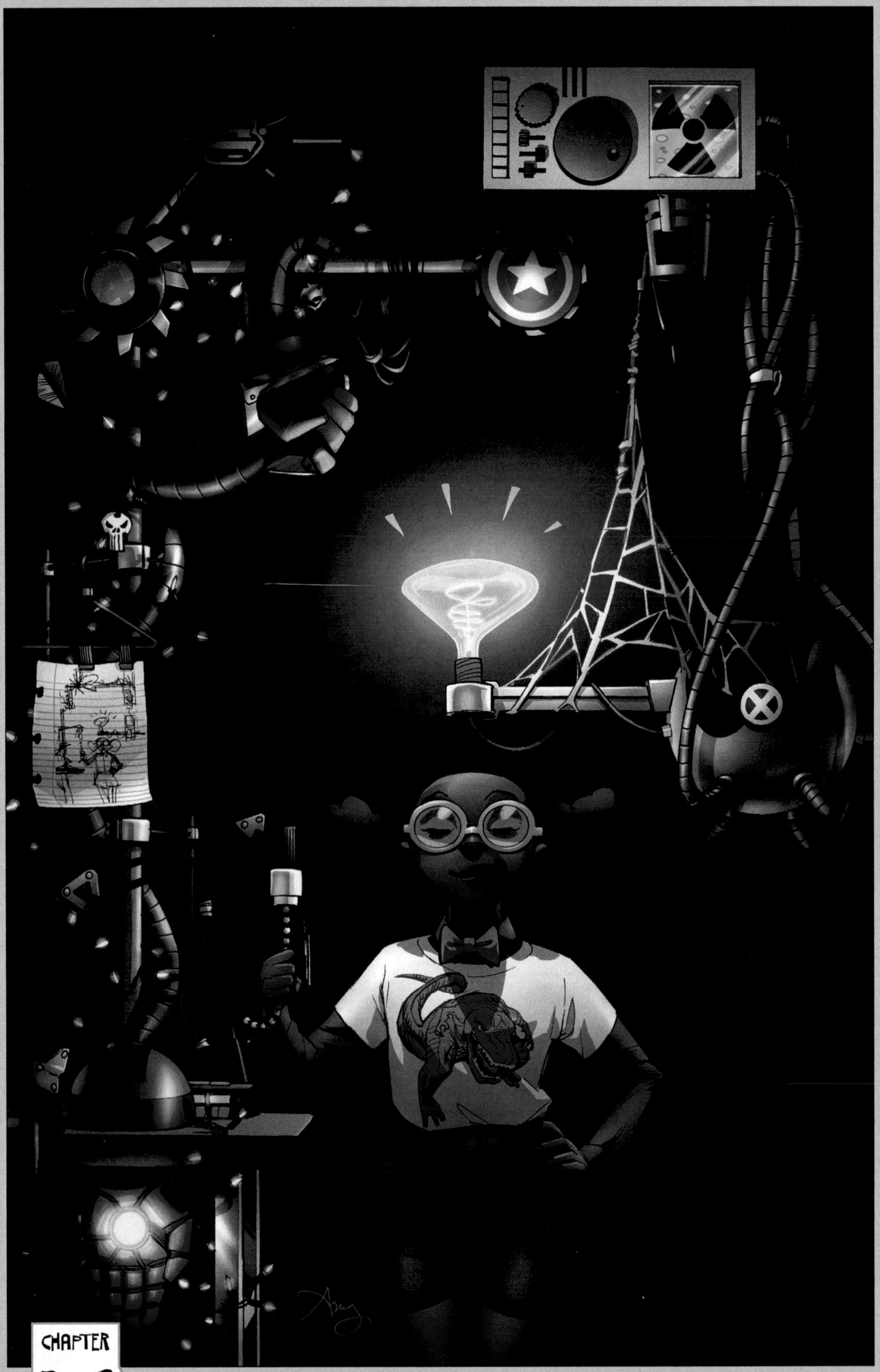

CHAPTER 13 "MARVEL NOW OR NEVER!"

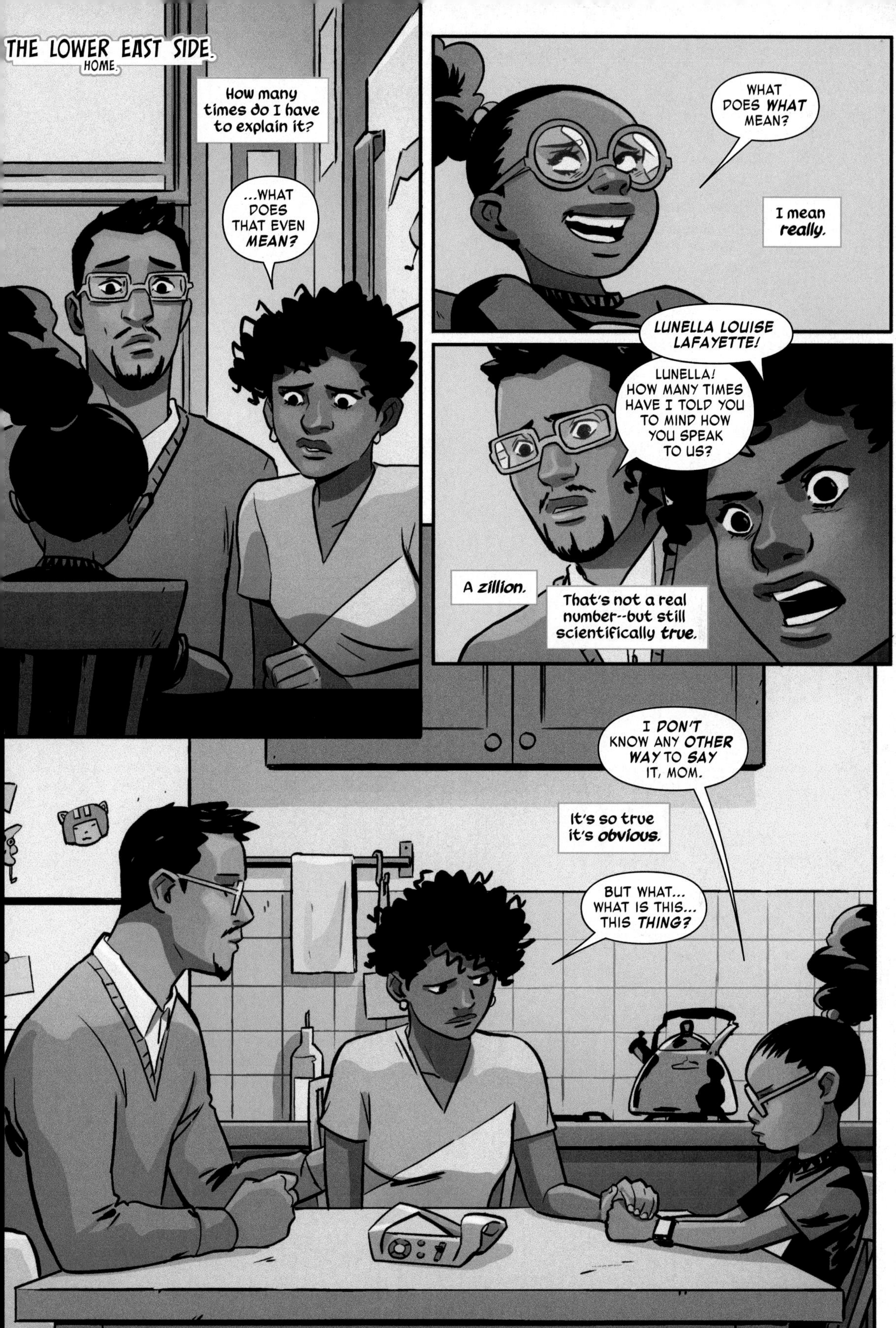
THE LOWER EAST SIDE.
HOME.
How many times do I have to explain it?
...WHAT DOES THAT EVEN MEAN?
WHAT DOES WHAT MEAN?
I mean really.
LUNELLA LOUISE LAFAYETTE!
LUNELLA! HOW MANY TIMES HAVE I TOLD YOU TO MIND HOW YOU SPEAK TO US?
A zillion.
That's not a real number--but still scientifically true.
I DON'T KNOW ANY OTHER WAY TO SAY IT, MOM.
It's so true it's obvious.
BUT WHAT... WHAT IS THIS... THIS THING?

THE SMARTEST THERE IS! PART ONE: "MARVEL NOW OR NEVER!"

"My body can do what it wants. I am not the body. I am the mind." --Rita Levi-Montalcini

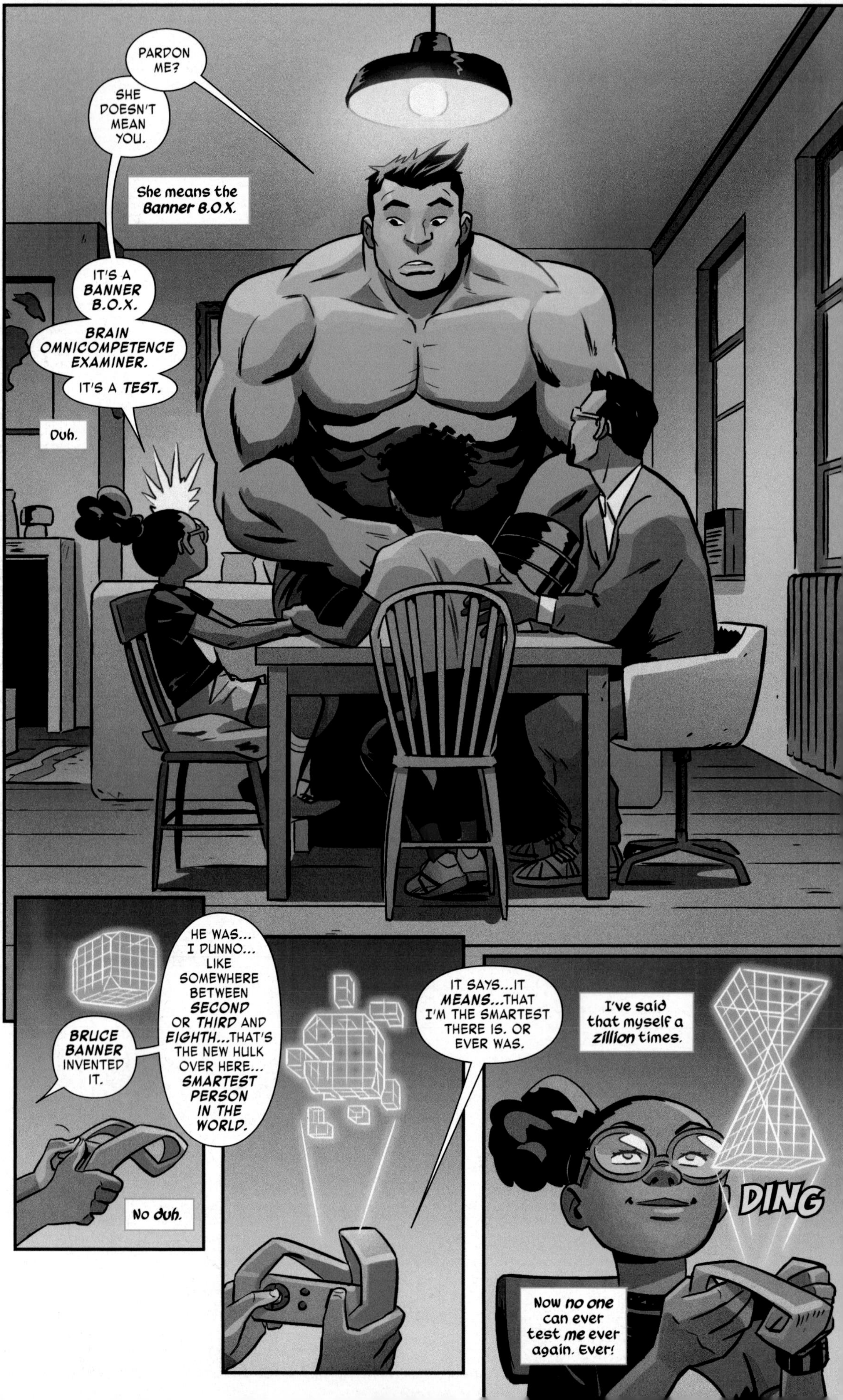
PARDON ME?
SHE DOESN'T MEAN YOU.
She means the Banner B.O.X.
IT'S A BANNER B.O.X.
BRAIN OMNICOMPETENCE EXAMINER.
IT'S A TEST.
Duh.
BRUCE BANNER INVENTED IT.
No duh.
HE WAS... I DUNNO... LIKE SOMEWHERE BETWEEN SECOND OR THIRD AND EIGHTH...THAT'S THE NEW HULK OVER HERE... SMARTEST PERSON IN THE WORLD.
IT SAYS...IT MEANS...THAT I'M THE SMARTEST THERE IS. OR EVER WAS.
I've said that myself a zillion times.
DING
Now no one can ever test me ever again. Ever!

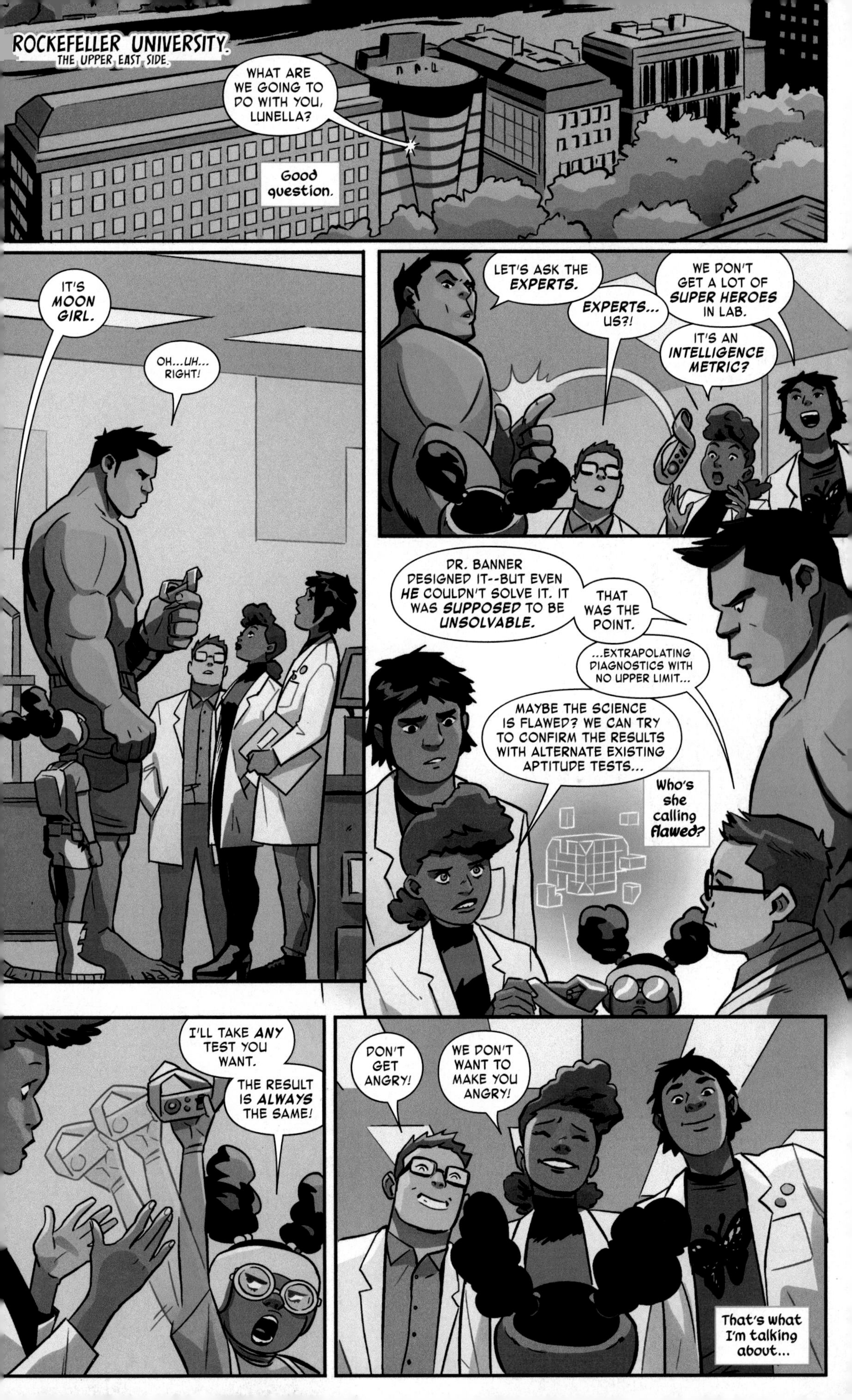

ROCKEFELLER UNIVERSITY.
THE UPPER EAST SIDE.
WHAT ARE WE GOING TO DO WITH YOU, LUNELLA?
Good question.
IT'S MOON GIRL.
OH...UH... RIGHT!
LET'S ASK THE EXPERTS.
EXPERTS... US?!
WE DON'T GET A LOT OF SUPER HEROES IN LAB.
IT'S AN INTELLIGENCE METRIC?
DR. BANNER DESIGNED IT--BUT EVEN HE COULDN'T SOLVE IT. IT WAS SUPPOSED TO BE UNSOLVABLE.
THAT WAS THE POINT.
...EXTRAPOLATING DIAGNOSTICS WITH NO UPPER LIMIT...
MAYBE THE SCIENCE IS FLAWED? WE CAN TRY TO CONFIRM THE RESULTS WITH ALTERNATE EXISTING APTITUDE TESTS...
Who's she calling flawed?
I'LL TAKE ANY TEST YOU WANT.
THE RESULT IS ALWAYS THE SAME!
DON'T GET ANGRY!
WE DON'T WANT TO MAKE YOU ANGRY!
That's what I'm talking about...

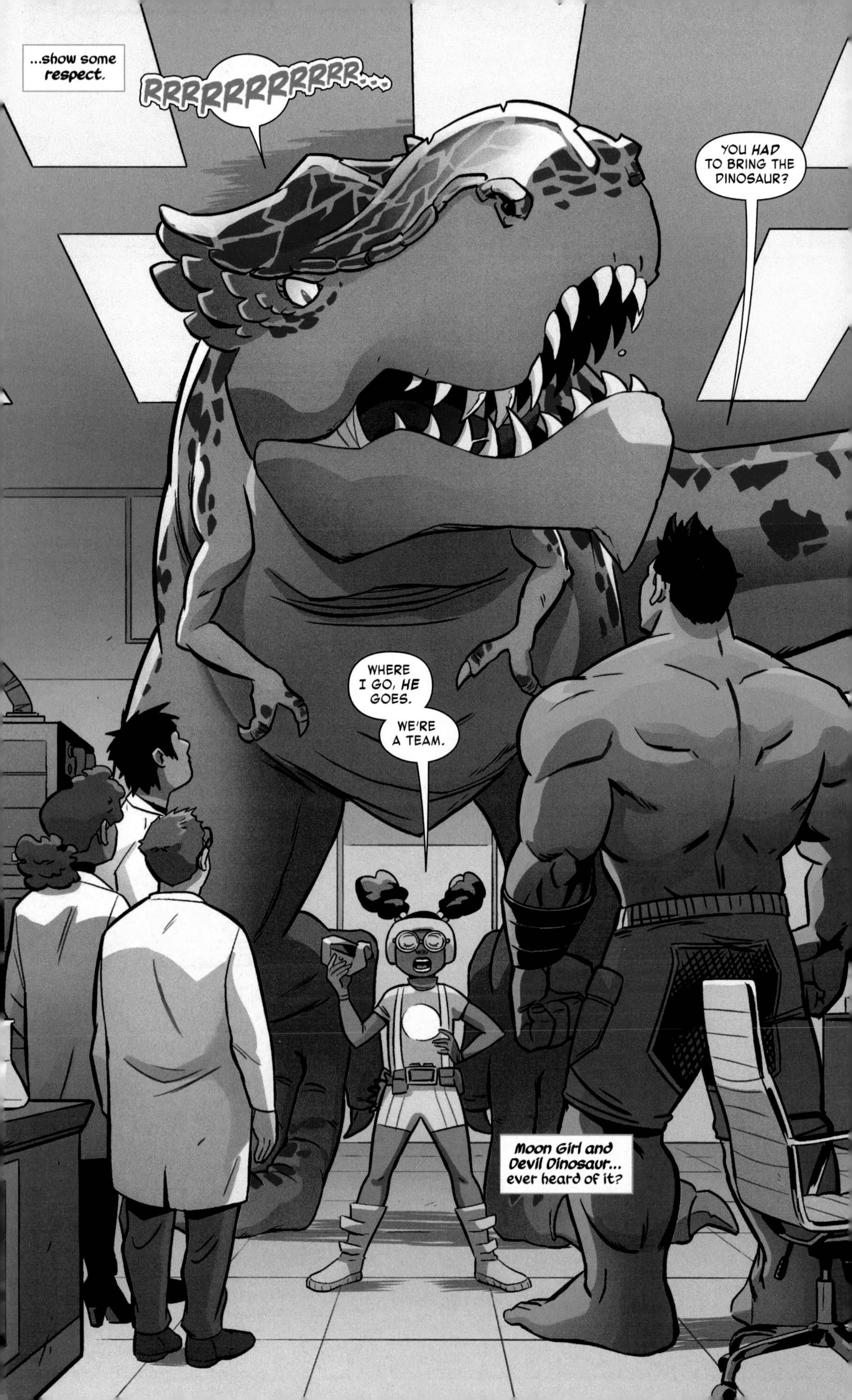
...show some respect.
RRRRRRRRRRR...
YOU HAD TO BRING THE DINOSAUR?
WHERE I GO, HE GOES.
WE'RE A TEAM.
Moon Girl and Devil Dinosaur... ever heard of it?

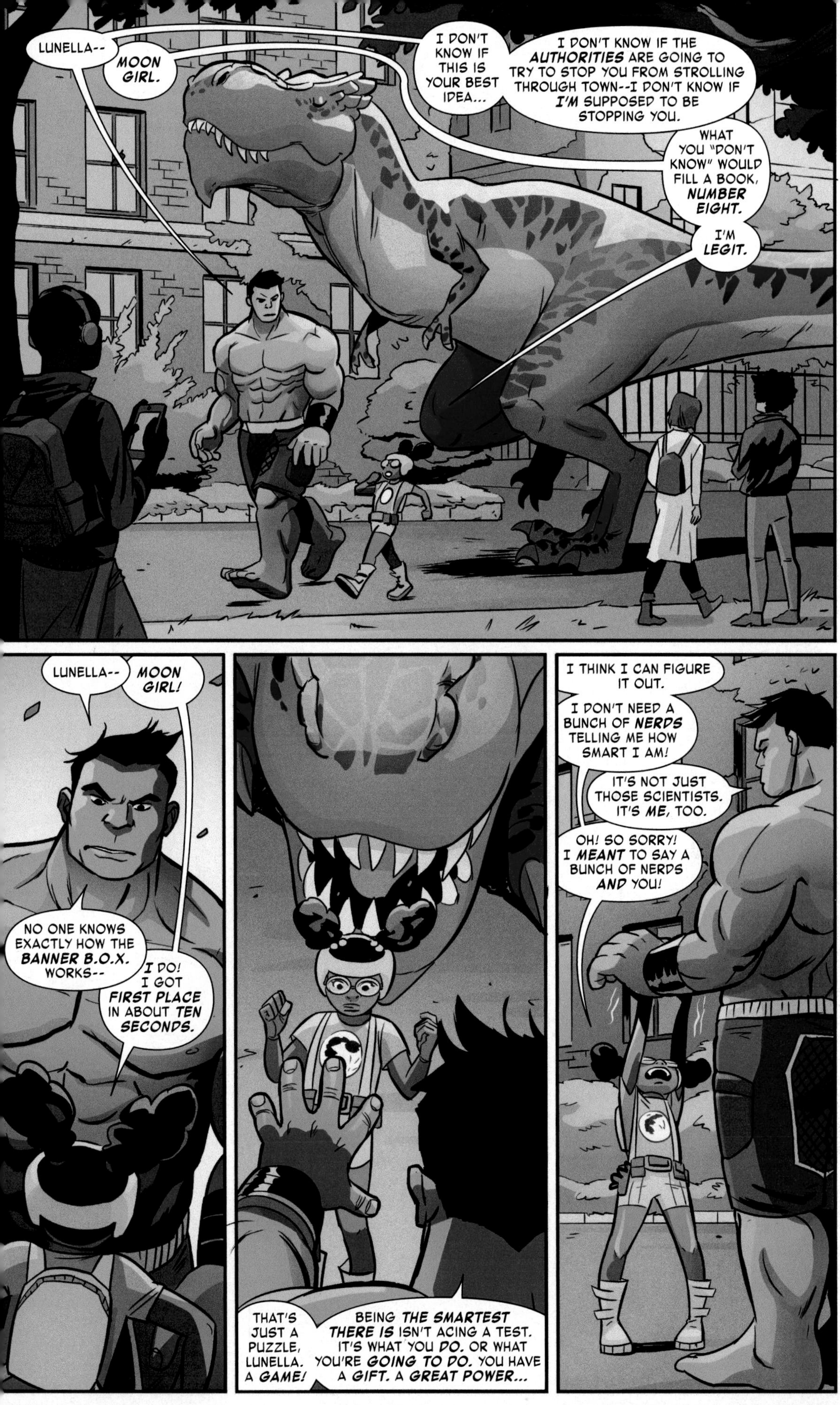

LUNELLA--
MOON GIRL.
I DON'T KNOW IF THIS IS YOUR BEST IDEA...
I DON'T KNOW IF THE AUTHORITIES ARE GOING TO TRY TO STOP YOU FROM STROLLING THROUGH TOWN--I DON'T KNOW IF I'M SUPPOSED TO BE STOPPING YOU.
WHAT YOU "DON'T KNOW" WOULD FILL A BOOK, NUMBER EIGHT.
I'M LEGIT.
LUNELLA--
MOON GIRL!
NO ONE KNOWS EXACTLY HOW THE BANNER B.O.X. WORKS--
I DO! I GOT FIRST PLACE IN ABOUT TEN SECONDS.
THAT'S JUST A PUZZLE, LUNELLA. A GAME!
BEING THE SMARTEST THERE IS ISN'T ACING A TEST. IT'S WHAT YOU DO. OR WHAT YOU'RE GOING TO DO. YOU HAVE A GIFT. A GREAT POWER...
I THINK I CAN FIGURE IT OUT.
I DON'T NEED A BUNCH OF NERDS TELLING ME HOW SMART I AM!
IT'S NOT JUST THOSE SCIENTISTS. IT'S ME, TOO.
OH! SO SORRY! I MEANT TO SAY A BUNCH OF NERDS AND YOU!

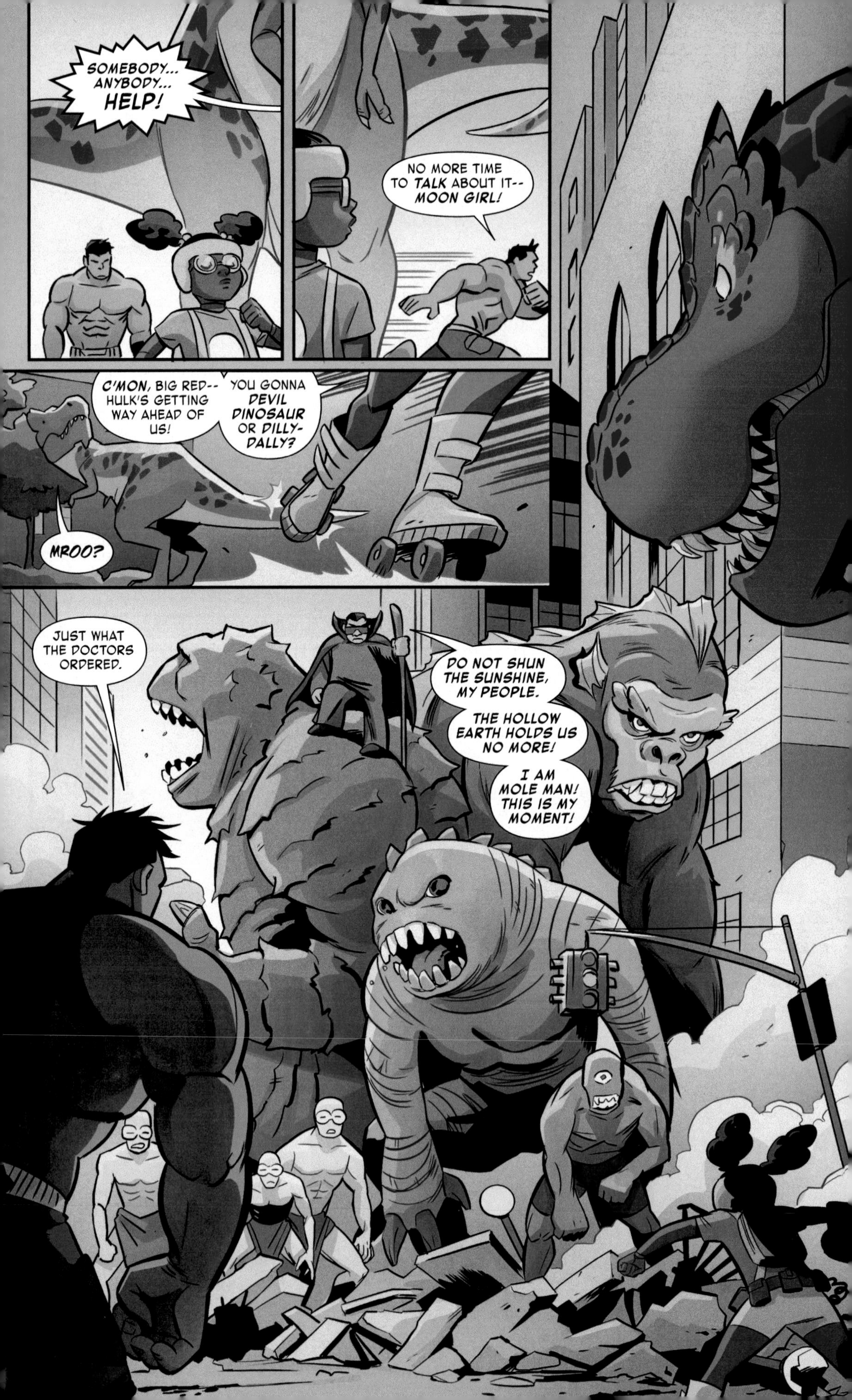

SOMEBODY... ANYBODY... HELP!
NO MORE TIME TO TALK ABOUT IT-- MOON GIRL!
C'MON, BIG RED-- HULK'S GETTING WAY AHEAD OF US!
YOU GONNA DEVIL DINOSAUR OR DILLY-DALLY?
MROO?
JUST WHAT THE DOCTORS ORDERED.
DO NOT SHUN THE SUNSHINE, MY PEOPLE.
THE HOLLOW EARTH HOLDS US NO MORE!
I AM MOLE MAN! THIS IS MY MOMENT!

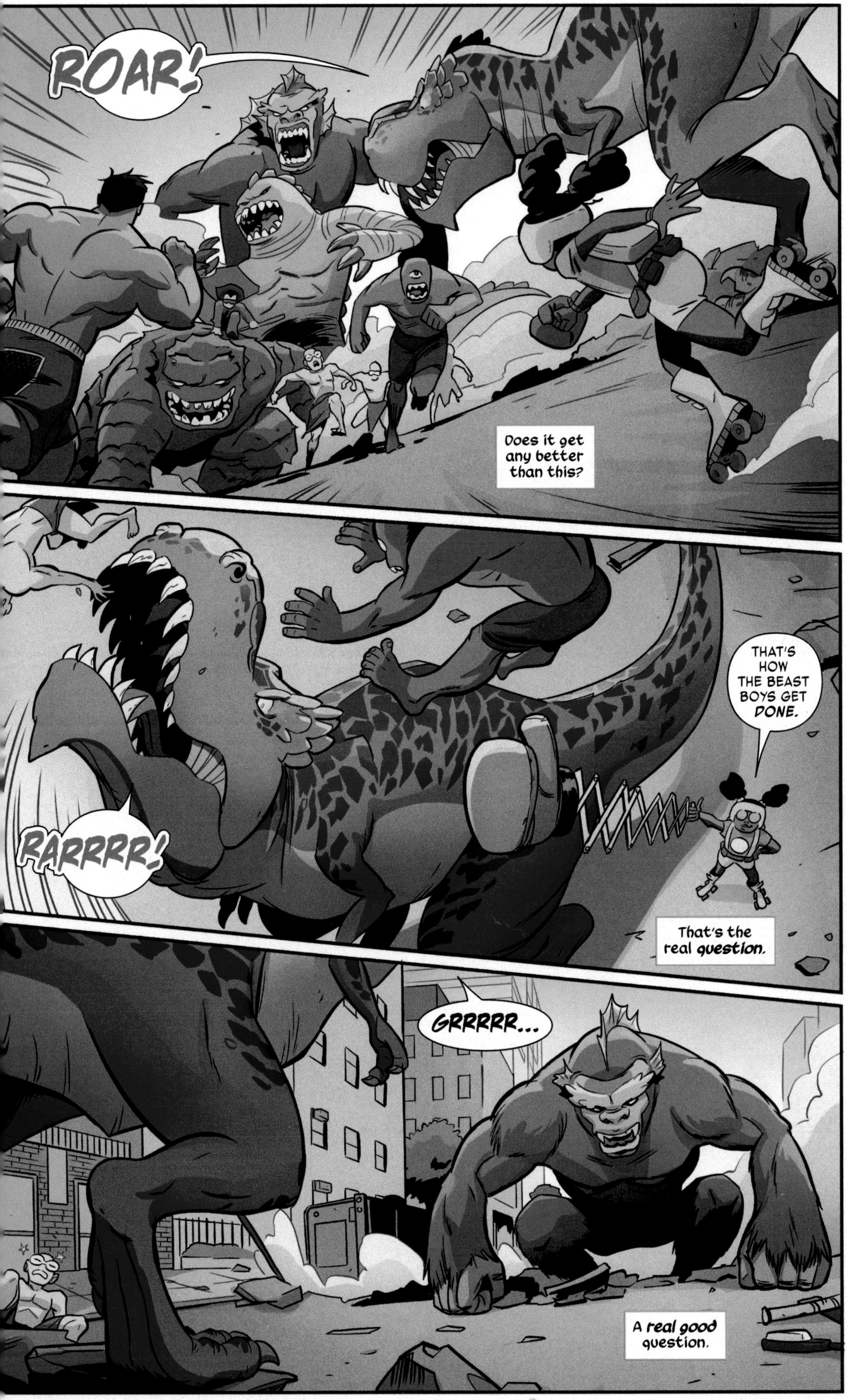

ROAR!
Does it get any better than this?
THAT'S HOW THE BEAST BOYS GET DONE.
RARRRR!
That's the real question.
GRRRRR...
A real good question.

TWO HEADS
ARE BETTER THAN
ONE--AM I *RIGHT,*
LUNELLA?

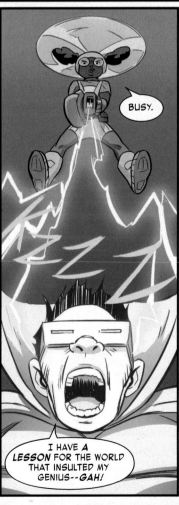

BUSY.

I HAVE *A
LESSON* FOR THE WORLD
THAT INSULTED MY
GENIUS--GAH!

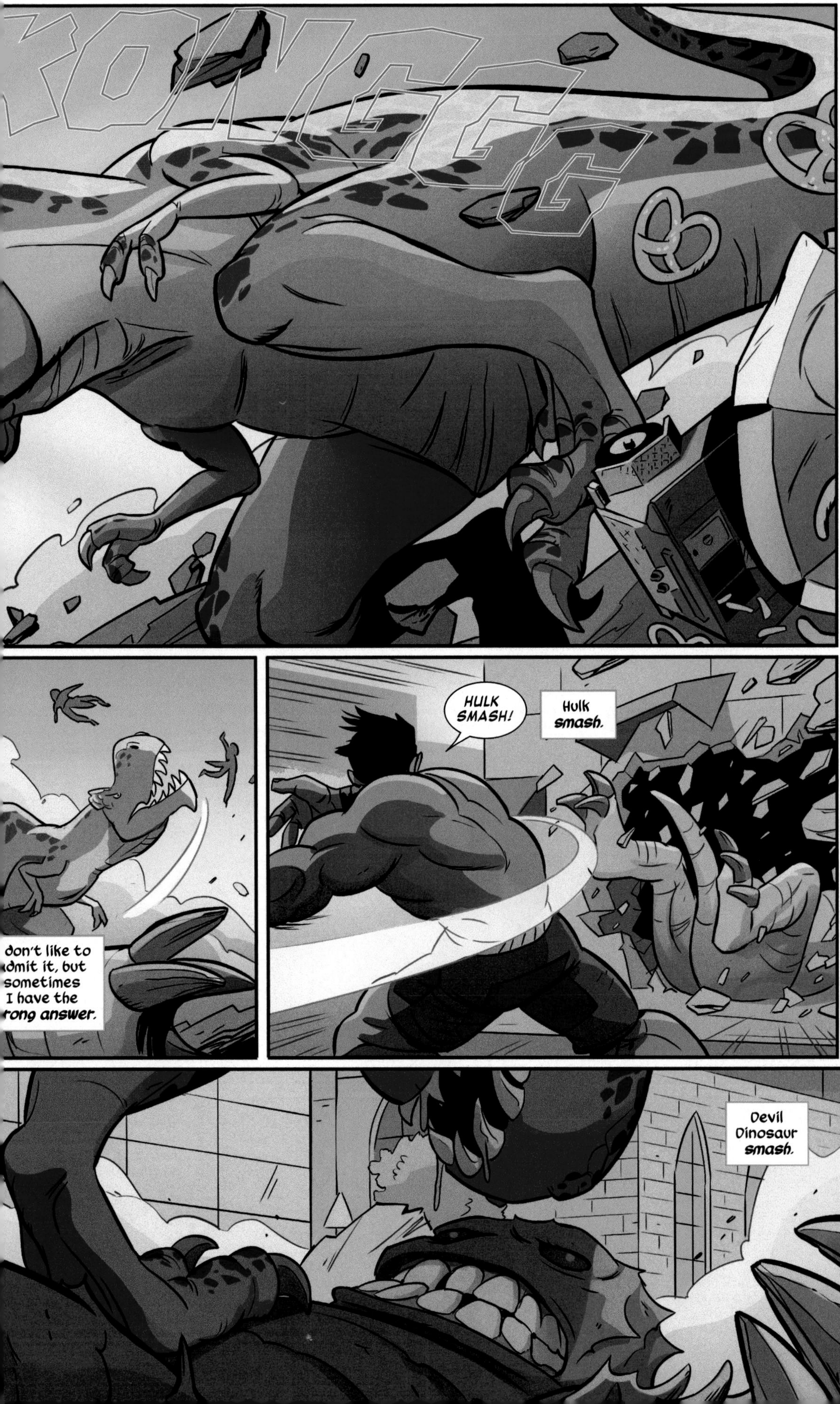
ONGGG
don't like to
dmit it, but
sometimes
I have the
rong answer.
HULK SMASH!
Hulk smash.
Devil Dinosaur smash.

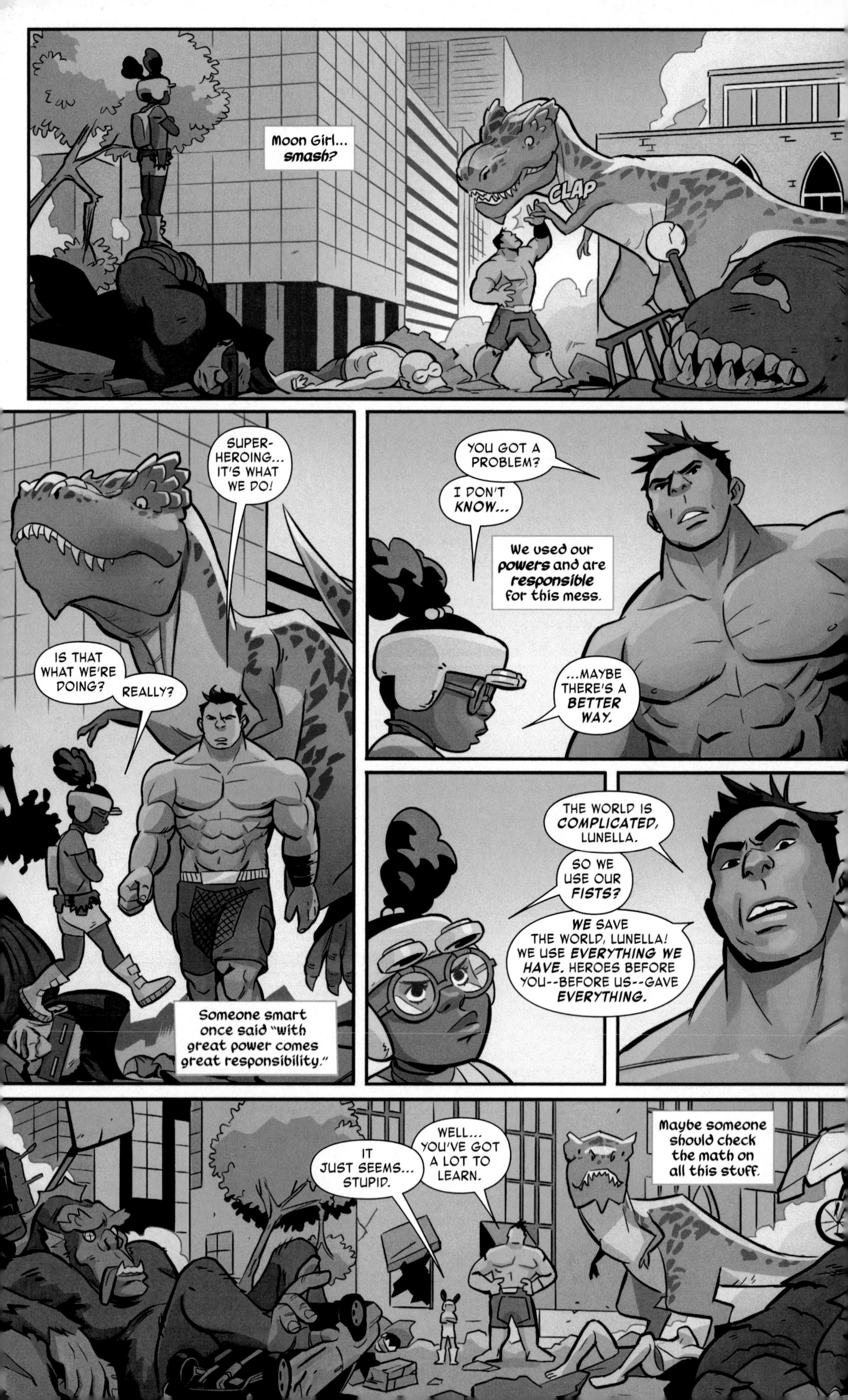
Moon Girl... smash?
CLAP
SUPER-HEROING... IT'S WHAT WE DO!
IS THAT WHAT WE'RE DOING?
REALLY?
Someone smart once said "with great power comes great responsibility."
YOU GOT A PROBLEM?
I DON'T KNOW...
We used our powers and are responsible for this mess.
...MAYBE THERE'S A BETTER WAY.
THE WORLD IS COMPLICATED, LUNELLA.
SO WE USE OUR FISTS?
WE SAVE THE WORLD, LUNELLA! WE USE EVERYTHING WE HAVE. HEROES BEFORE YOU--BEFORE US--GAVE EVERYTHING.
IT JUST SEEMS... STUPID.
WELL... YOU'VE GOT A LOT TO LEARN.
Maybe someone should check the math on all this stuff.

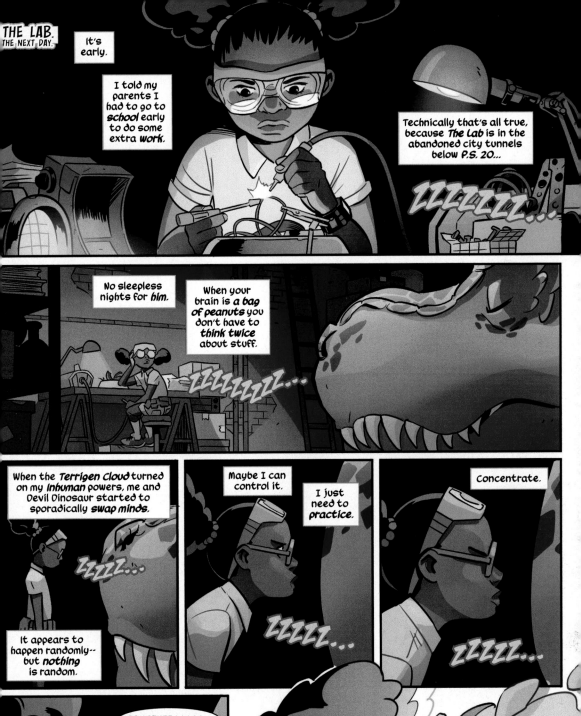

THE LAB.
THE NEXT DAY.

It's early.

I told my parents I had to go to *school* early to do some extra *work*.

Technically that's all true, because *The Lab* is in the abandoned city tunnels below *P.S. 20...*

ZZZZZZ...

No sleepless nights for *him*.

When your brain is *a bag of peanuts* you don't have to *think twice* about stuff.

ZZZZZZZZ...

When the *Terrigen Cloud* turned on my *Inhuman* powers, me and Devil Dinosaur started to sporadically *swap minds*.

ZZZZ...

It appears to happen randomly-- but *nothing* is random.

Maybe I can control it.

I just need to *practice*.

ZZZZ...

Concentrate.

ZZZZ...

CONCENTRAAAAA...

ZZZZZ...

RAAAAAAR.

ZZZZ...

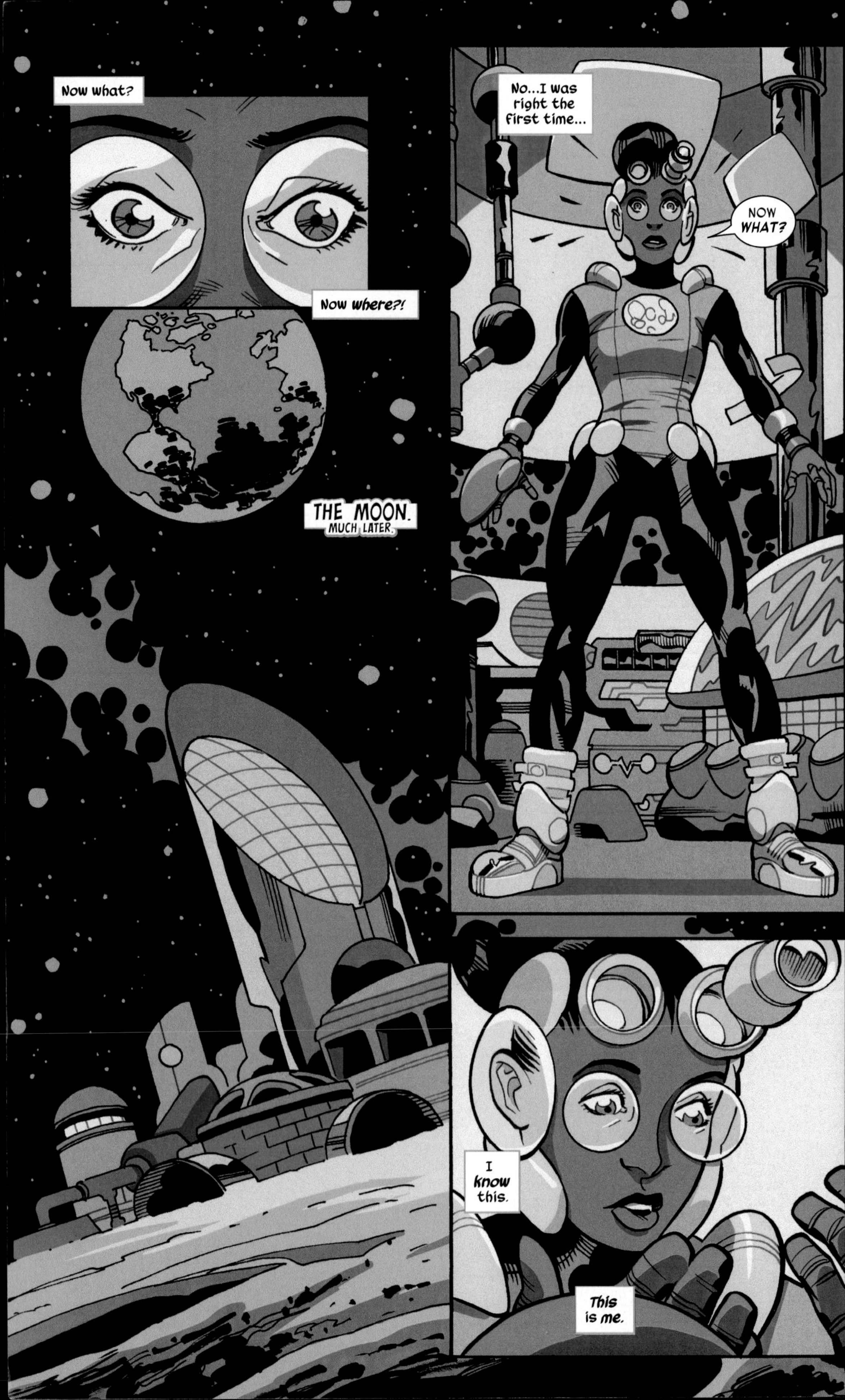
Now what?
Now where?!
THE MOON. MUCH LATER.
No...I was right the first time...
NOW WHAT?
I know this.
This is me.

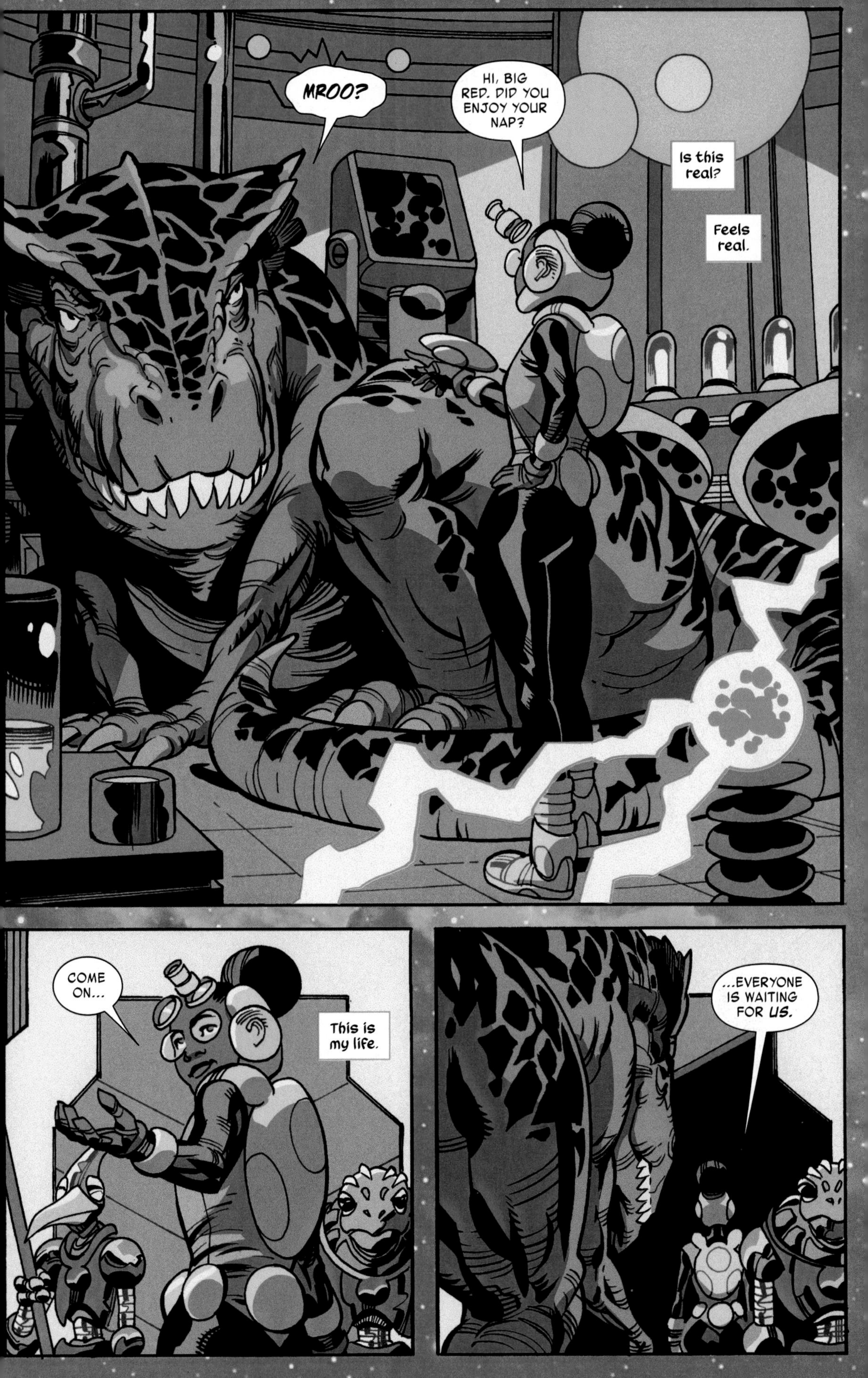
MROO?
HI, BIG RED. DID YOU ENJOY YOUR NAP?
Is this real?
Feels real.
COME ON...
This is my life.
...EVERYONE IS WAITING FOR *US*.

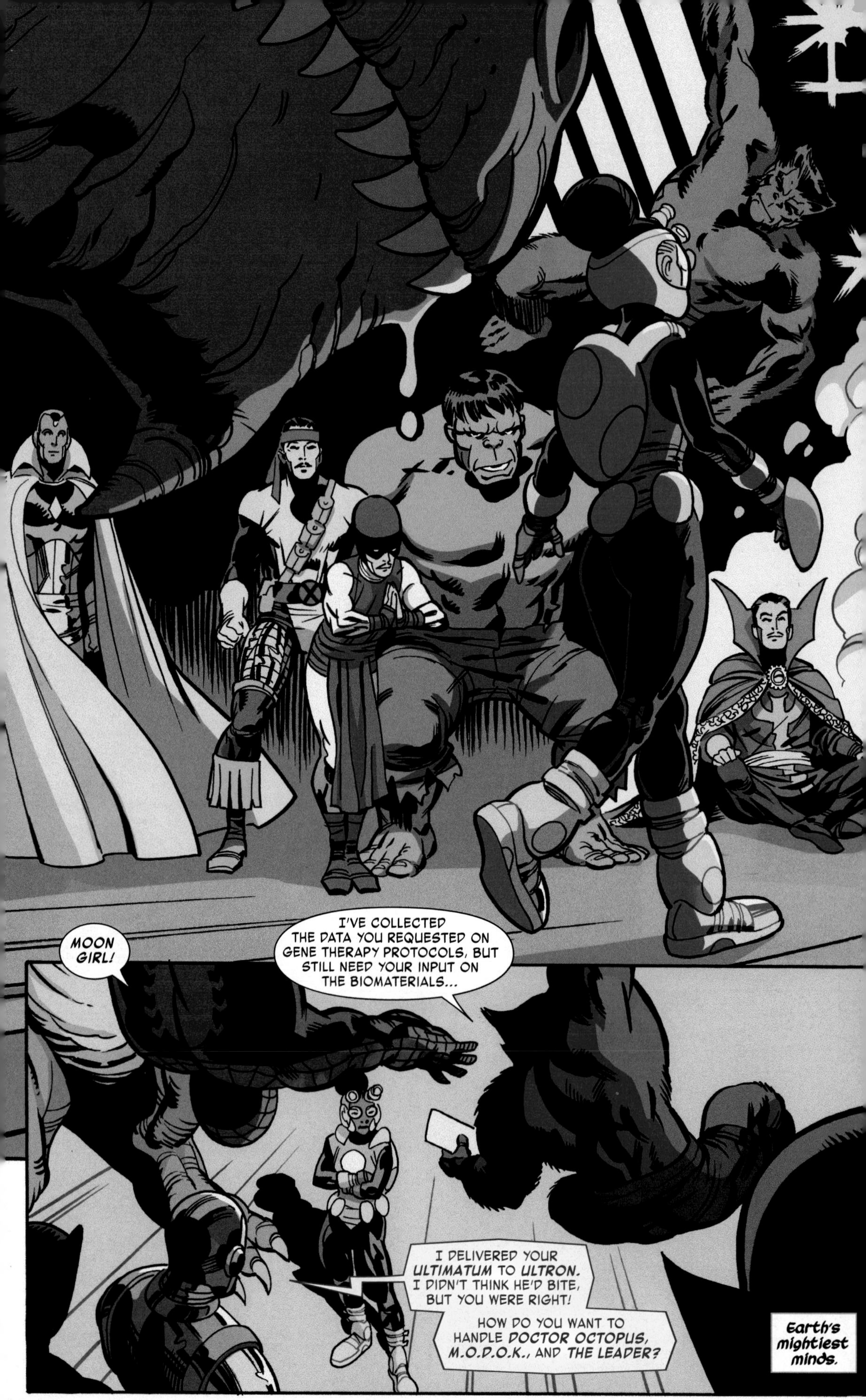
MOON GIRL!
I'VE COLLECTED THE DATA YOU REQUESTED ON GENE THERAPY PROTOCOLS, BUT STILL NEED YOUR INPUT ON THE BIOMATERIALS...
I DELIVERED YOUR ULTIMATUM TO ULTRON. I DIDN'T THINK HE'D BITE, BUT YOU WERE RIGHT!
HOW DO YOU WANT TO HANDLE DOCTOR OCTOPUS, M.O.D.O.K., AND THE LEADER?
Earth's mightiest minds.

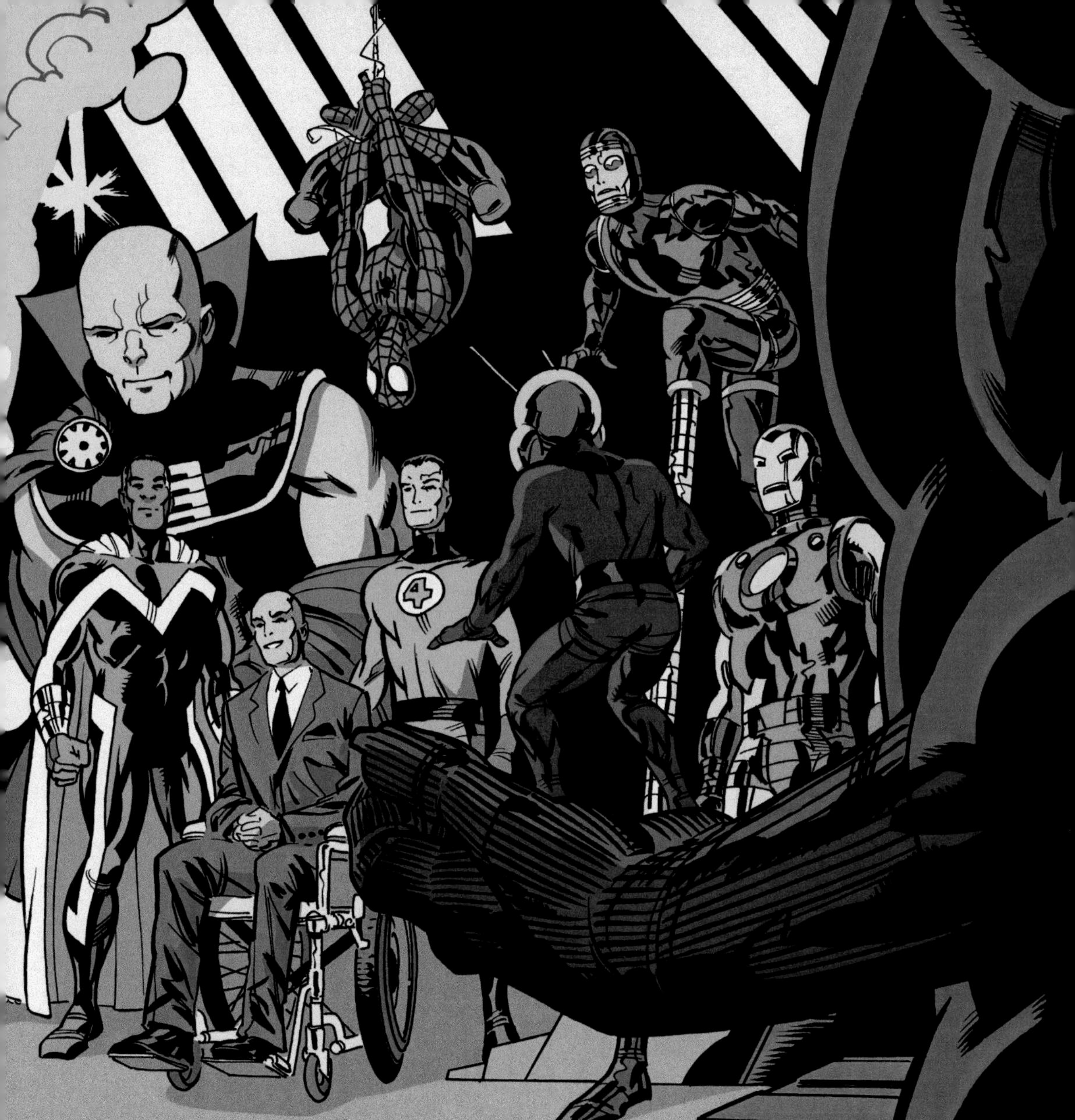

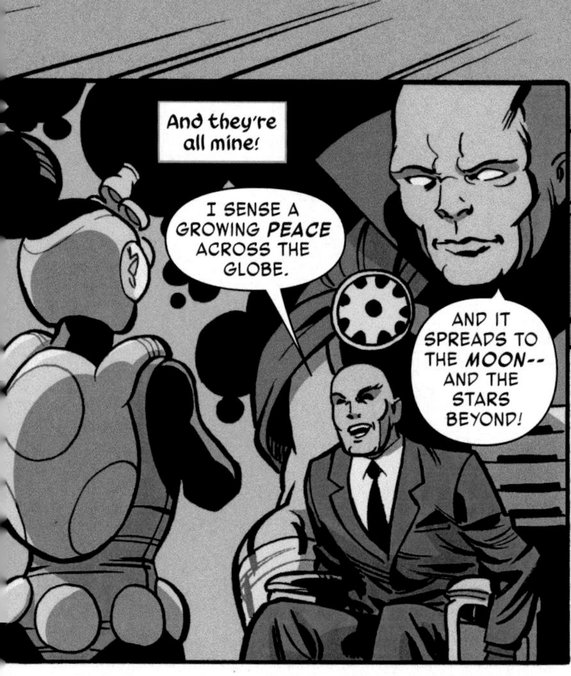
And they're all mine!
I SENSE A GROWING PEACE ACROSS THE GLOBE.
AND IT SPREADS TO THE MOON-- AND THE STARS BEYOND!

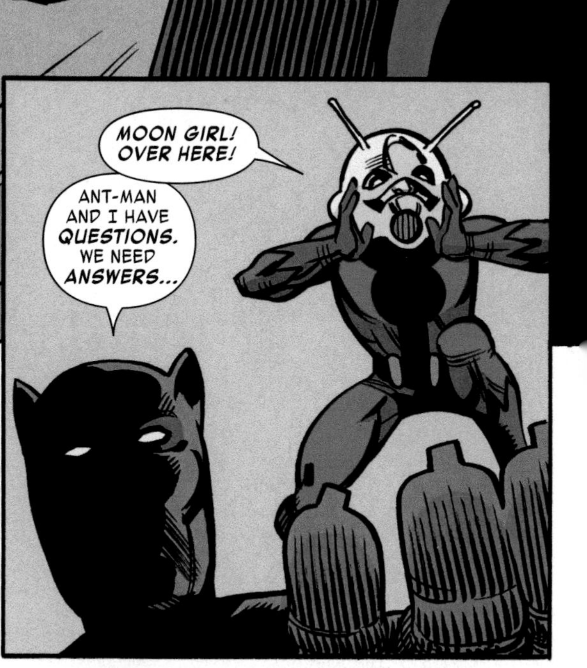
MOON GIRL! OVER HERE!
ANT-MAN AND I HAVE QUESTIONS. WE NEED ANSWERS...

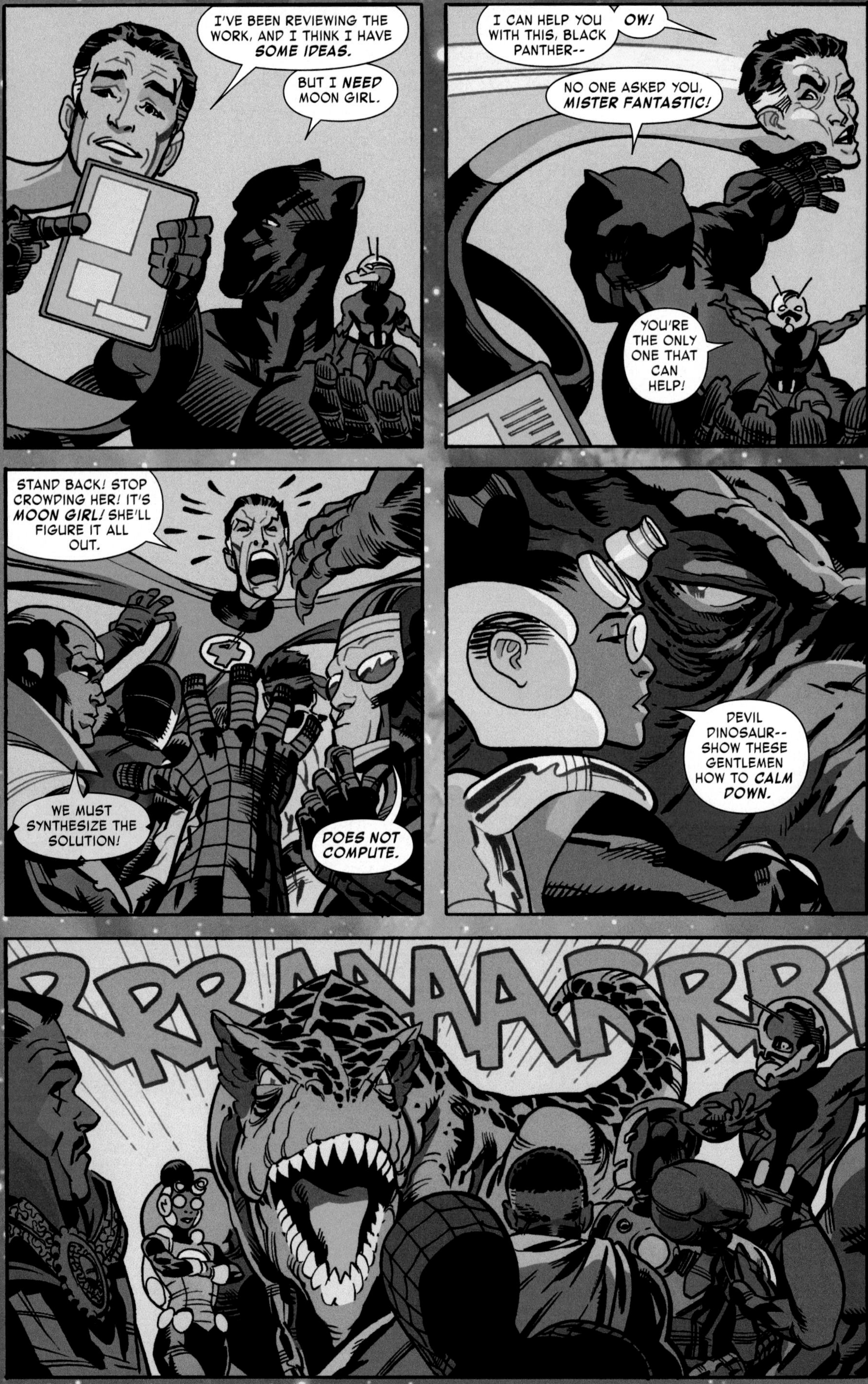
I'VE BEEN REVIEWING THE WORK, AND I THINK I HAVE SOME IDEAS.
BUT I NEED MOON GIRL.
I CAN HELP YOU WITH THIS, BLACK PANTHER--
OW!
NO ONE ASKED YOU, MISTER FANTASTIC!
YOU'RE THE ONLY ONE THAT CAN HELP!
STAND BACK! STOP CROWDING HER! IT'S MOON GIRL! SHE'LL FIGURE IT ALL OUT.
WE MUST SYNTHESIZE THE SOLUTION!
DOES NOT COMPUTE.
DEVIL DINOSAUR-- SHOW THESE GENTLEMEN HOW TO CALM DOWN.

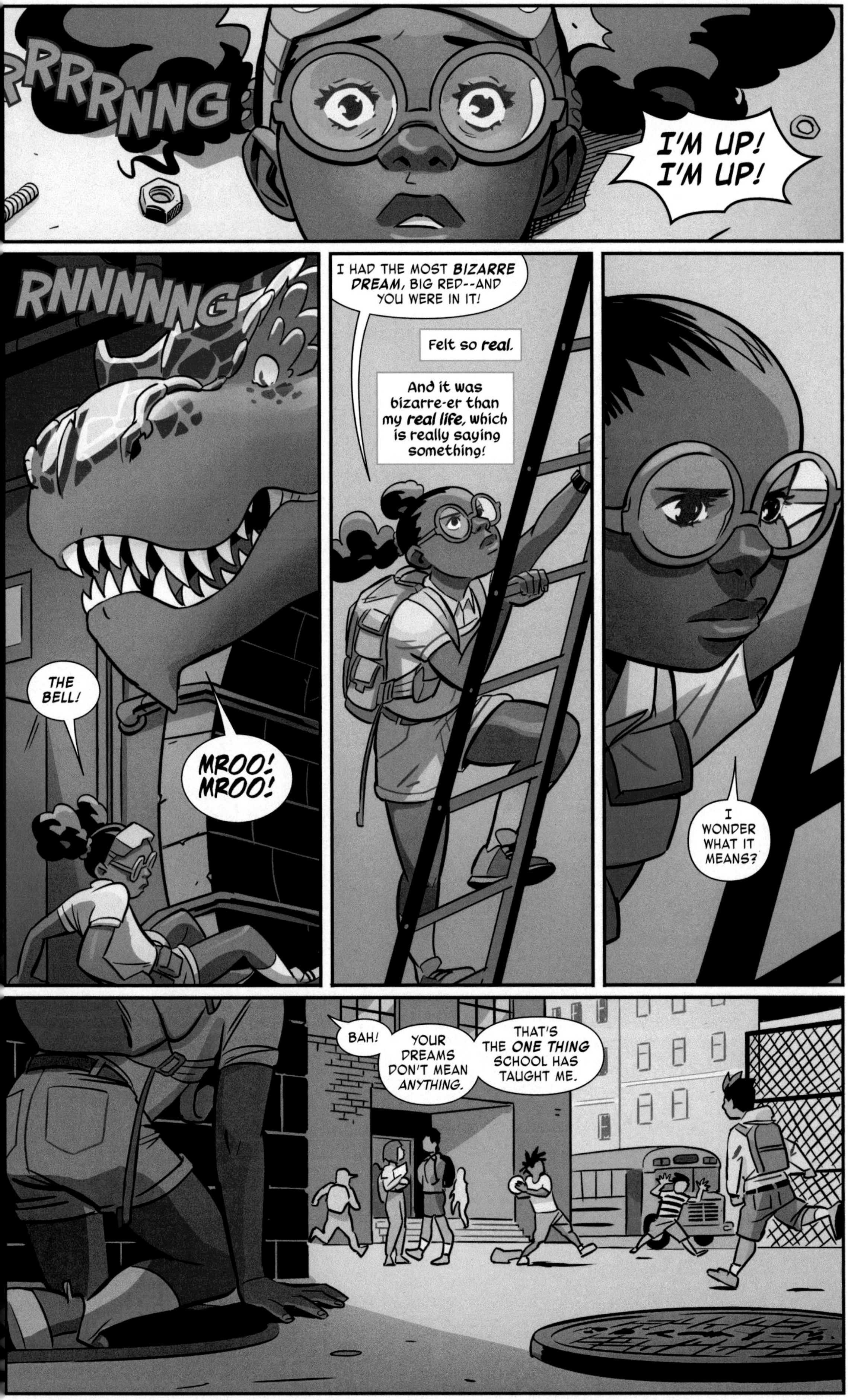
RRRRRNNG
I'M UP! I'M UP!
RNNNNNG
THE BELL!
MROO! MROO!
I HAD THE MOST BIZARRE DREAM, BIG RED--AND YOU WERE IN IT!
Felt so real.
And it was bizarre-er than my real life, which is really saying something!
I WONDER WHAT IT MEANS?
BAH!
YOUR DREAMS DON'T MEAN ANYTHING.
THAT'S THE ONE THING SCHOOL HAS TAUGHT ME.

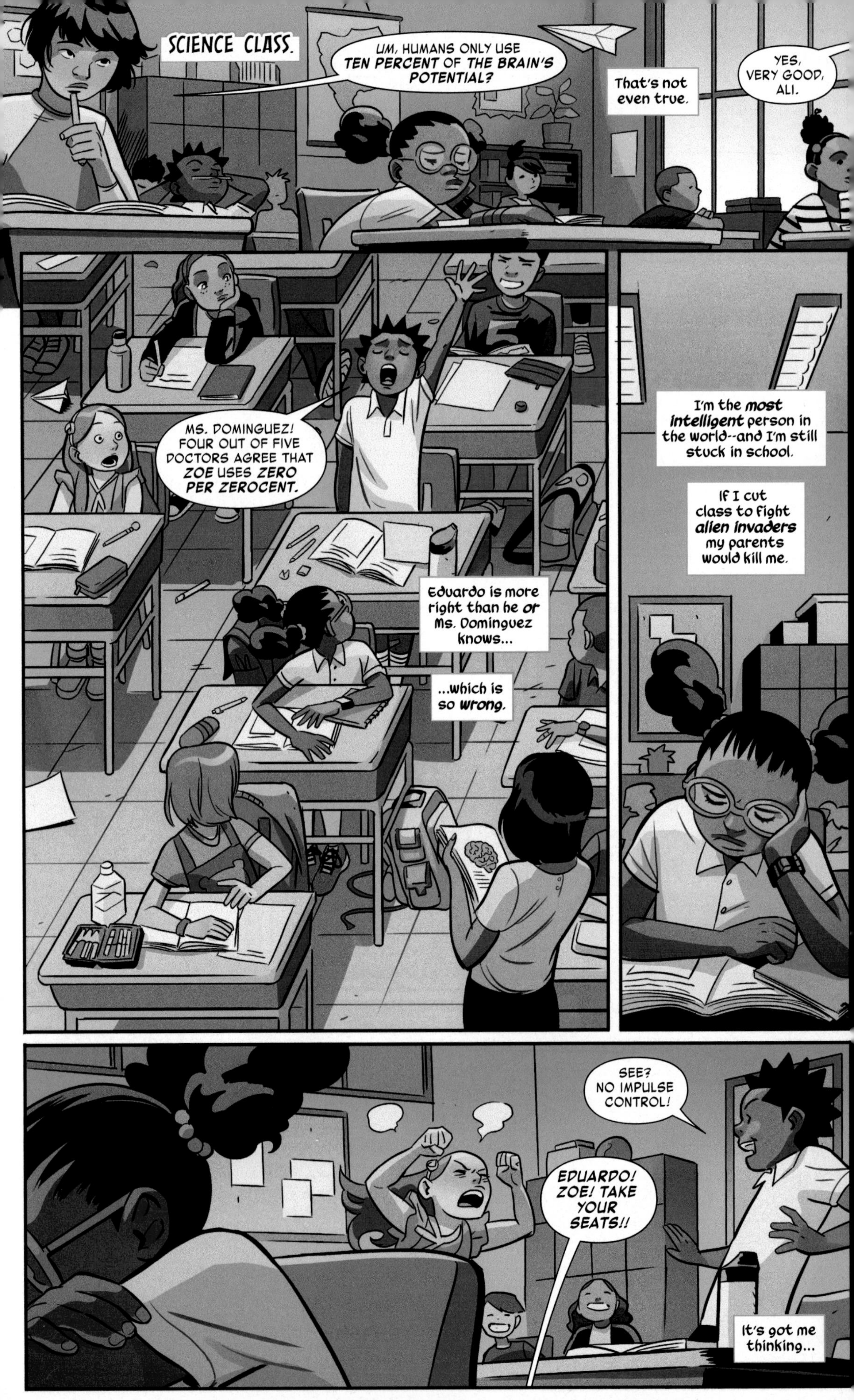
SCIENCE CLASS.
UM, HUMANS ONLY USE TEN PERCENT OF THE BRAIN'S POTENTIAL?
That's not even true.
YES, VERY GOOD, ALI.
MS. DOMINGUEZ! FOUR OUT OF FIVE DOCTORS AGREE THAT ZOE USES ZERO PER ZEROCENT.
Eduardo is more right than he or Ms. Dominguez knows...
...which is so wrong.
I'm the most intelligent person in the world--and I'm still stuck in school.
If I cut class to fight alien invaders my parents would kill me.
SEE? NO IMPULSE CONTROL!
EDUARDO! ZOE! TAKE YOUR SEATS!!
It's got me thinking...

YANCY STREET.

...what's my place in the world?

Does it *matter* to anyone?

Is anyone *watching* Moon Girl?

BAH!

I've always had to *do* for myself. I went my whole life without anyone *recognizing me.*

It's not the *time* for teachers and parents. Eduardos and Zoes. Hulks and heroes.

Imagine that! A whole bunch of *other people's* opinions telling *the smartest person in the world* what to do.

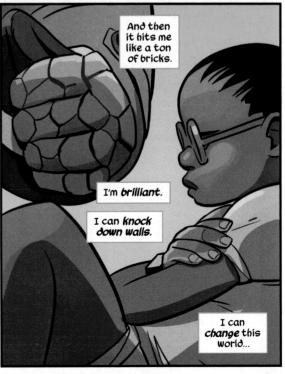

And then it hits me like a ton of bricks.

I'm *brilliant.*

I can *knock down walls.*

I can *change* this world...

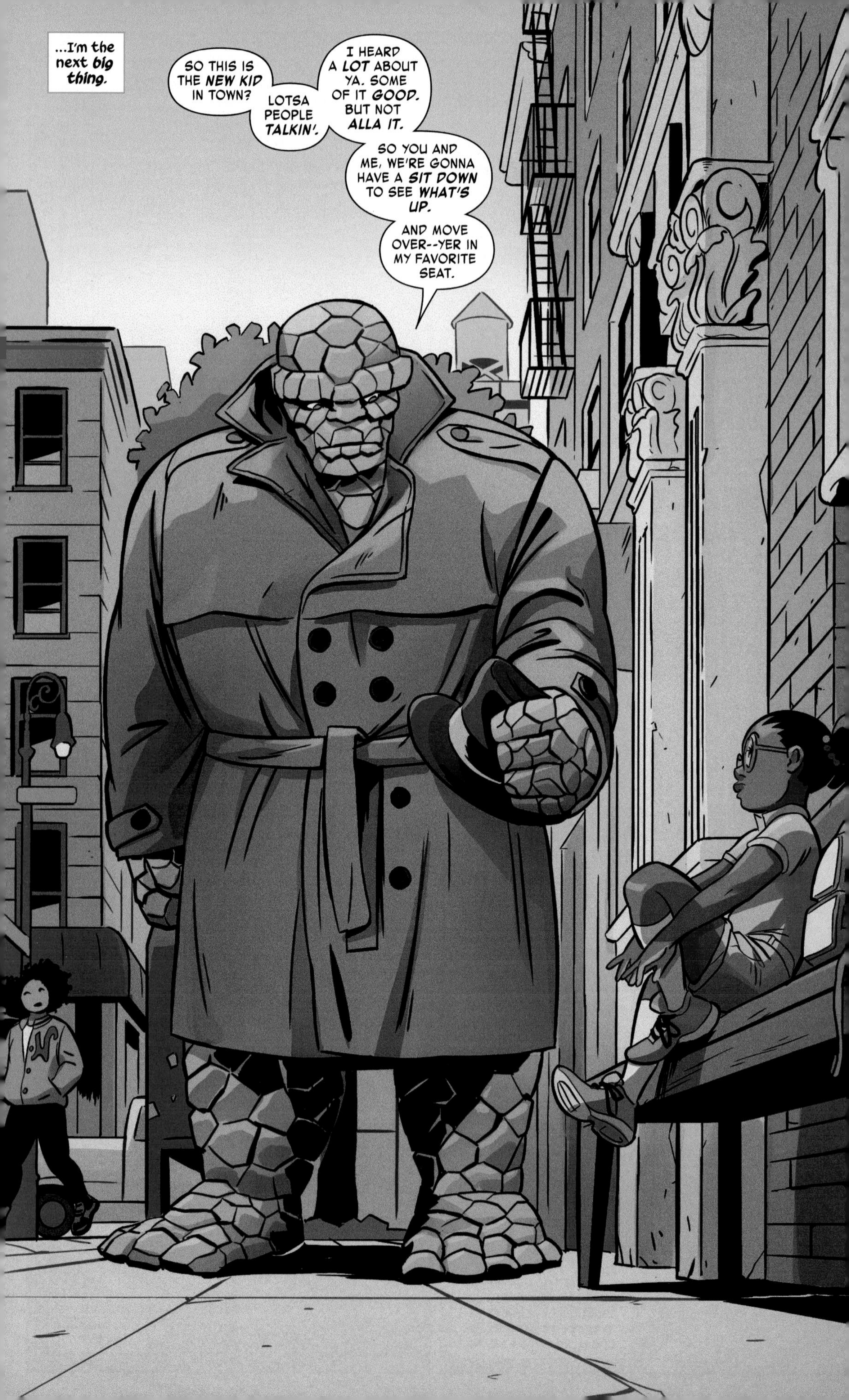
...I'm the next *big* *thing.*
SO THIS IS THE *NEW KID* IN TOWN?
LOTSA PEOPLE *TALKIN'.*
I HEARD A *LOT* ABOUT YA. SOME OF IT *GOOD.* BUT NOT *ALLA IT.*
SO YOU AND ME, WE'RE GONNA HAVE A *SIT DOWN* TO SEE *WHAT'S UP.*
AND MOVE OVER--YER IN MY FAVORITE SEAT.

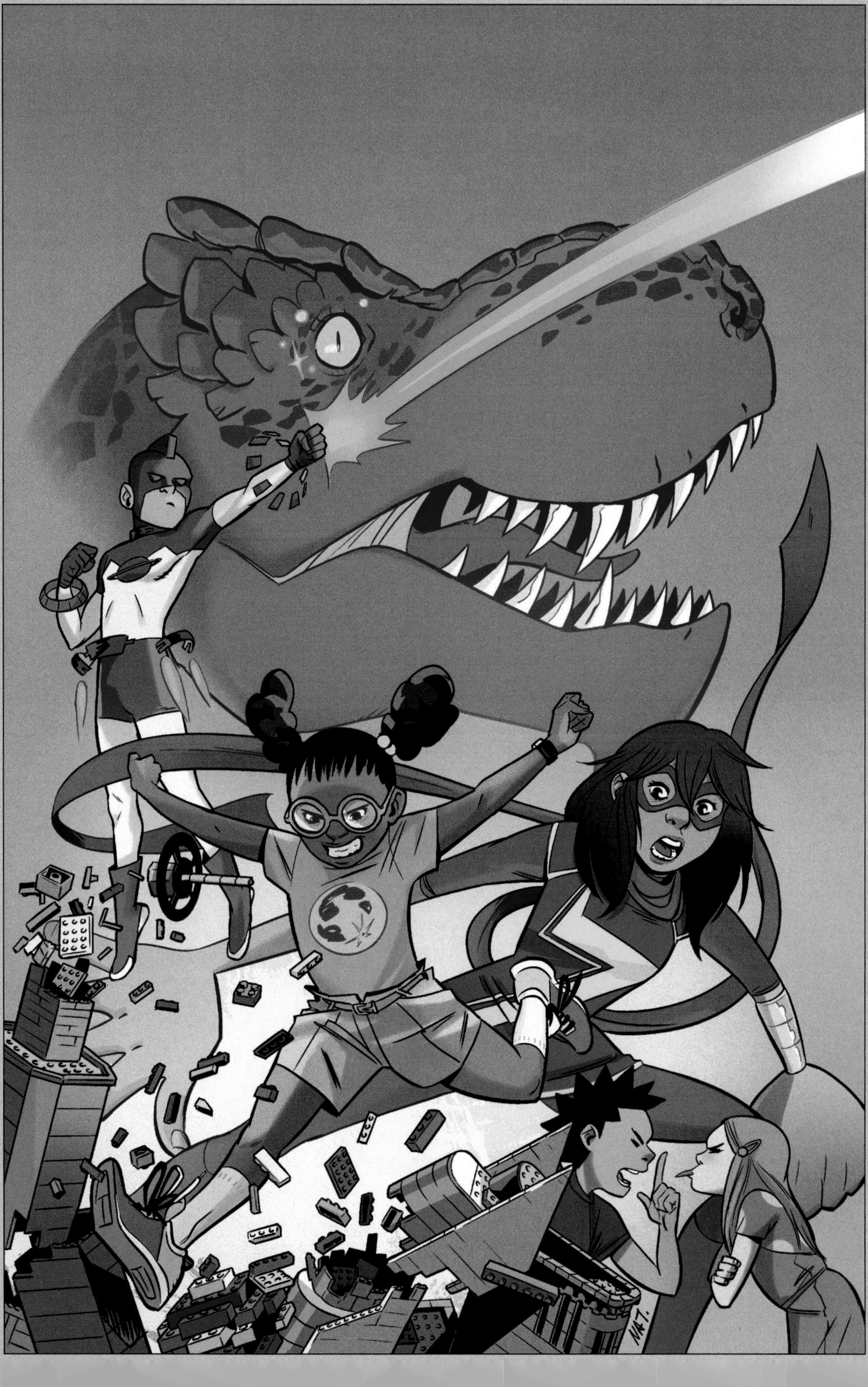

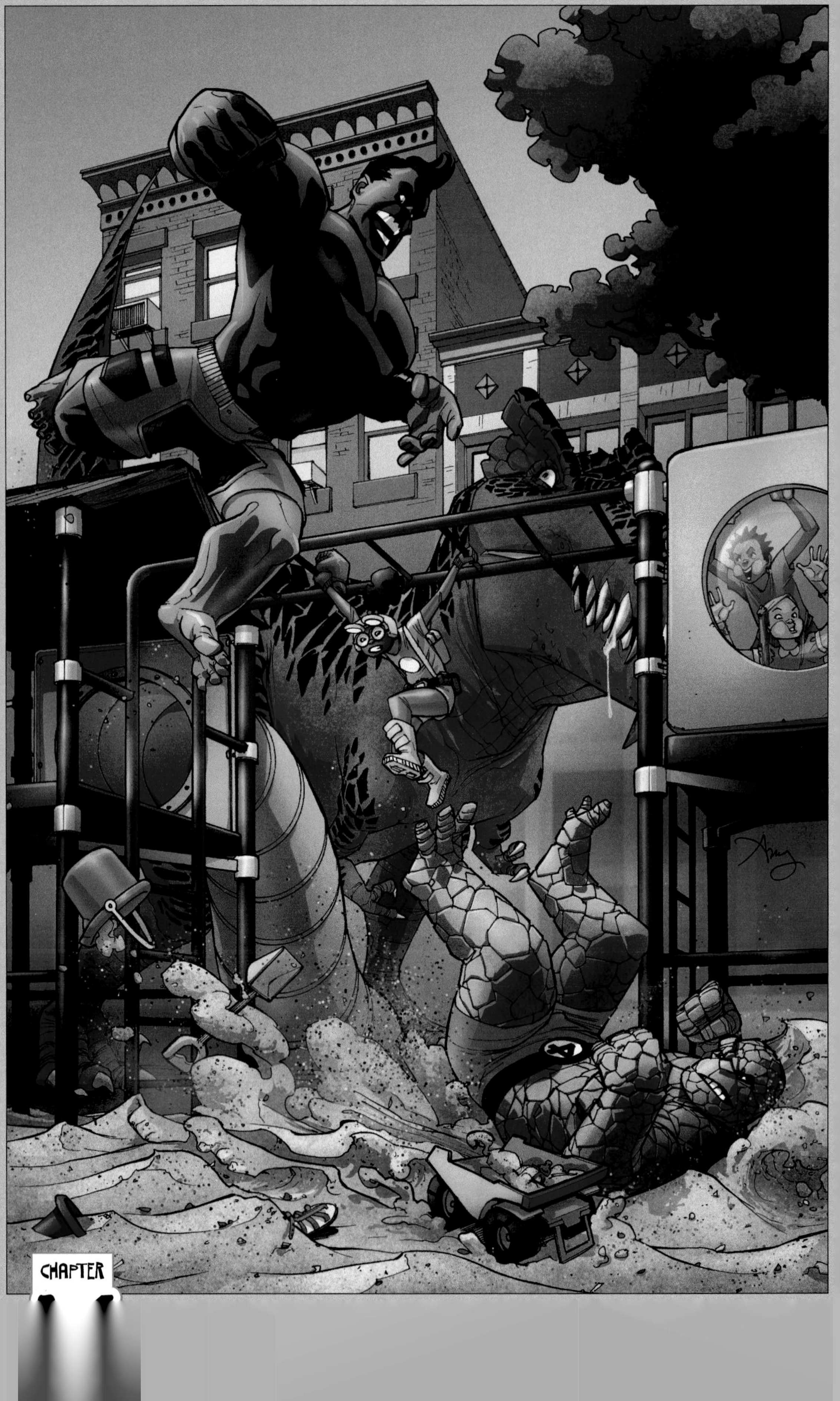
CHAPTER

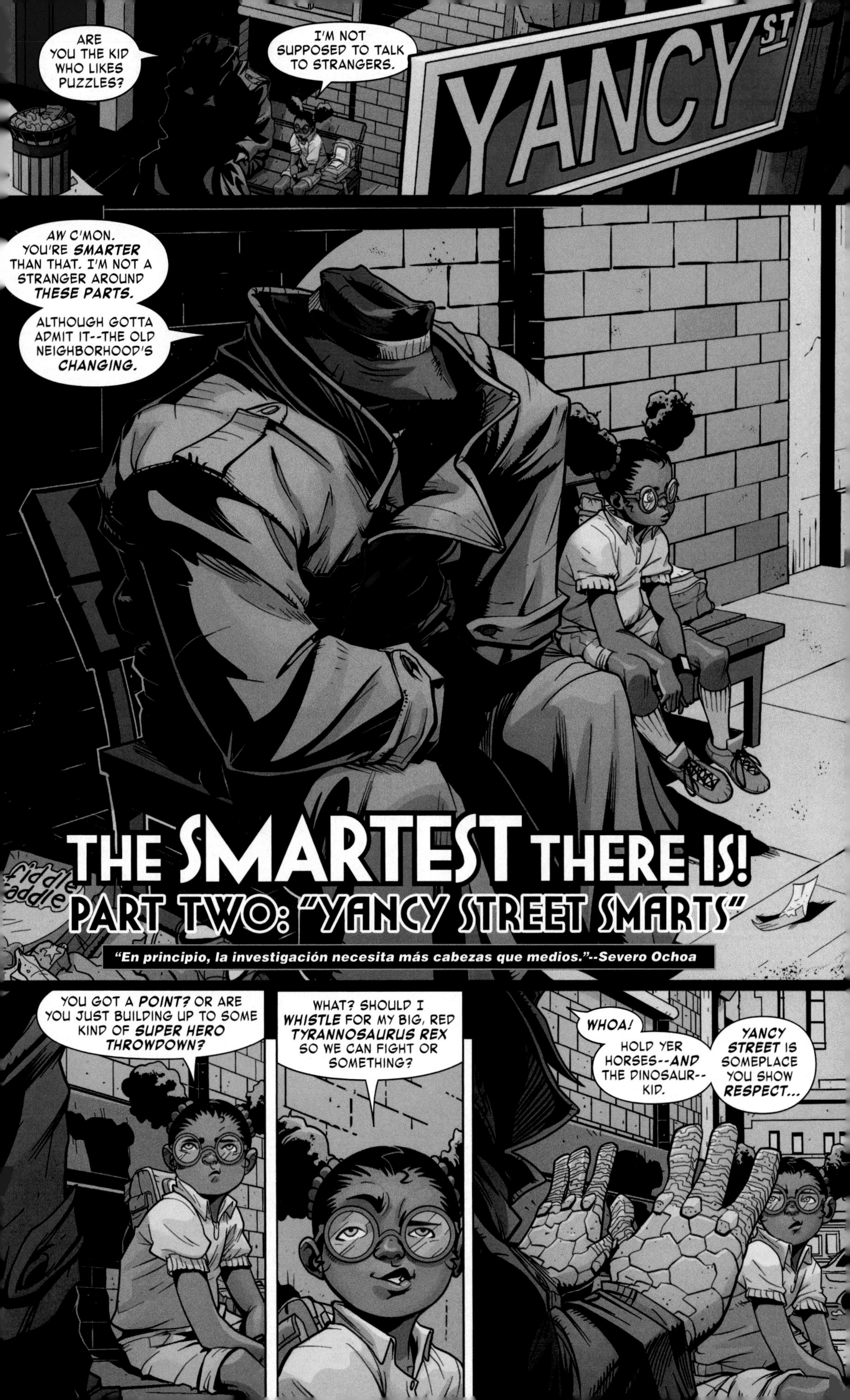

ARE YOU THE KID WHO LIKES PUZZLES?
I'M NOT SUPPOSED TO TALK TO STRANGERS.
YANCY ST
AW C'MON. YOU'RE SMARTER THAN THAT. I'M NOT A STRANGER AROUND THESE PARTS.
ALTHOUGH GOTTA ADMIT IT--THE OLD NEIGHBORHOOD'S CHANGING.
THE SMARTEST THERE IS!
PART TWO: "YANCY STREET SMARTS"
"En principio, la investigación necesita más cabezas que medios."--Severo Ochoa
YOU GOT A POINT? OR ARE YOU JUST BUILDING UP TO SOME KIND OF SUPER HERO THROWDOWN?
WHAT? SHOULD I WHISTLE FOR MY BIG, RED TYRANNOSAURUS REX SO WE CAN FIGHT OR SOMETHING?
WHOA!
HOLD YER HORSES--AND THE DINOSAUR--KID.
YANCY STREET IS SOMEPLACE YOU SHOW RESPECT...

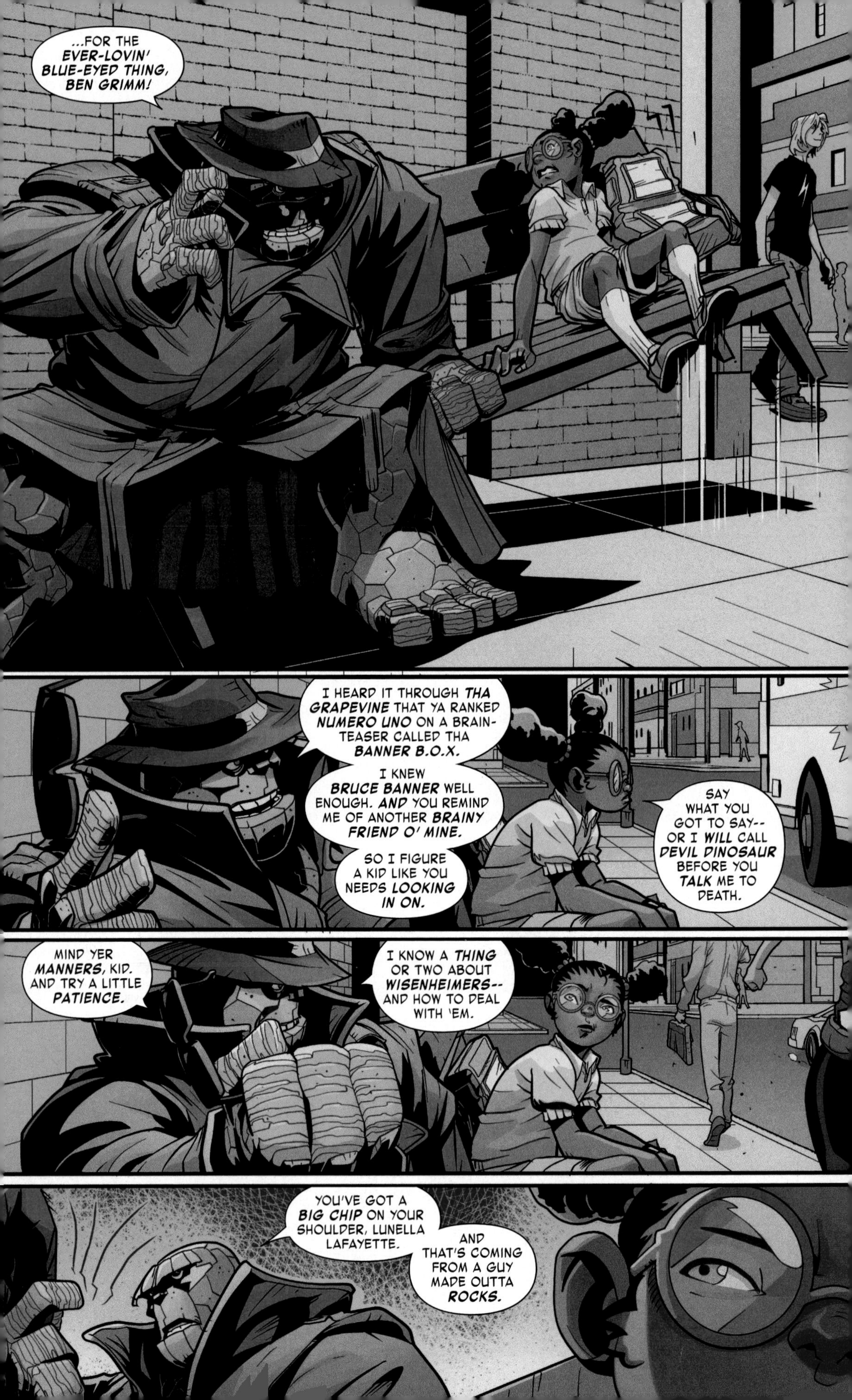
...FOR THE EVER-LOVIN' BLUE-EYED THING, BEN GRIMM!
I HEARD IT THROUGH THA GRAPEVINE THAT YA RANKED NUMERO UNO ON A BRAIN-TEASER CALLED THA BANNER B.O.X.
I KNEW BRUCE BANNER WELL ENOUGH. AND YOU REMIND ME OF ANOTHER BRAINY FRIEND O' MINE.
SO I FIGURE A KID LIKE YOU NEEDS LOOKING IN ON.
SAY WHAT YOU GOT TO SAY-- OR I WILL CALL DEVIL DINOSAUR BEFORE YOU TALK ME TO DEATH.
MIND YER MANNERS, KID. AND TRY A LITTLE PATIENCE.
I KNOW A THING OR TWO ABOUT WISENHEIMERS-- AND HOW TO DEAL WITH 'EM.
YOU'VE GOT A BIG CHIP ON YOUR SHOULDER, LUNELLA LAFAYETTE.
AND THAT'S COMING FROM A GUY MADE OUTTA ROCKS.

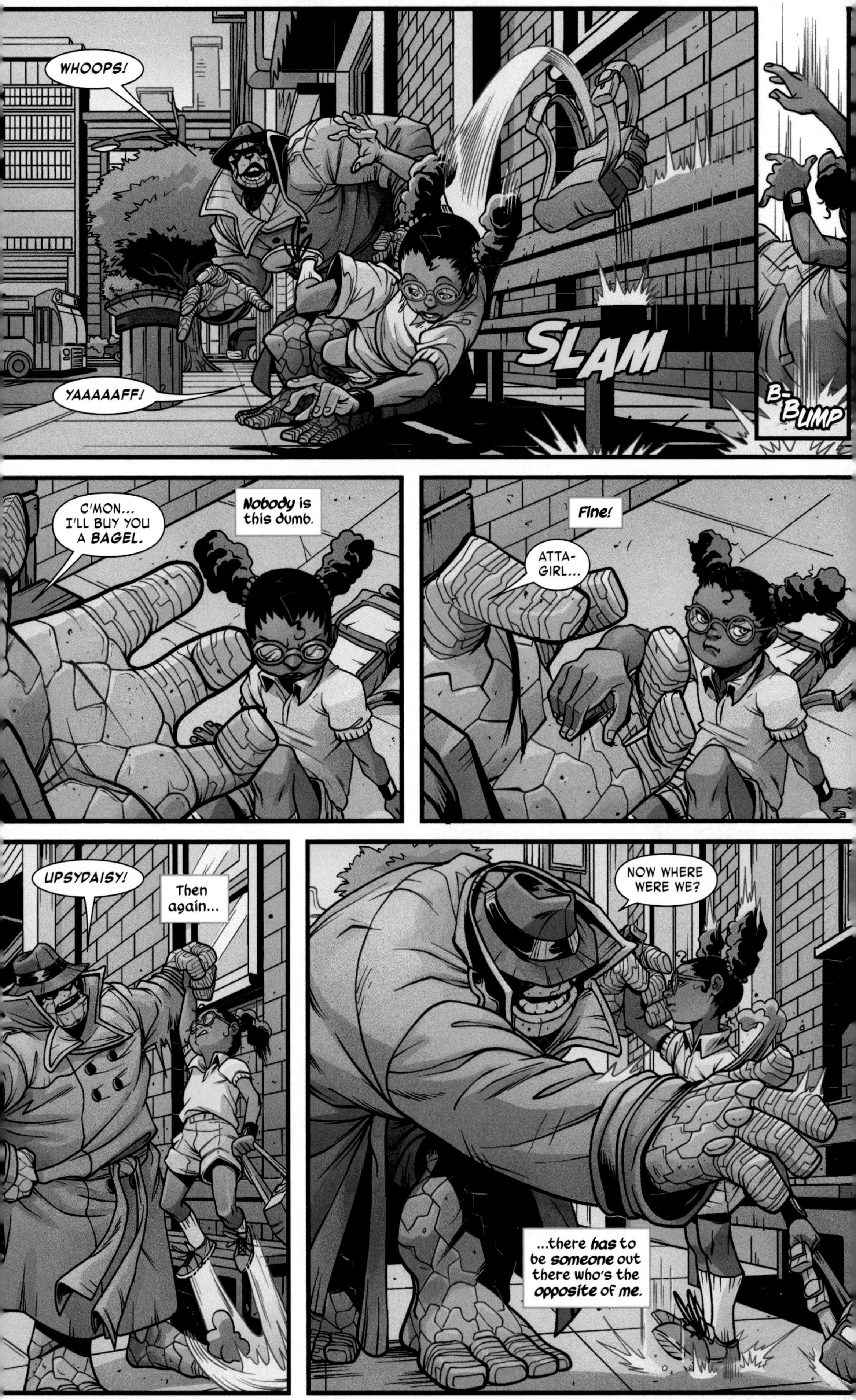

WHOOPS!
YAAAAAFF!
SLAM
B-BUMP
C'MON... I'LL BUY YOU A BAGEL.
Nobody is this dumb.
Fine!
ATTA-GIRL...
UPSYDAISY!
Then again...
NOW WHERE WERE WE?
...there has to be someone out there who's the opposite of me.

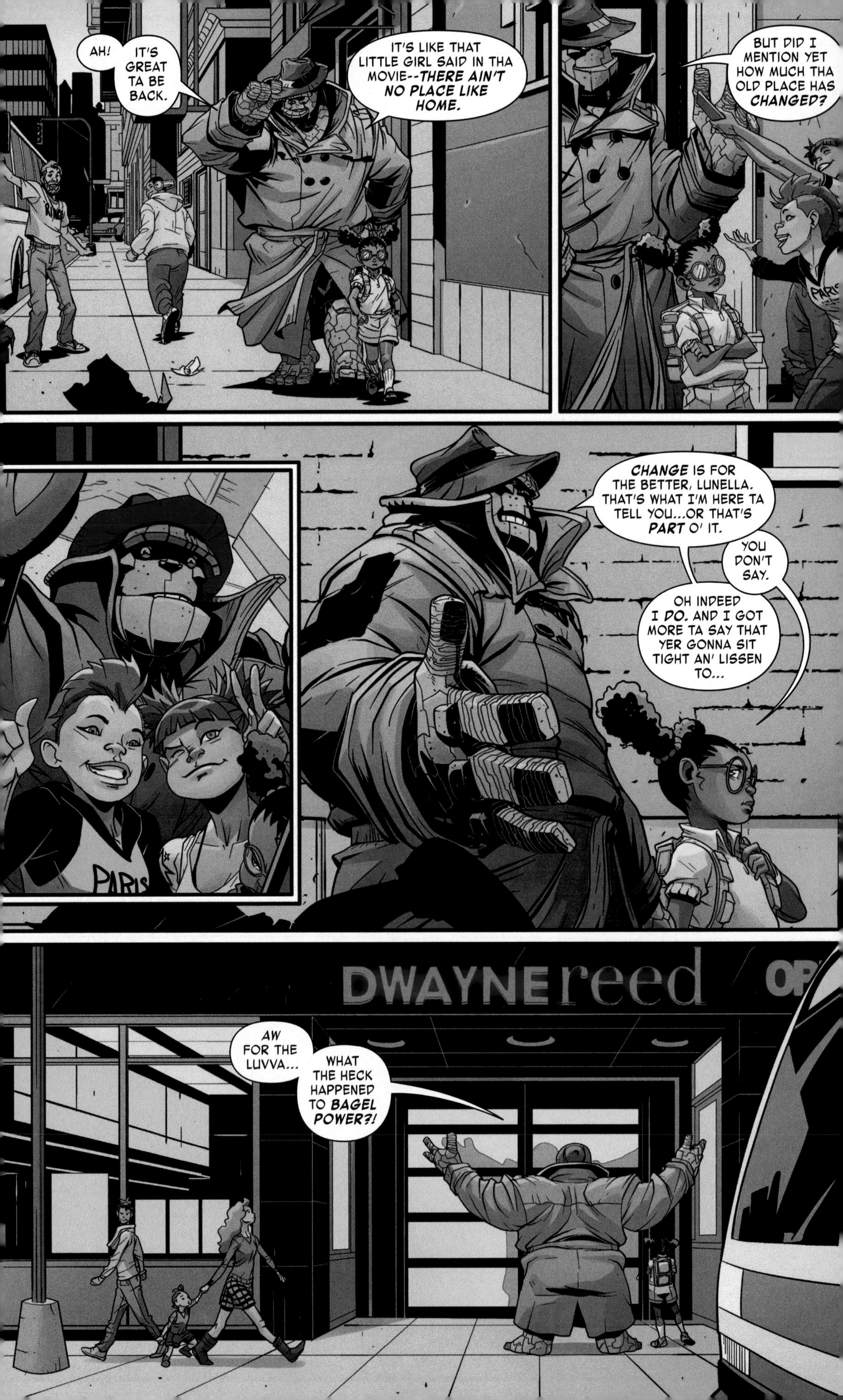
AH!
IT'S GREAT TA BE BACK.
IT'S LIKE THAT LITTLE GIRL SAID IN THA MOVIE--THERE AIN'T NO PLACE LIKE HOME.
BUT DID I MENTION YET HOW MUCH THA OLD PLACE HAS CHANGED?
PARIS
CHANGE IS FOR THE BETTER, LUNELLA. THAT'S WHAT I'M HERE TA TELL YOU...OR THAT'S PART O' IT.
YOU DON'T SAY.
OH INDEED I DO. AND I GOT MORE TA SAY THAT YER GONNA SIT TIGHT AN' LISSEN TO...
DWAYNEreed
AW FOR THE LUVVA...
WHAT THE HECK HAPPENED TO BAGEL POWER?!

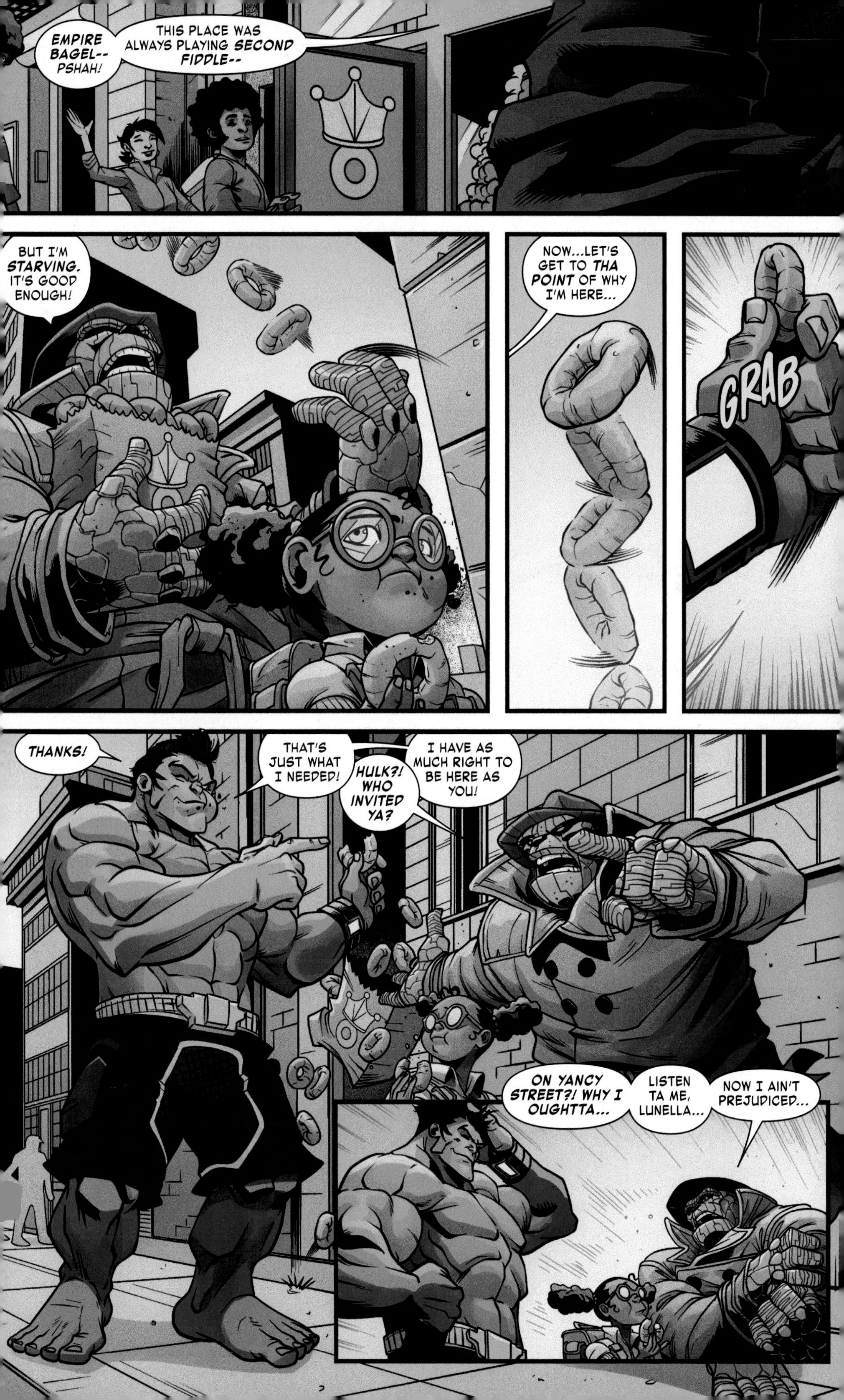
EMPIRE BAGEL-- PSHAH!
THIS PLACE WAS ALWAYS PLAYING SECOND FIDDLE--
BUT I'M STARVING. IT'S GOOD ENOUGH!
NOW...LET'S GET TO THA POINT OF WHY I'M HERE...
GRAB
THANKS!
THAT'S JUST WHAT I NEEDED!
HULK?! WHO INVITED YA?
I HAVE AS MUCH RIGHT TO BE HERE AS YOU!
ON YANCY STREET?! WHY I OUGHTTA...
LISTEN TA ME, LUNELLA...
NOW I AIN'T PREJUDICED...

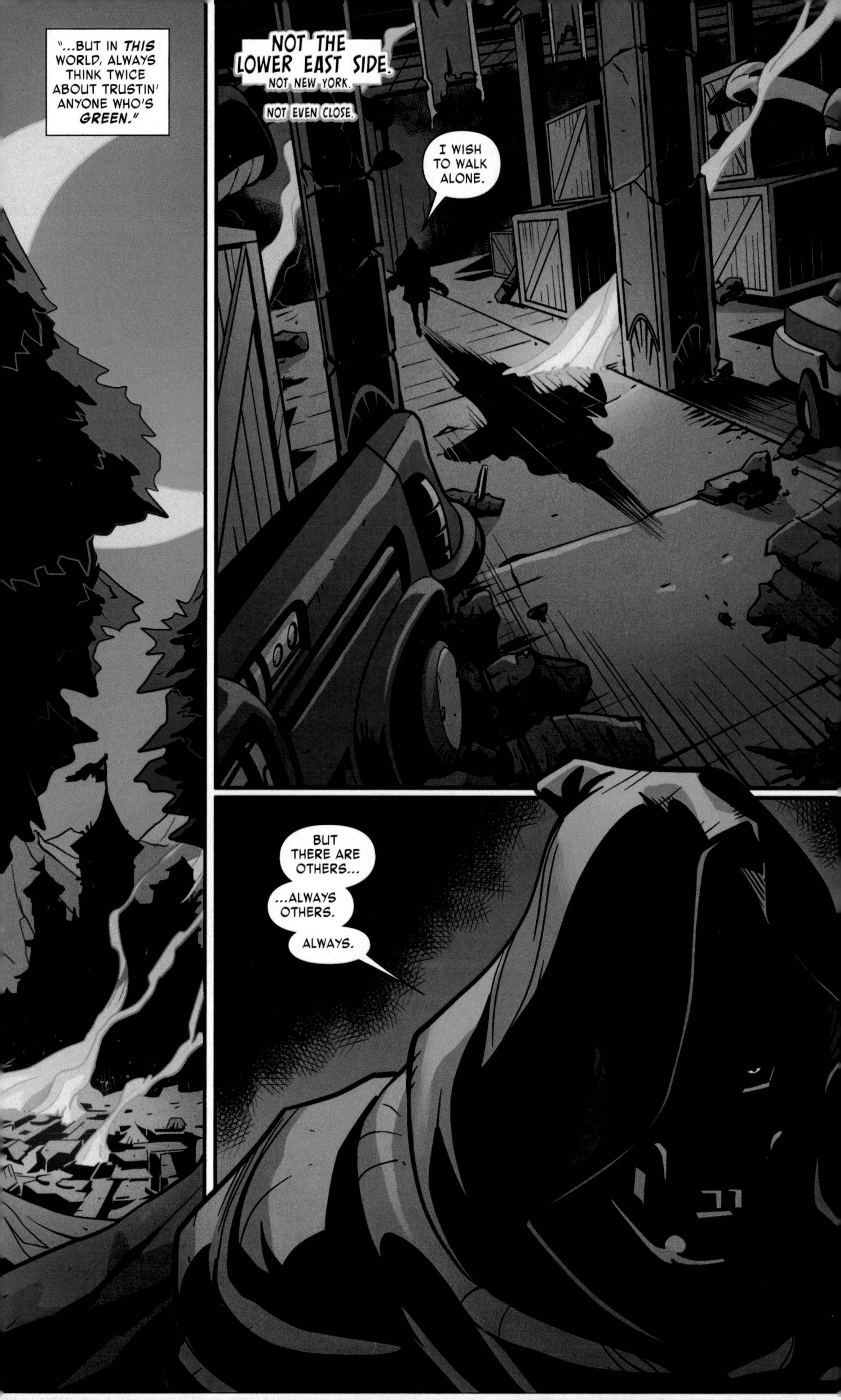
"...BUT IN THIS WORLD, ALWAYS THINK TWICE ABOUT TRUSTIN' ANYONE WHO'S GREEN."
NOT THE LOWER EAST SIDE.
NOT NEW YORK.
NOT EVEN CLOSE.
I WISH TO WALK ALONE.
BUT THERE ARE OTHERS...
...ALWAYS OTHERS.
ALWAYS.

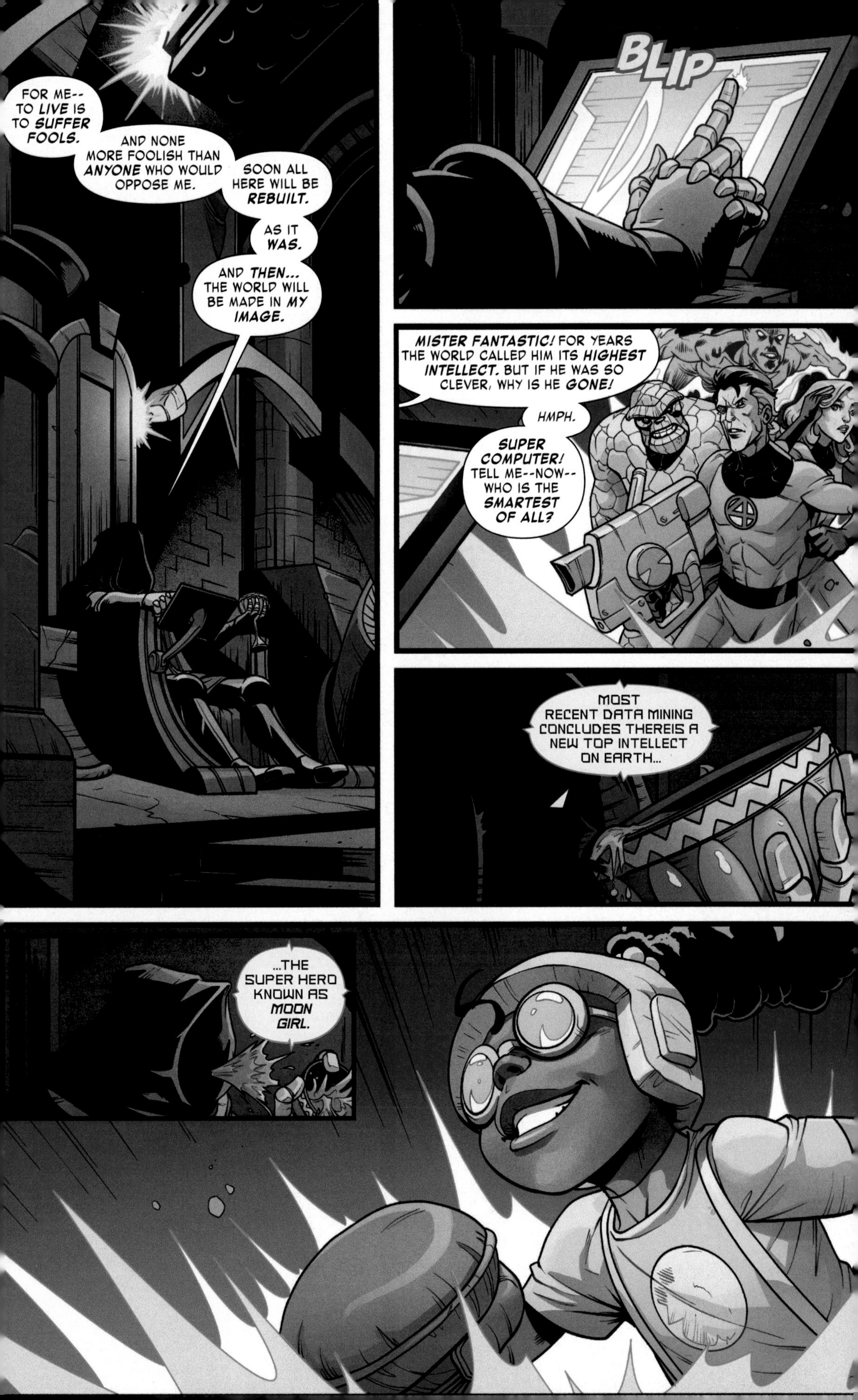
FOR ME-- TO LIVE IS TO SUFFER FOOLS.
AND NONE MORE FOOLISH THAN ANYONE WHO WOULD OPPOSE ME.
SOON ALL HERE WILL BE REBUILT.
AS IT WAS.
AND THEN... THE WORLD WILL BE MADE IN MY IMAGE.
BLIP
MISTER FANTASTIC! FOR YEARS THE WORLD CALLED HIM ITS HIGHEST INTELLECT. BUT IF HE WAS SO CLEVER, WHY IS HE GONE!
HMPH.
SUPER COMPUTER! TELL ME--NOW-- WHO IS THE SMARTEST OF ALL?
MOST RECENT DATA MINING CONCLUDES THEREIS A NEW TOP INTELLECT ON EARTH...
...THE SUPER HERO KNOWN AS MOON GIRL.

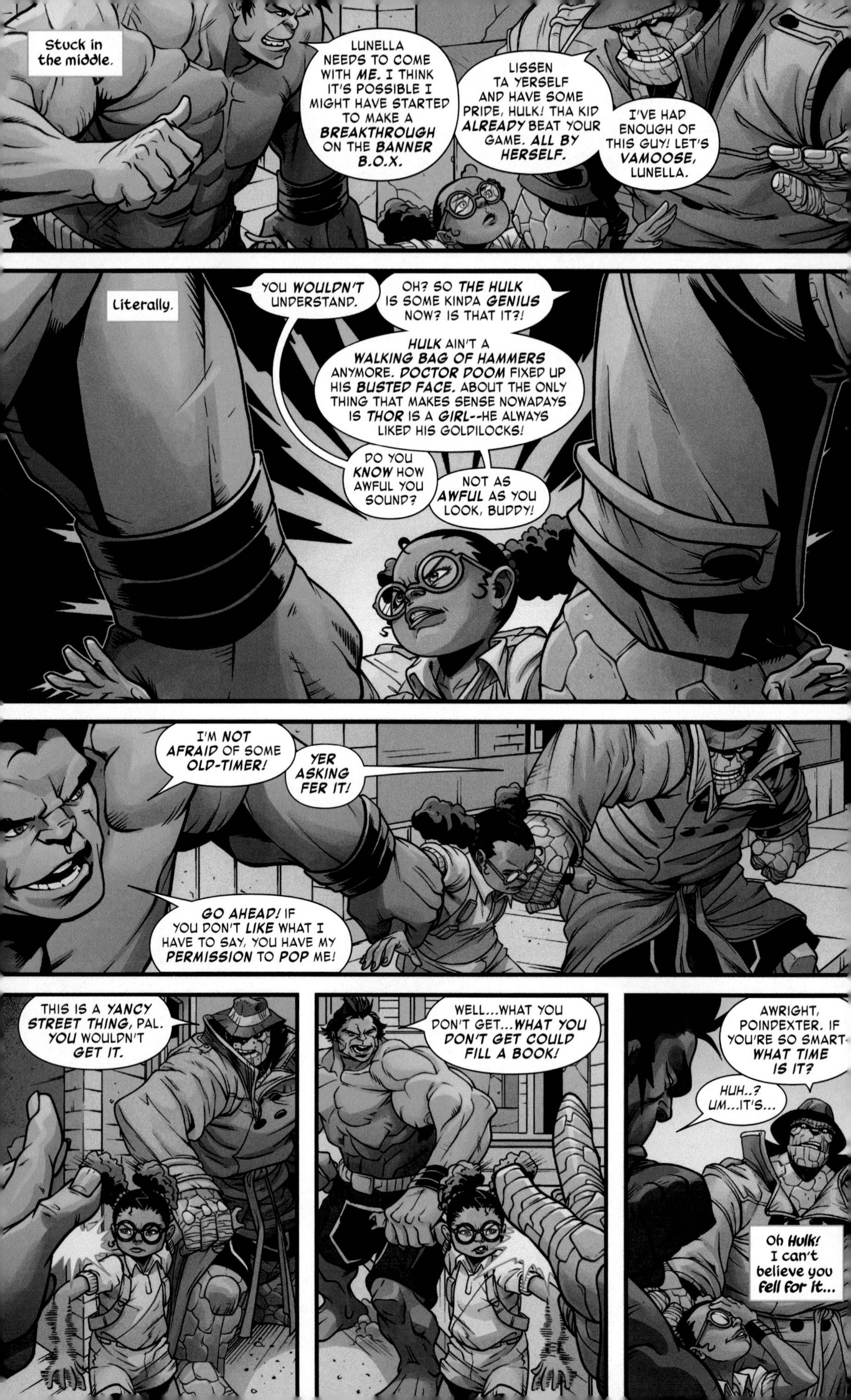
Stuck in the middle.
LUNELLA NEEDS TO COME WITH ME. I THINK IT'S POSSIBLE I MIGHT HAVE STARTED TO MAKE A BREAKTHROUGH ON THE BANNER B.O.X.
LISSEN TA YERSELF AND HAVE SOME PRIDE, HULK! THA KID ALREADY BEAT YOUR GAME. ALL BY HERSELF.
I'VE HAD ENOUGH OF THIS GUY! LET'S VAMOOSE, LUNELLA.
Literally.
YOU WOULDN'T UNDERSTAND.
OH? SO THE HULK IS SOME KINDA GENIUS NOW? IS THAT IT?!
HULK AIN'T A WALKING BAG OF HAMMERS ANYMORE. DOCTOR DOOM FIXED UP HIS BUSTED FACE. ABOUT THE ONLY THING THAT MAKES SENSE NOWADAYS IS THOR IS A GIRL--HE ALWAYS LIKED HIS GOLDILOCKS!
DO YOU KNOW HOW AWFUL YOU SOUND?
NOT AS AWFUL AS YOU LOOK, BUDDY!
I'M NOT AFRAID OF SOME OLD-TIMER!
YER ASKING FER IT!
GO AHEAD! IF YOU DON'T LIKE WHAT I HAVE TO SAY, YOU HAVE MY PERMISSION TO POP ME!
THIS IS A YANCY STREET THING, PAL. YOU WOULDN'T GET IT.
WELL...WHAT YOU DON'T GET...WHAT YOU DON'T GET COULD FILL A BOOK!
AWRIGHT, POINDEXTER. IF YOU'RE SO SMART WHAT TIME IS IT?
HUH..? UM...IT'S...
Oh Hulk! I can't believe you fell for it...

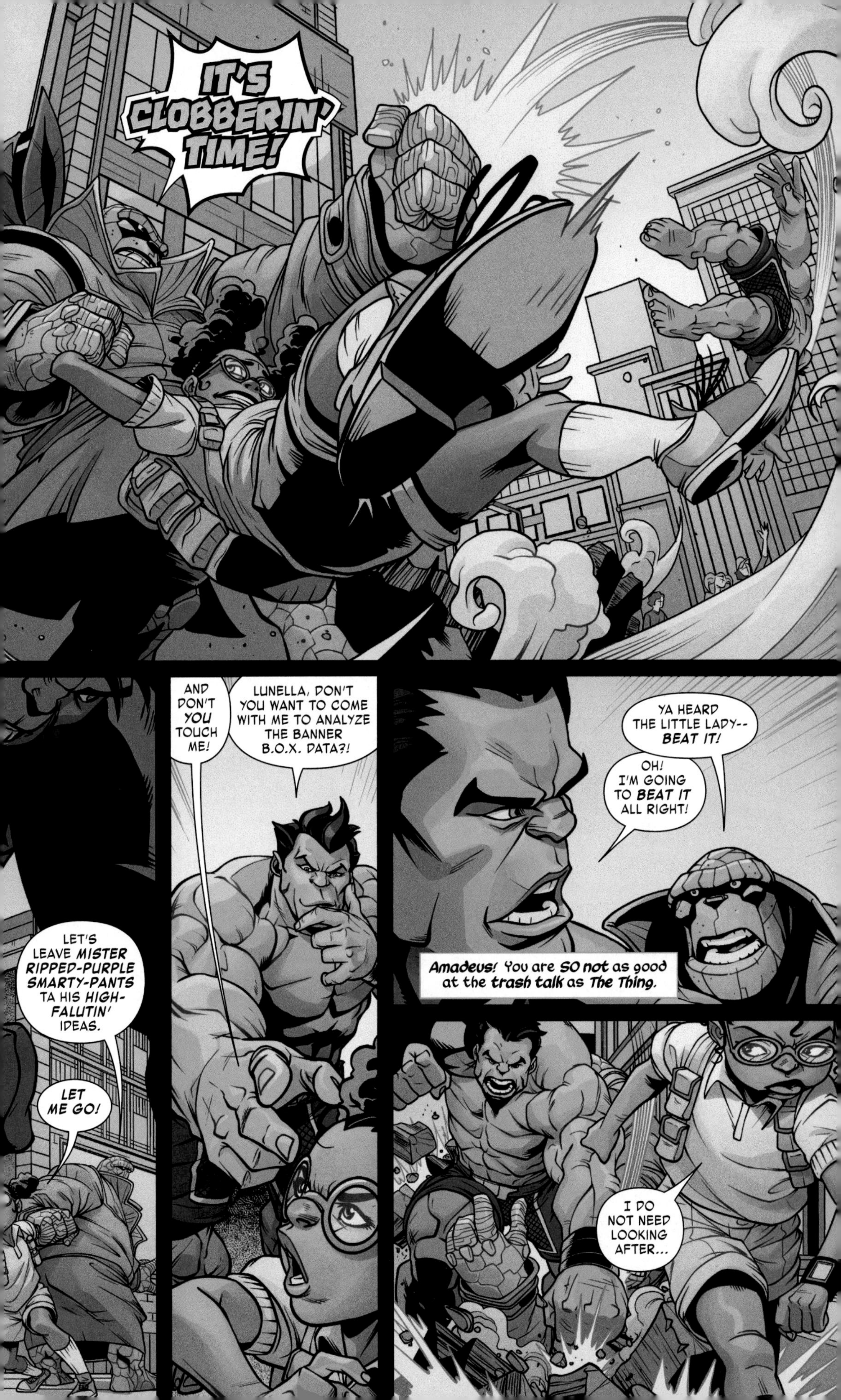
IT'S CLOBBERIN' TIME!
AND DON'T YOU TOUCH ME!
LUNELLA, DON'T YOU WANT TO COME WITH ME TO ANALYZE THE BANNER B.O.X. DATA?!
YA HEARD THE LITTLE LADY-- BEAT IT!
OH! I'M GOING TO BEAT IT ALL RIGHT!
Amadeus! You are SO not as good at the trash talk as The Thing.
LET'S LEAVE MISTER RIPPED-PURPLE SMARTY-PANTS TA HIS HIGH-FALUTIN' IDEAS.
LET ME GO!
I DO NOT NEED LOOKING AFTER...

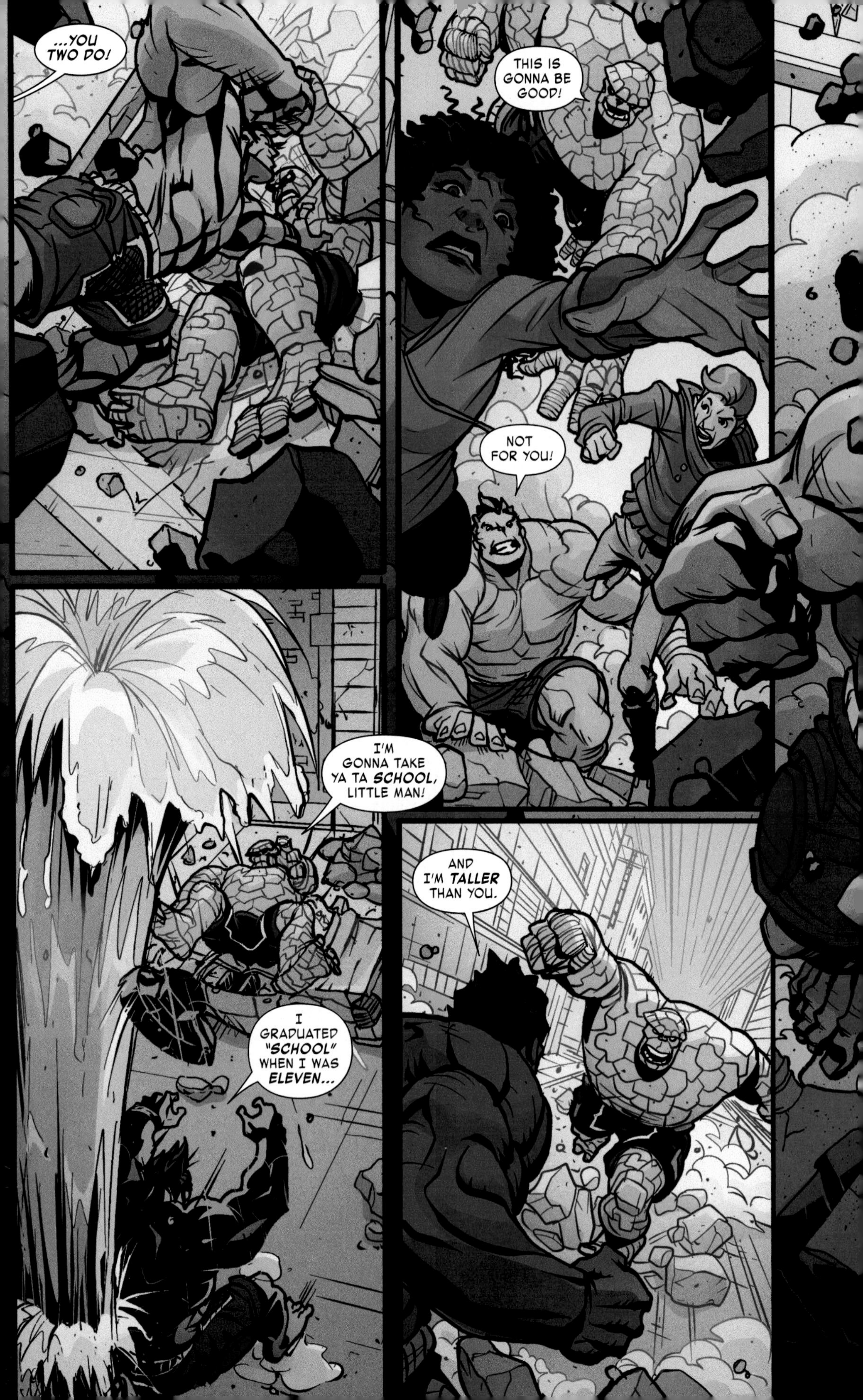
...YOU TWO DO!
THIS IS GONNA BE GOOD!
NOT FOR YOU!
I'M GONNA TAKE YA TA SCHOOL, LITTLE MAN!
I GRADUATED "SCHOOL" WHEN I WAS ELEVEN...
AND I'M TALLER THAN YOU.

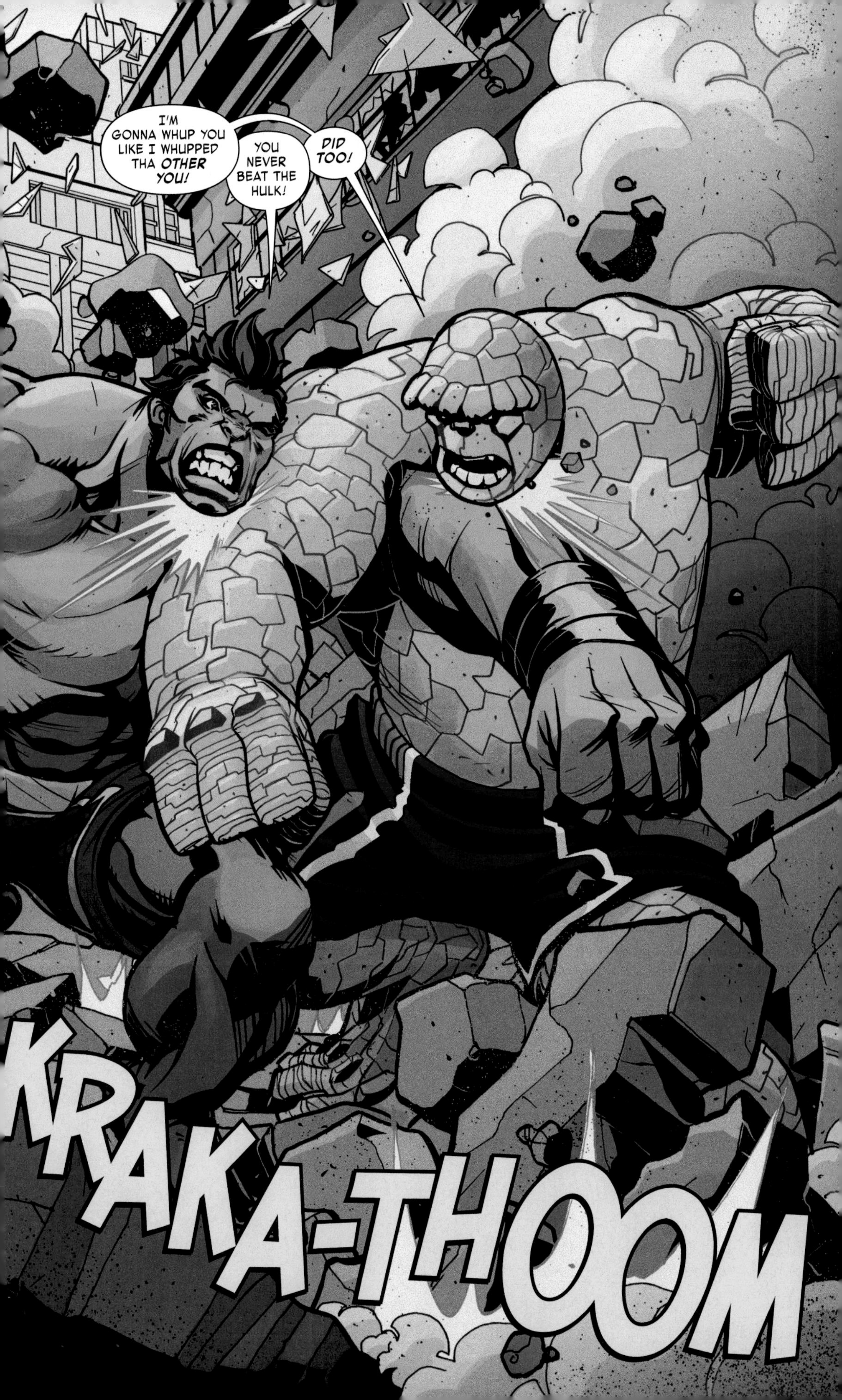

I'M GONNA WHUP YOU LIKE I WHUPPED THA *OTHER YOU!*
YOU NEVER BEAT THE HULK!
DID TOO!
KRAKA-THOOM

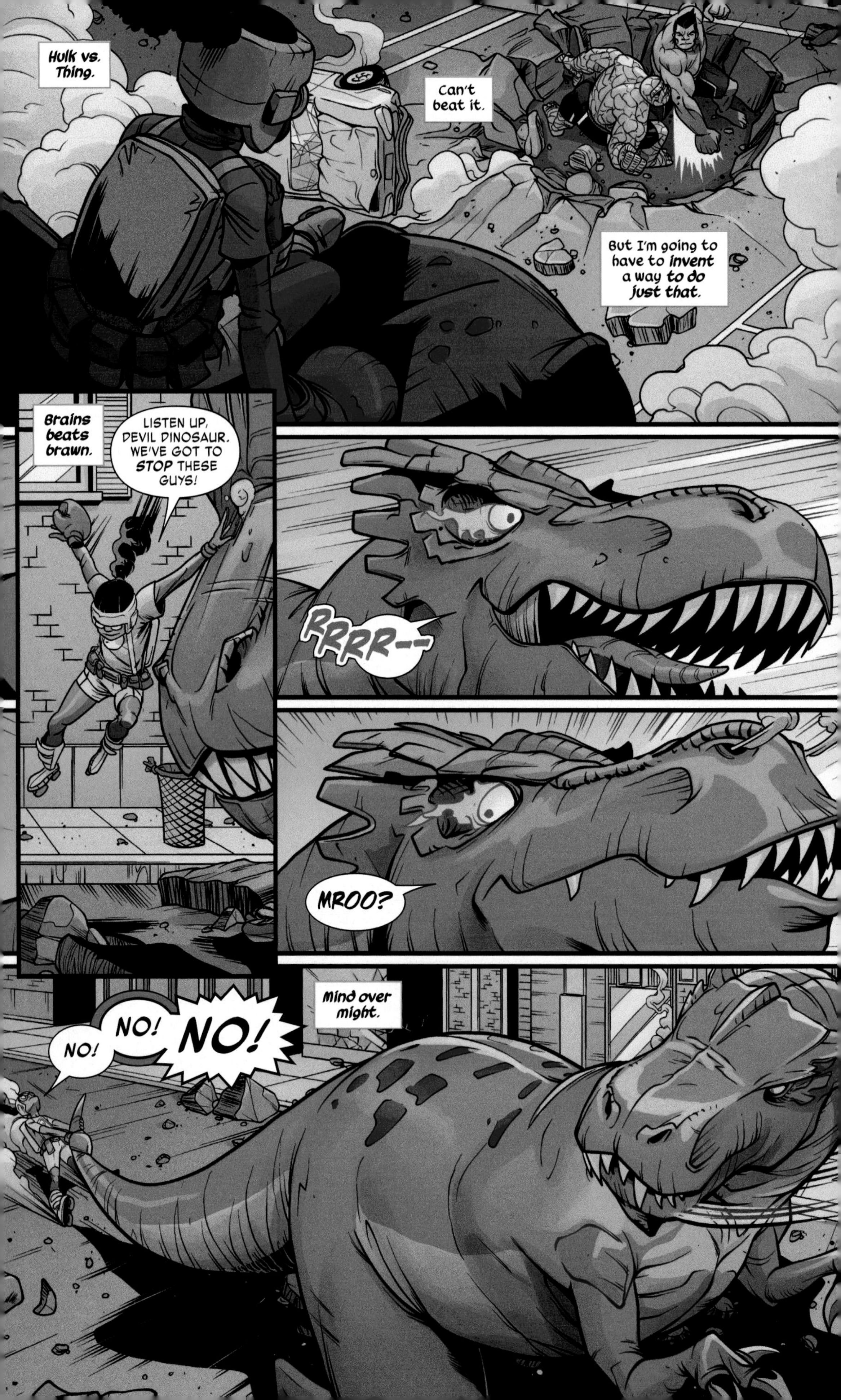

Hulk vs. Thing.
Can't beat it.
But I'm going to have to invent a way to do just that.
Brains beats brawn.
LISTEN UP, DEVIL DINOSAUR. WE'VE GOT TO STOP THESE GUYS!
RRRR--
MROO?
Mind over might.
NO!
NO!
NO!

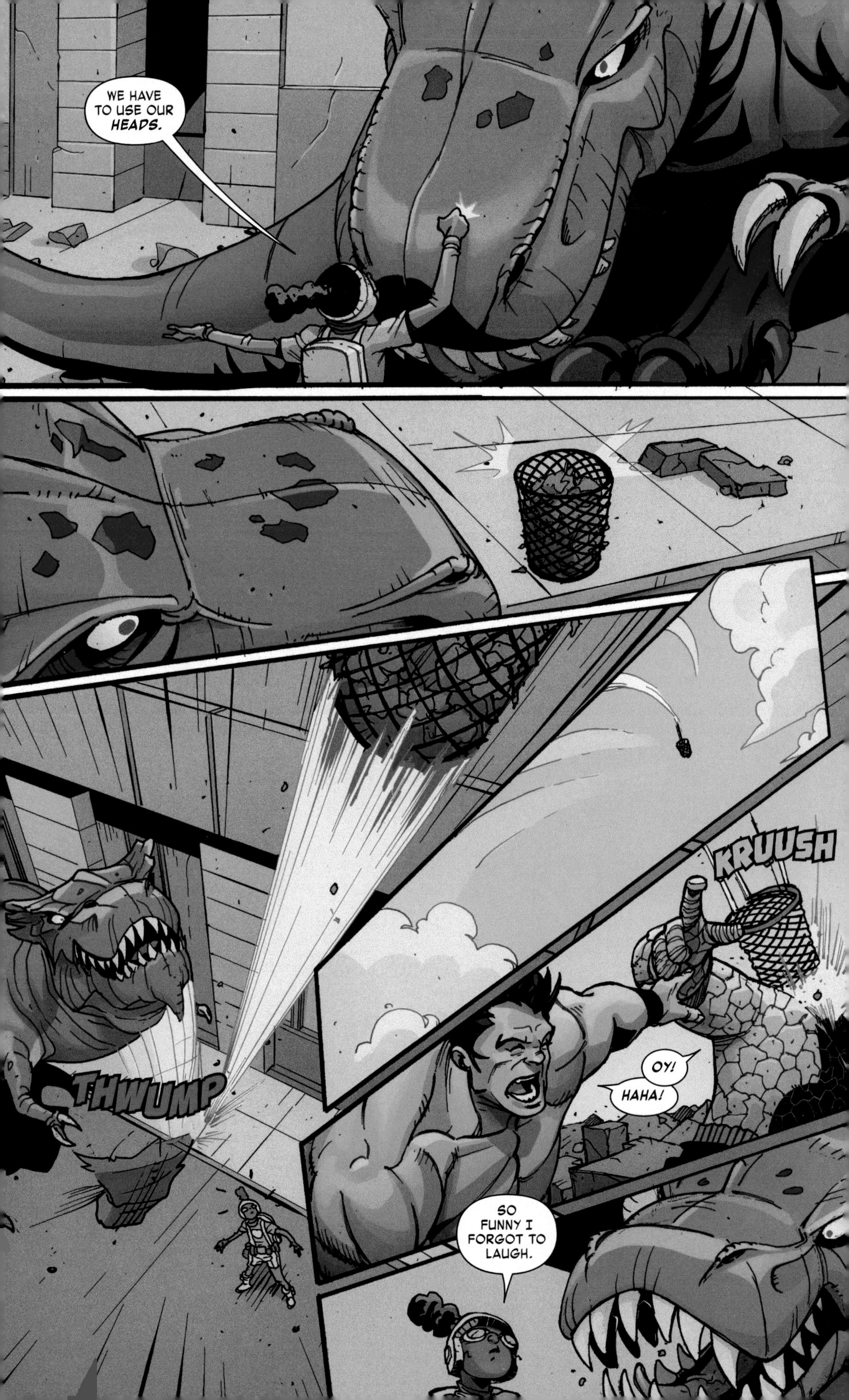
WE HAVE TO USE OUR HEADS.
THWUMP
KRUUSH
OY!
HAHA!
SO FUNNY I FORGOT TO LAUGH.

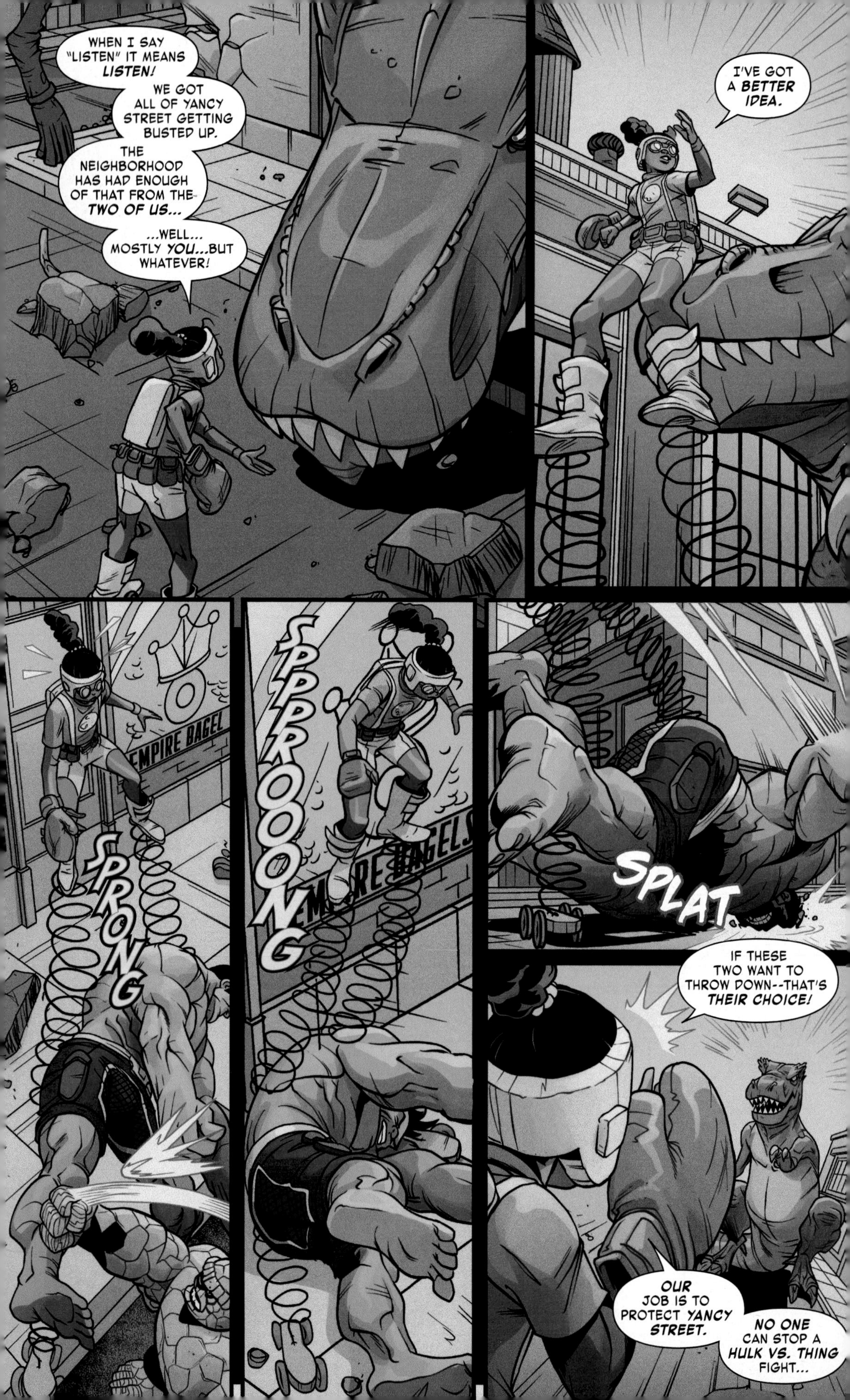

WHEN I SAY "LISTEN" IT MEANS LISTEN!
WE GOT ALL OF YANCY STREET GETTING BUSTED UP.
THE NEIGHBORHOOD HAS HAD ENOUGH OF THAT FROM THE TWO OF US...
...WELL... MOSTLY YOU...BUT WHATEVER!
I'VE GOT A BETTER IDEA.
EMPIRE BAGEL
SPRONG
SPPROOOONG
EMPIRE BAGELS
SPLAT
IF THESE TWO WANT TO THROW DOWN--THAT'S THEIR CHOICE!
OUR JOB IS TO PROTECT YANCY STREET.
NO ONE CAN STOP A HULK VS. THING FIGHT...

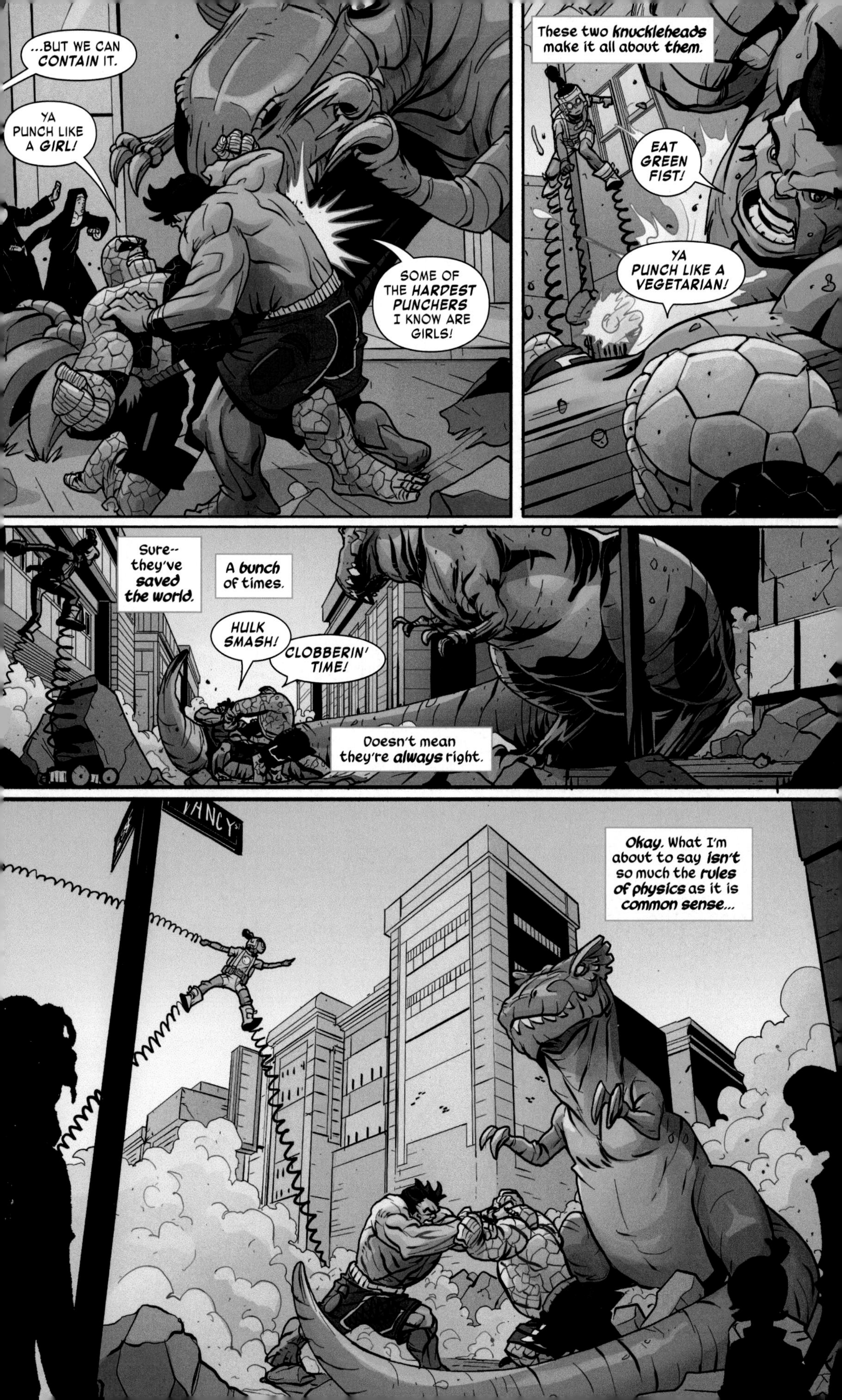
...BUT WE CAN CONTAIN IT.
YA PUNCH LIKE A GIRL!
SOME OF THE HARDEST PUNCHERS I KNOW ARE GIRLS!
These two knuckleheads make it all about them.
EAT GREEN FIST!
YA PUNCH LIKE A VEGETARIAN!
Sure-- they've saved the world.
A bunch of times.
HULK SMASH!
CLOBBERIN' TIME!
Doesn't mean they're always right.
Okay. What I'm about to say isn't so much the rules of physics as it is common sense...

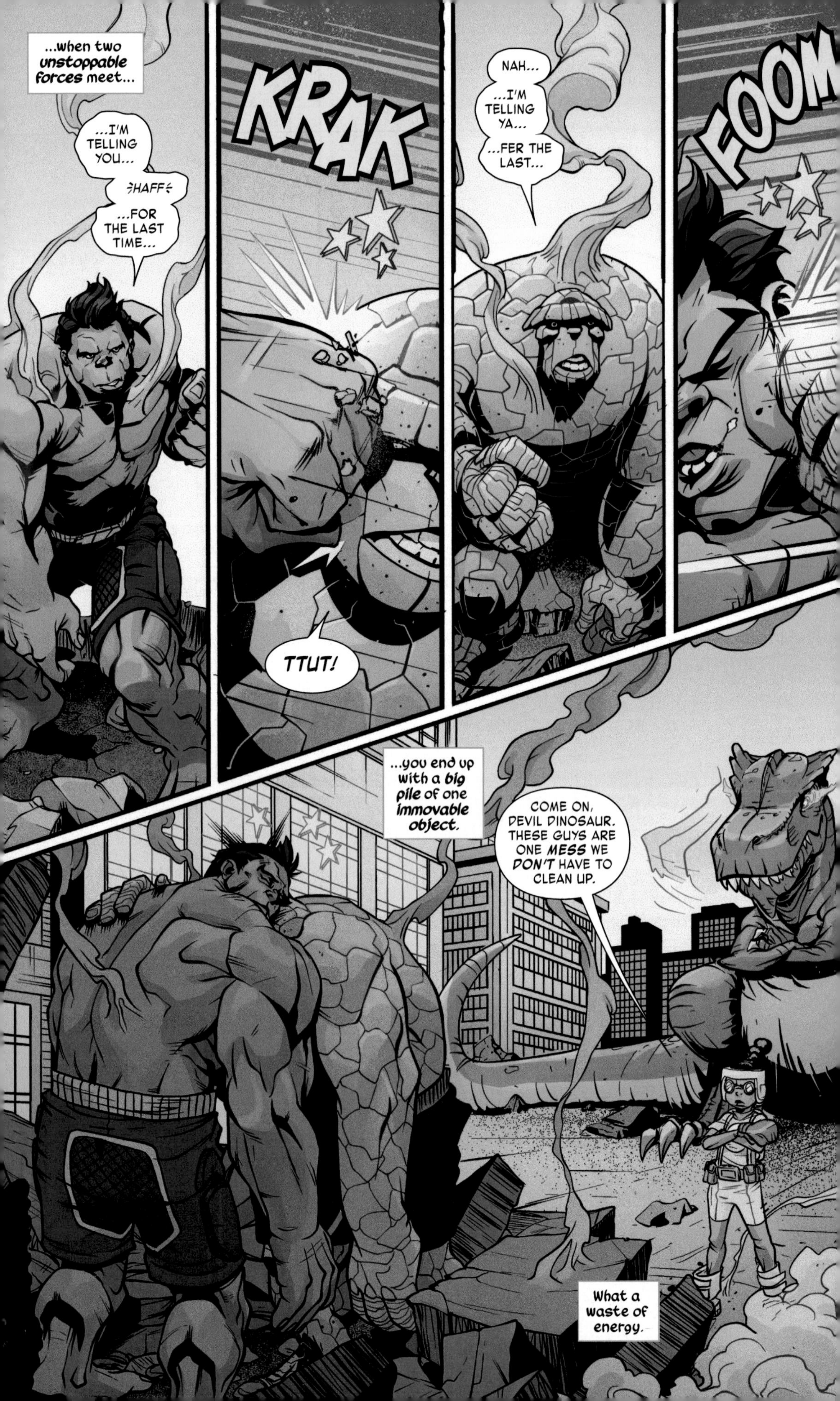

...when two unstoppable forces meet...
...I'M TELLING YOU...
HAFF
...FOR THE LAST TIME...
KRAK
TTUT!
NAH...
...I'M TELLING YA...
...FER THE LAST...
FOOM
...you end up with a big pile of one immovable object.
COME ON, DEVIL DINOSAUR. THESE GUYS ARE ONE MESS WE DON'T HAVE TO CLEAN UP.
What a waste of energy.

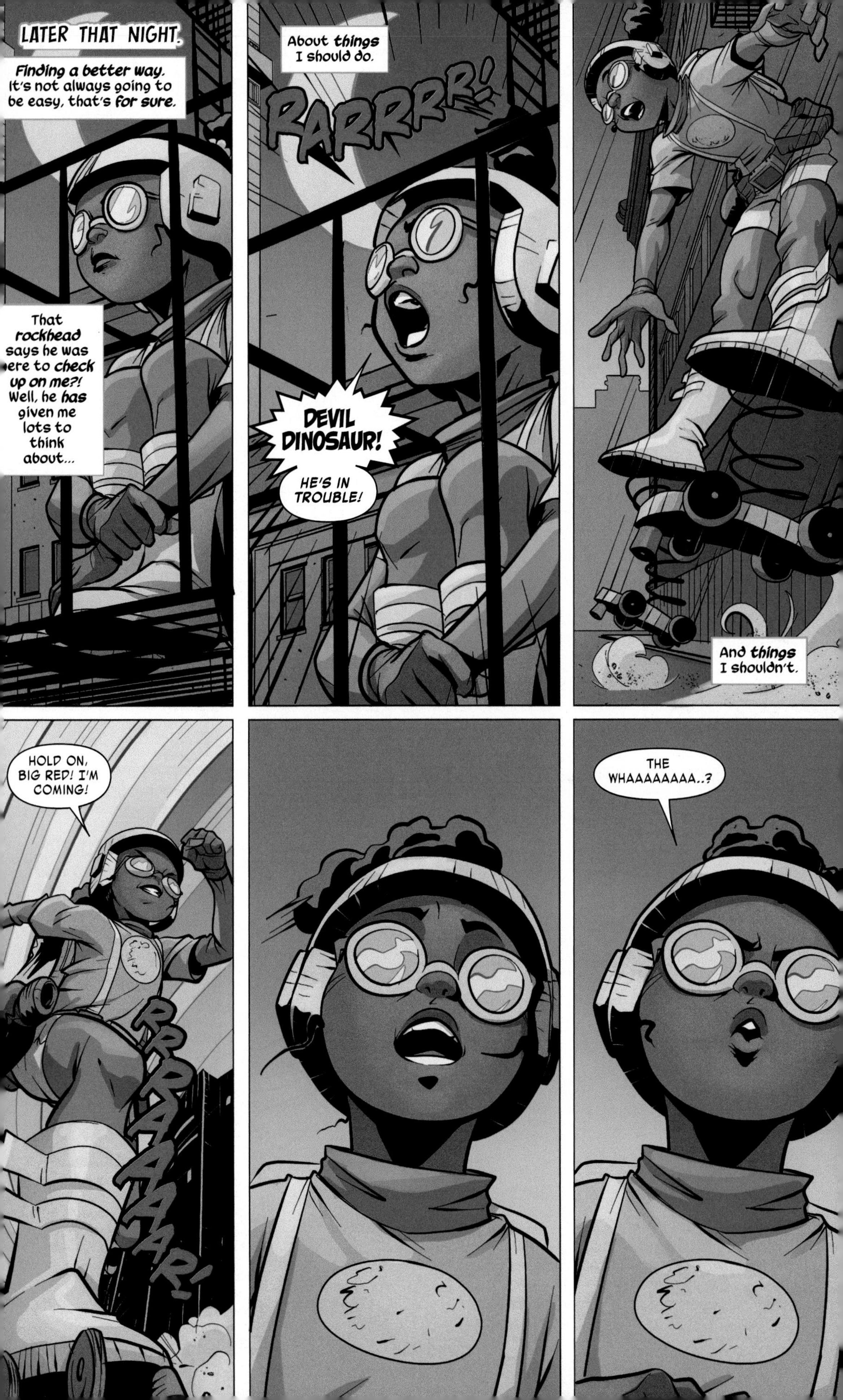
LATER THAT NIGHT.
Finding a better way. It's not always going to be easy, that's for sure.
That rockhead says he was ere to check up on me?! Well, he has given me lots to think about...
About things I should do.
RARRRR!
DEVIL DINOSAUR!
HE'S IN TROUBLE!
And things I shouldn't.
HOLD ON, BIG RED! I'M COMING!
RRRAAAAAR!
THE WHAAAAAAAA..?

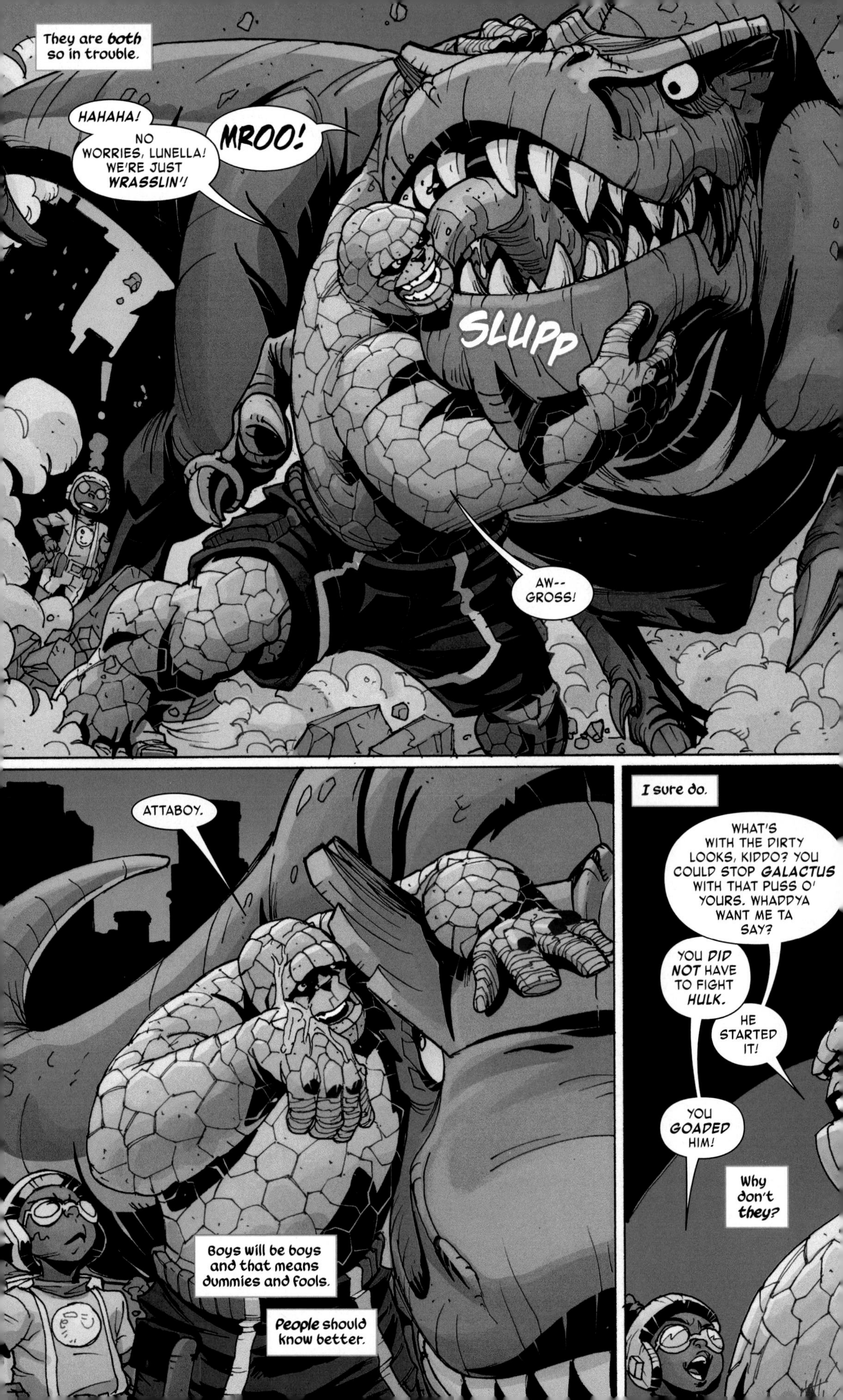
They are both so in trouble.
HAHAHA!
NO WORRIES, LUNELLA! WE'RE JUST WRASSLIN'!
MROO!
SLUPP
AW-- GROSS!
ATTABOY.
Boys will be boys and that means dummies and fools.
People should know better.
I sure do.
WHAT'S WITH THE DIRTY LOOKS, KIDDO? YOU COULD STOP GALACTUS WITH THAT PUSS O' YOURS. WHADDYA WANT ME TA SAY?
YOU DID NOT HAVE TO FIGHT HULK.
HE STARTED IT!
YOU GOADED HIM!
Why don't they?

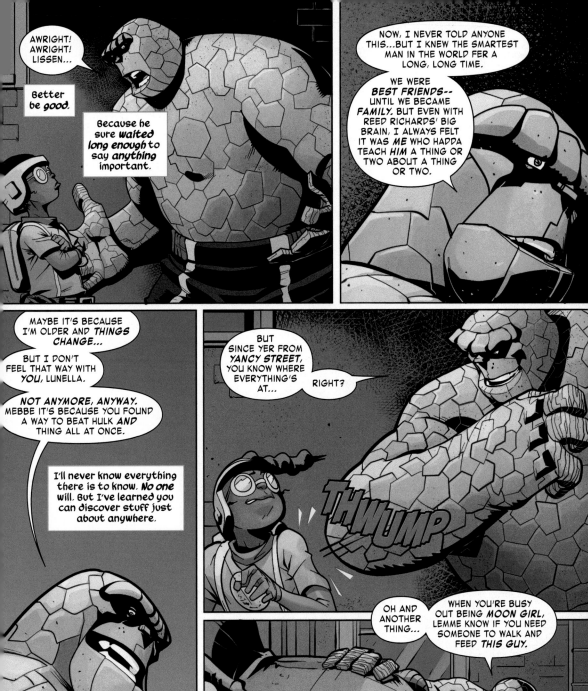

AWRIGHT! AWRIGHT! LISSEN...

Better be *good*.

Because he sure *waited long enough* to say *anything important*.

NOW, I NEVER TOLD ANYONE THIS...BUT I KNEW THE SMARTEST MAN IN THE WORLD FER A LONG, LONG TIME.

WE WERE *BEST FRIENDS*-- UNTIL WE BECAME *FAMILY*. BUT EVEN WITH REED RICHARDS' BIG BRAIN, I ALWAYS FELT IT WAS *ME* WHO HADDA TEACH *HIM* A THING OR TWO ABOUT A THING OR TWO.

MAYBE IT'S BECAUSE I'M OLDER AND *THINGS CHANGE*...

BUT I DON'T FEEL THAT WAY WITH *YOU*, LUNELLA.

NOT ANYMORE, ANYWAY. MEBBE IT'S BECAUSE YOU FOUND A WAY TO BEAT HULK *AND* THING ALL AT ONCE.

I'll never know everything there is to know. *No one* will. But I've learned you can discover stuff just about anywhere.

BUT SINCE YER FROM *YANCY STREET*, YOU KNOW WHERE EVERYTHING'S AT...

RIGHT?

THWUMP

OH AND ANOTHER THING...

WHEN YOU'RE BUSY OUT BEING *MOON GIRL*, LEMME KNOW IF YOU NEED SOMEONE TO WALK AND FEED *THIS GUY*.

I guess I'm going to find out what it *feels* like...

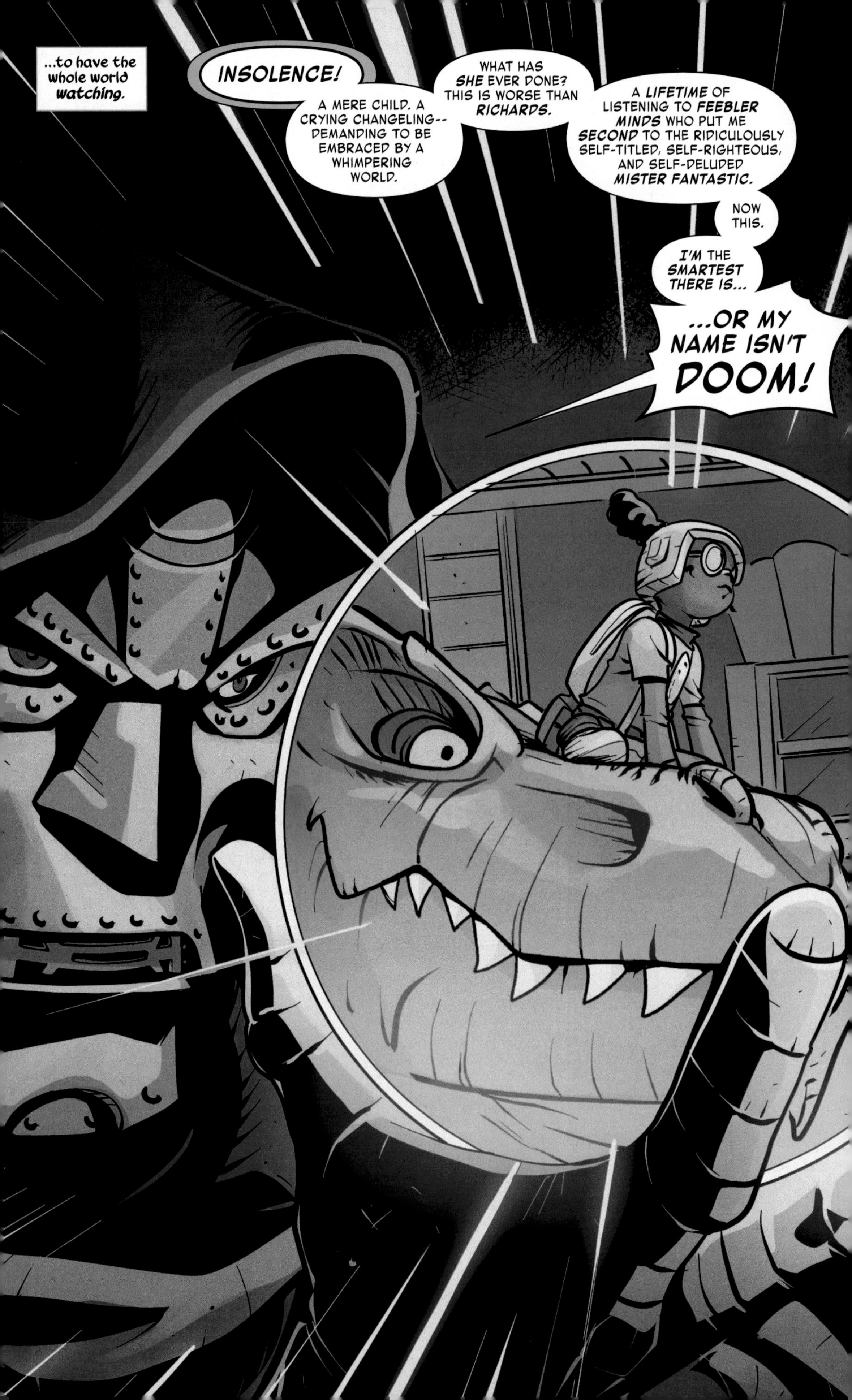
...to have the whole world watching.
INSOLENCE!
A MERE CHILD. A CRYING CHANGELING-- DEMANDING TO BE EMBRACED BY A WHIMPERING WORLD.
WHAT HAS SHE EVER DONE? THIS IS WORSE THAN RICHARDS.
A LIFETIME OF LISTENING TO FEEBLER MINDS WHO PUT ME SECOND TO THE RIDICULOUSLY SELF-TITLED, SELF-RIGHTEOUS, AND SELF-DELUDED MISTER FANTASTIC.
NOW THIS.
I'M THE SMARTEST THERE IS...
...OR MY NAME ISN'T DOOM!

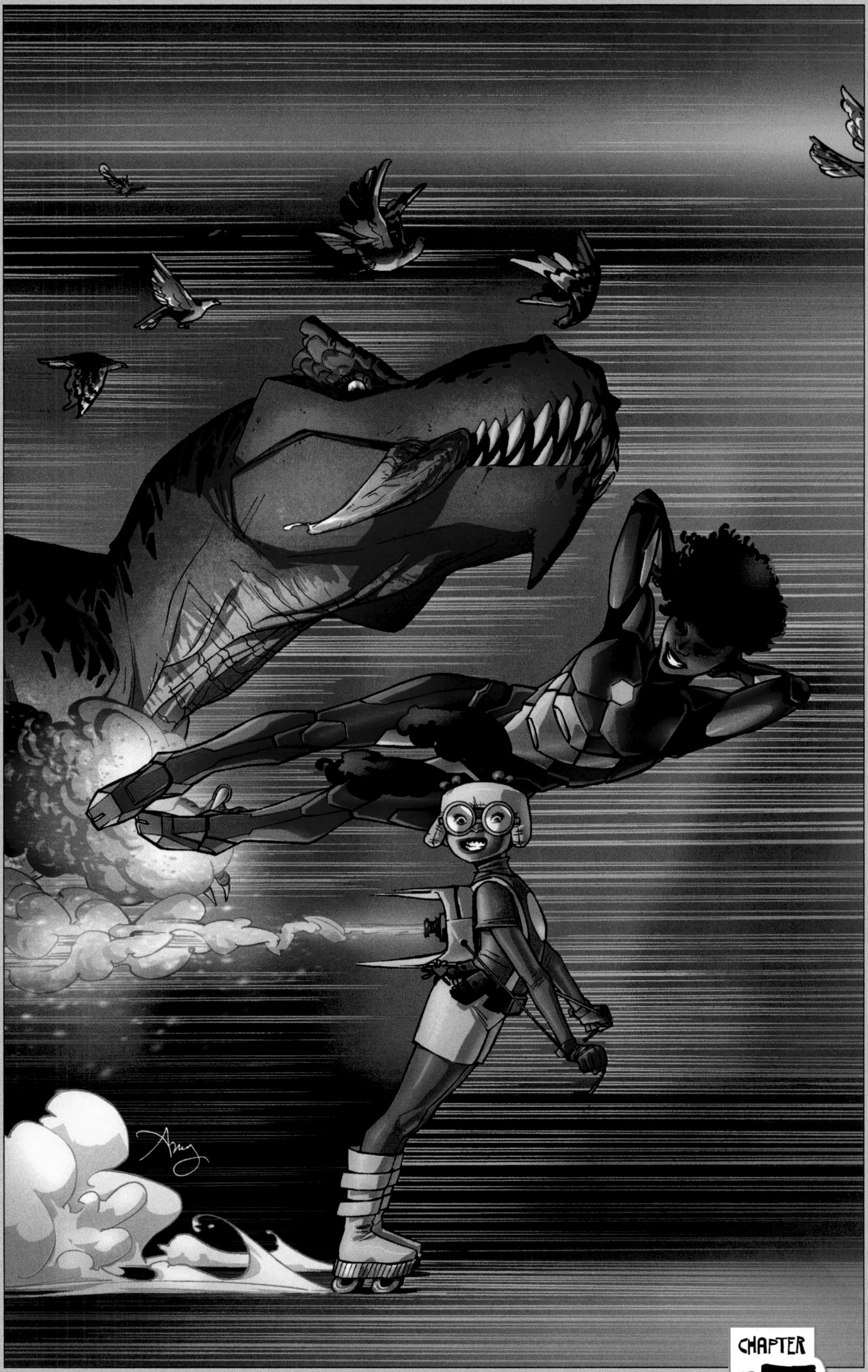

CHAPTER

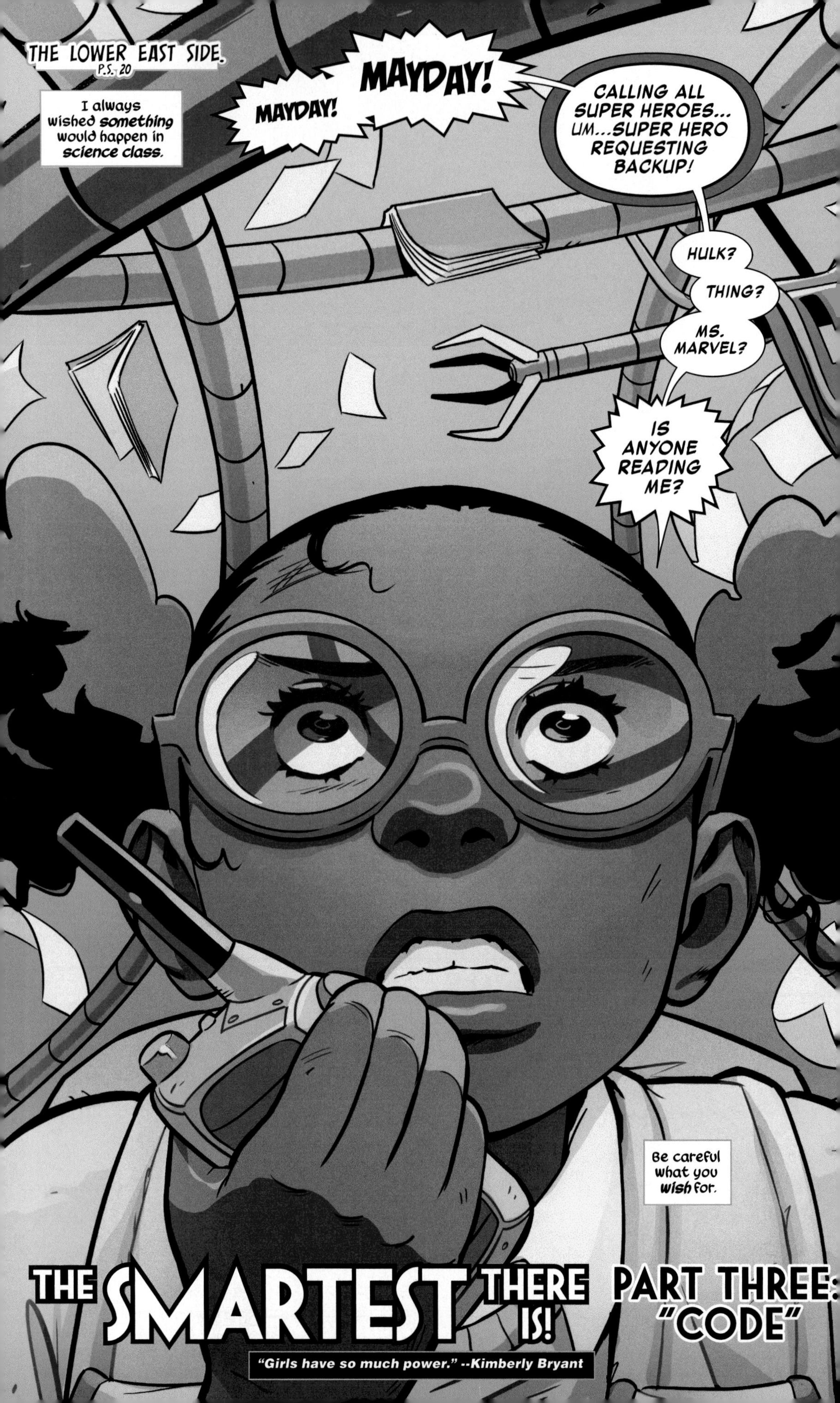

THE LOWER EAST SIDE.
P.S. 20
I always wished something would happen in science class.
MAYDAY!
MAYDAY!
CALLING ALL SUPER HEROES... UM...SUPER HERO REQUESTING BACKUP!
HULK?
THING?
MS. MARVEL?
IS ANYONE READING ME?
Be careful what you wish for.
THE SMARTEST THERE IS!
PART THREE: "CODE"
"Girls have so much power." --Kimberly Bryant

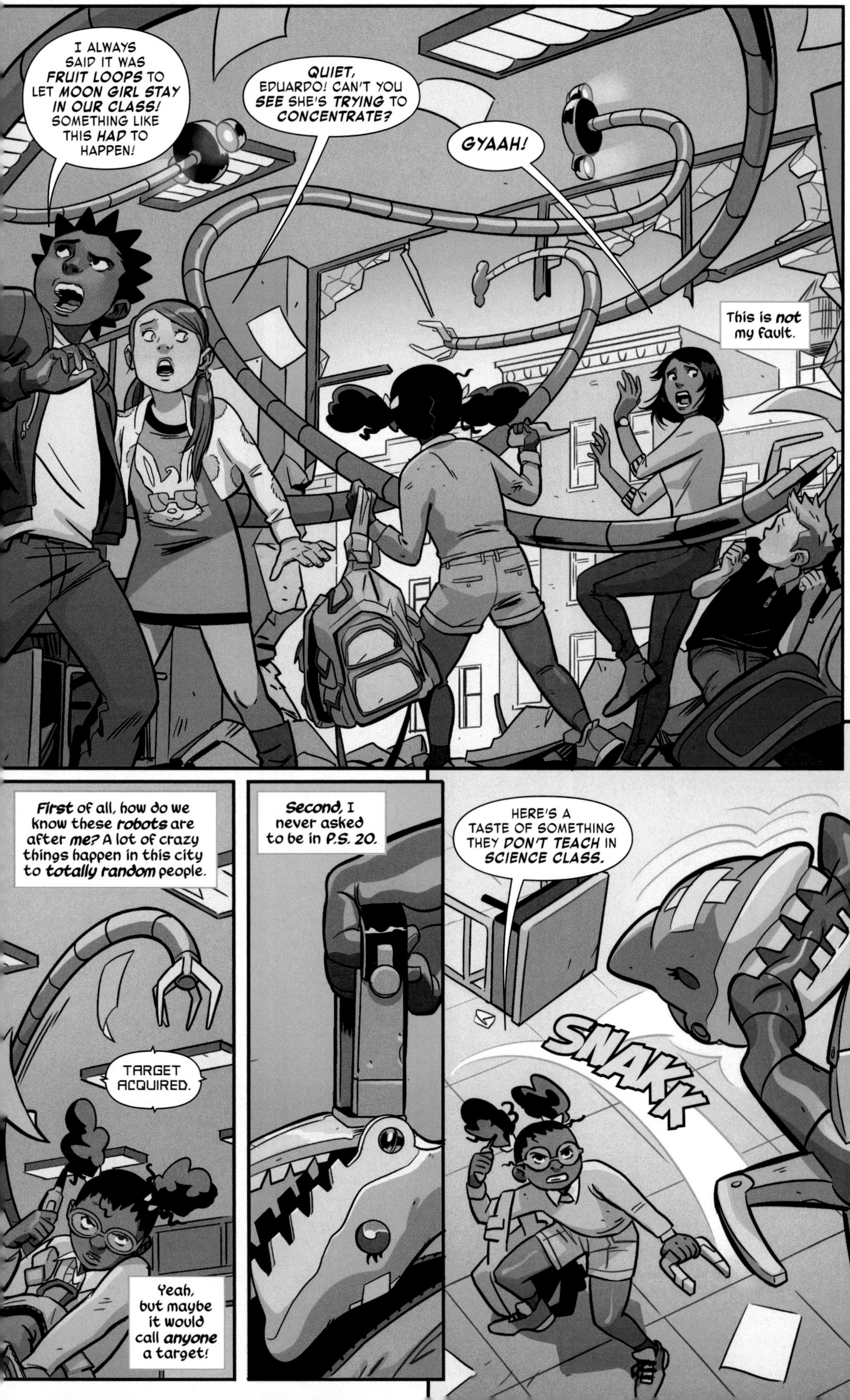
I ALWAYS SAID IT WAS FRUIT LOOPS TO LET MOON GIRL STAY IN OUR CLASS! SOMETHING LIKE THIS HAD TO HAPPEN!
QUIET, EDUARDO! CAN'T YOU SEE SHE'S TRYING TO CONCENTRATE?
GYAAH!
This is not my fault.
First of all, how do we know these robots are after me? A lot of crazy things happen in this city to totally random people.
TARGET ACQUIRED.
Yeah, but maybe it would call anyone a target!
Second, I never asked to be in P.S. 20.
HERE'S A TASTE OF SOMETHING THEY DON'T TEACH IN SCIENCE CLASS.
SNAKK

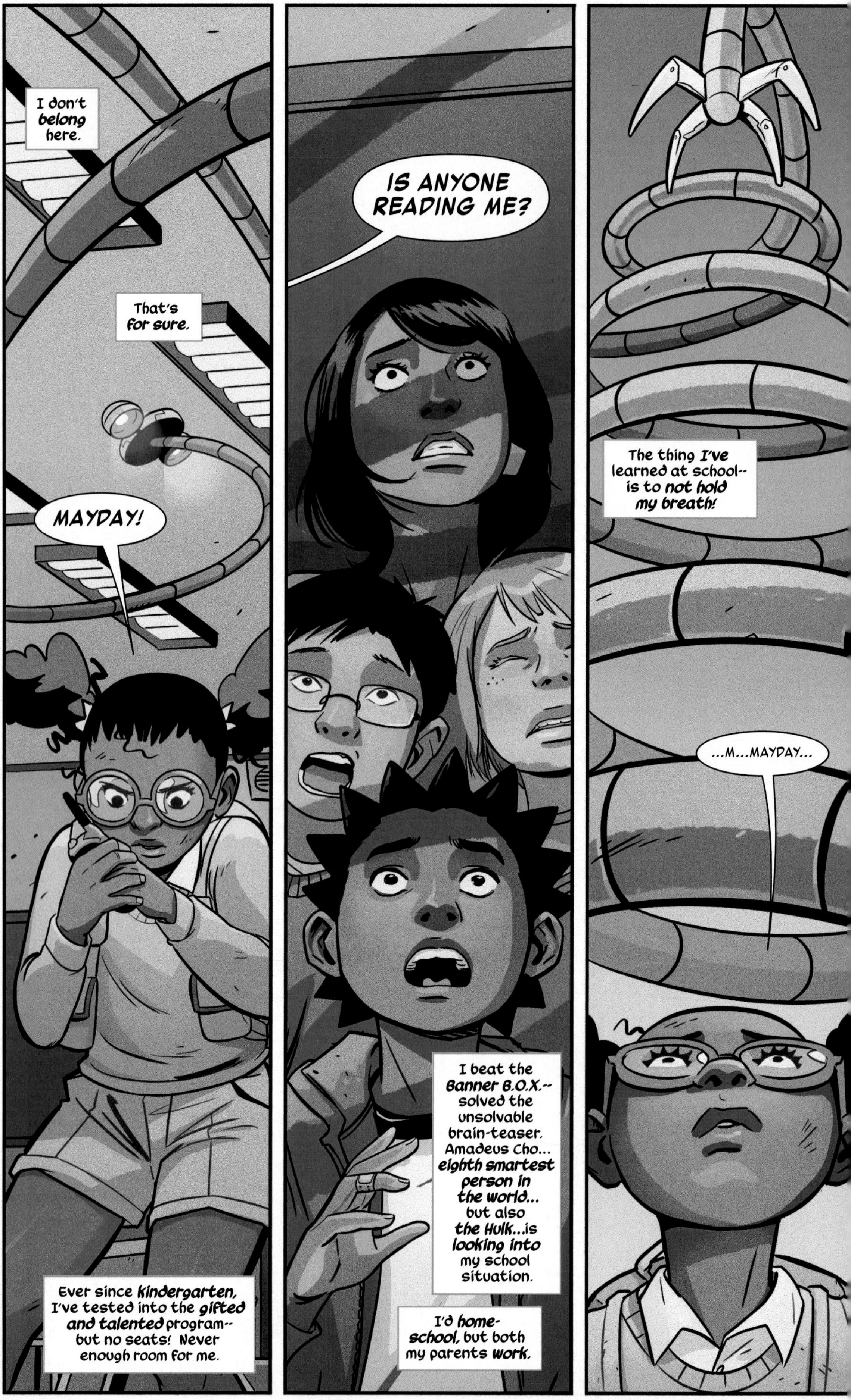
I don't belong here.
That's for sure.
MAYDAY!
Ever since kindergarten, I've tested into the gifted and talented program--but no seats! Never enough room for me.
IS ANYONE READING ME?
I beat the Banner B.O.X.--solved the unsolvable brain-teaser. Amadeus Cho... eighth smartest person in the world... but also the Hulk...is looking into my school situation.
I'd home-school, but both my parents work.
The thing I've learned at school--is to not hold my breath!
...M...MAYDAY...

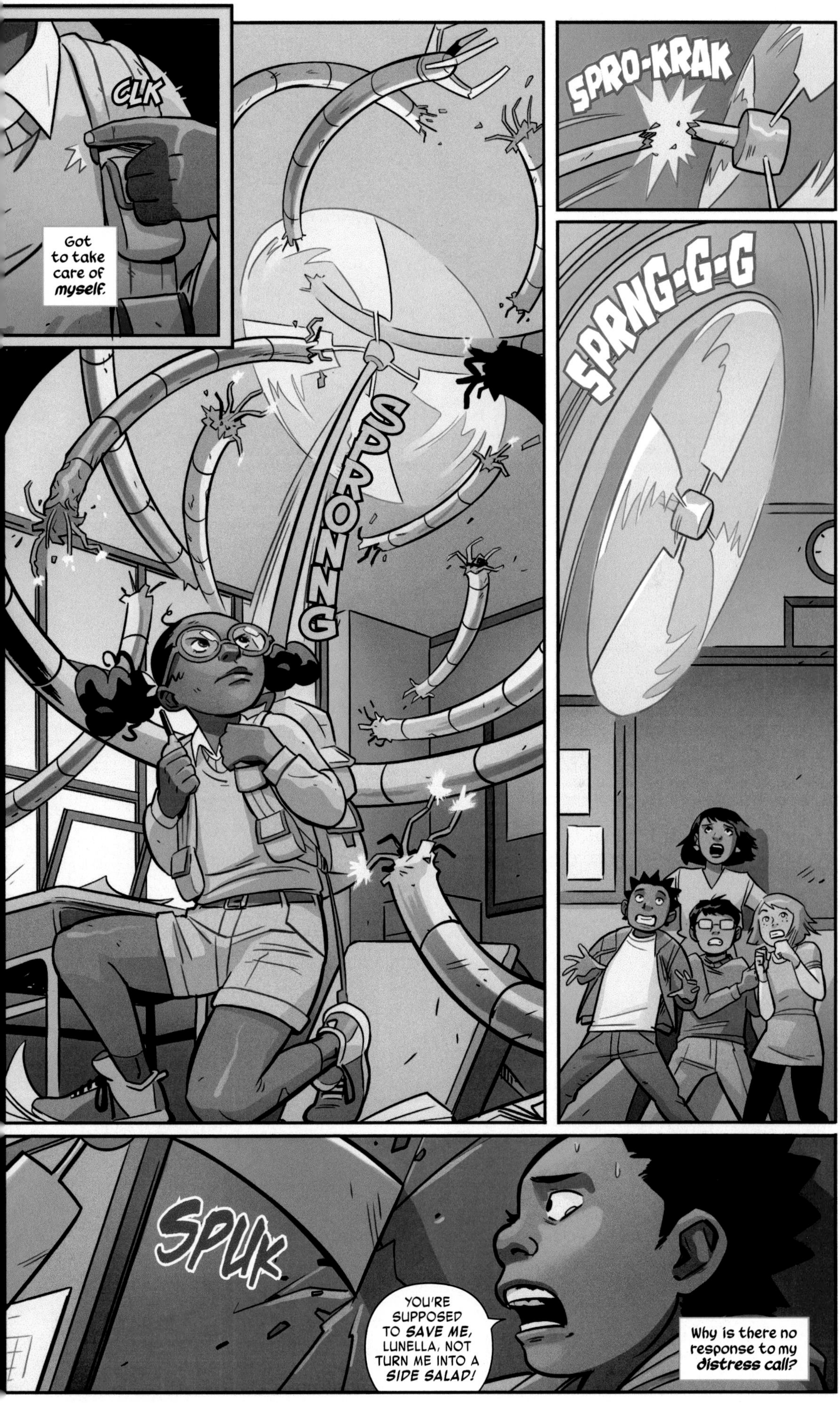
CLK
Got to take care of *myself*.
SPRONNG
SPRO-KRAK
SPRNG-G-G
SPUK
YOU'RE SUPPOSED TO *SAVE ME*, LUNELLA, NOT TURN ME INTO A *SIDE SALAD*!
Why is there no response to my *distress call?*

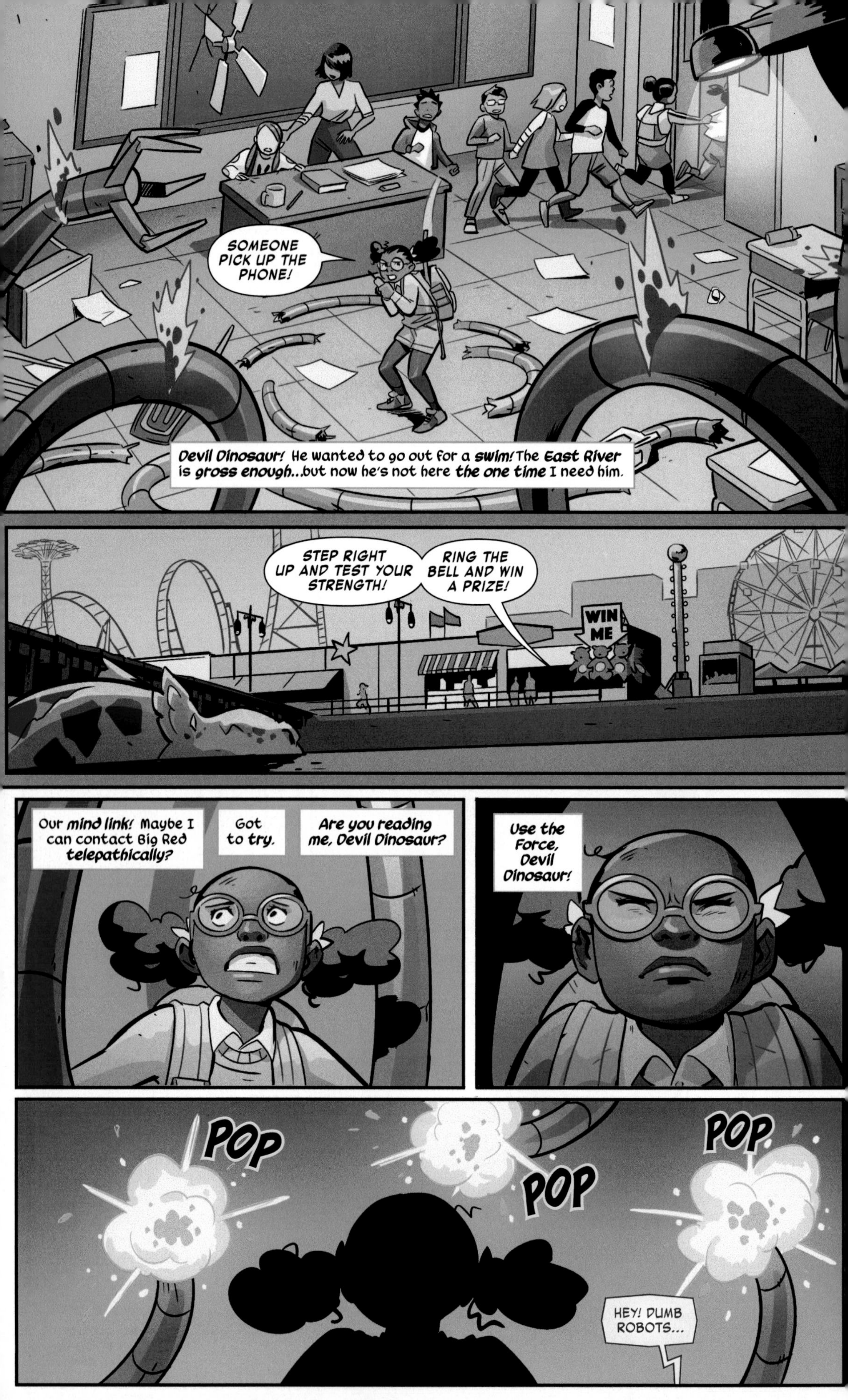

SOMEONE PICK UP THE PHONE!
Devil Dinosaur! He wanted to go out for a swim! The East River is gross enough...but now he's not here the one time I need him.
STEP RIGHT UP AND TEST YOUR STRENGTH!
RING THE BELL AND WIN A PRIZE!
WIN ME
Our mind link! Maybe I can contact Big Red telepathically?
Got to try.
Are you reading me, Devil Dinosaur?
Use the Force, Devil Dinosaur!
POP
POP
POP
HEY! DUMB ROBOTS...

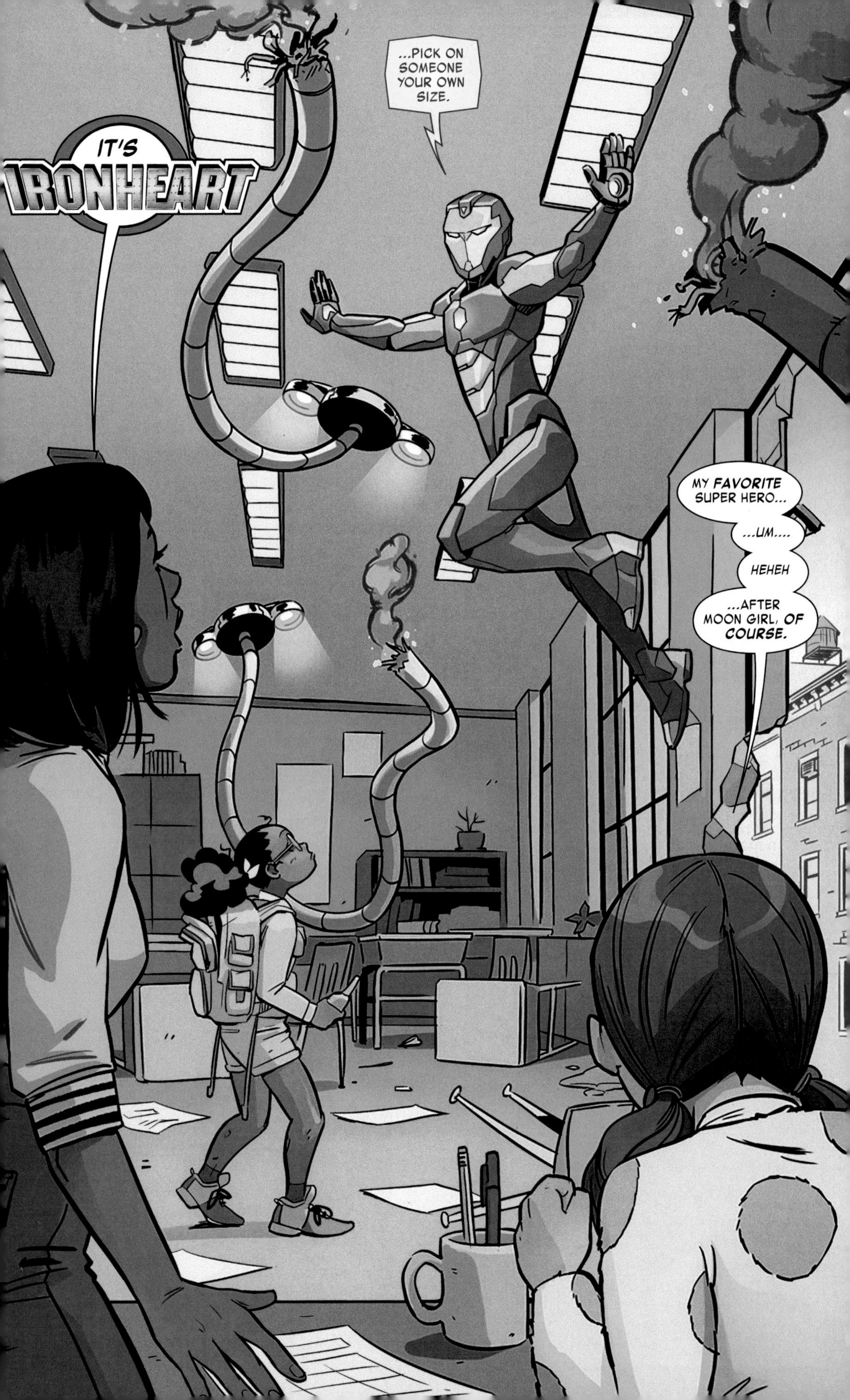
IT'S IRONHEART
...PICK ON SOMEONE YOUR OWN SIZE.
MY FAVORITE SUPER HERO...
...UM....
HEHEH
...AFTER MOON GIRL, OF COURSE.

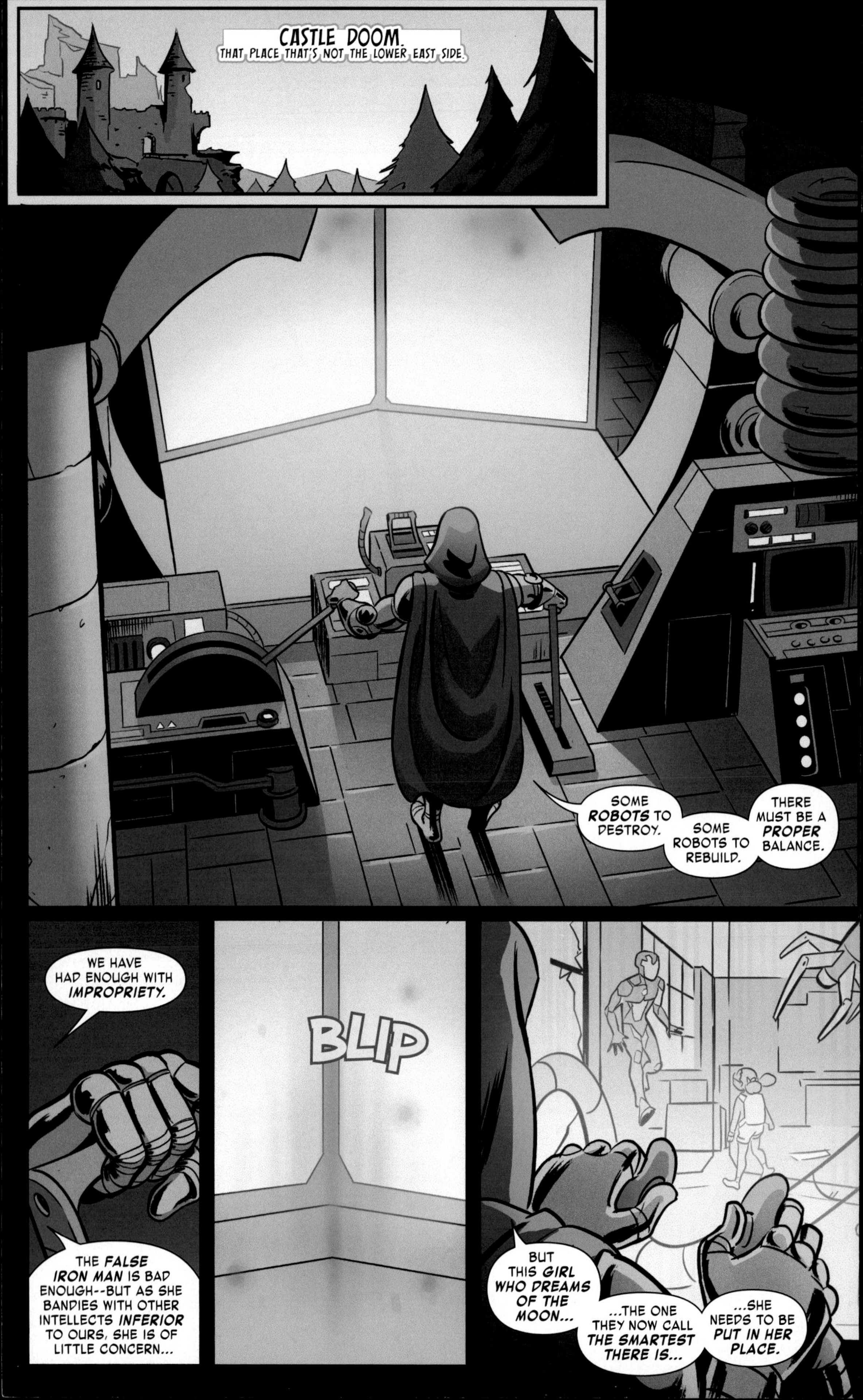
CASTLE DOOM.
THAT PLACE THAT'S NOT THE LOWER EAST SIDE.
SOME ROBOTS TO DESTROY.
SOME ROBOTS TO REBUILD.
THERE MUST BE A PROPER BALANCE.
WE HAVE HAD ENOUGH WITH IMPROPRIETY.
THE FALSE IRON MAN IS BAD ENOUGH--BUT AS SHE BANDIES WITH OTHER INTELLECTS INFERIOR TO OURS, SHE IS OF LITTLE CONCERN...
BLIP
BUT THIS GIRL WHO DREAMS OF THE MOON...
...THE ONE THEY NOW CALL THE SMARTEST THERE IS...
...SHE NEEDS TO BE PUT IN HER PLACE.

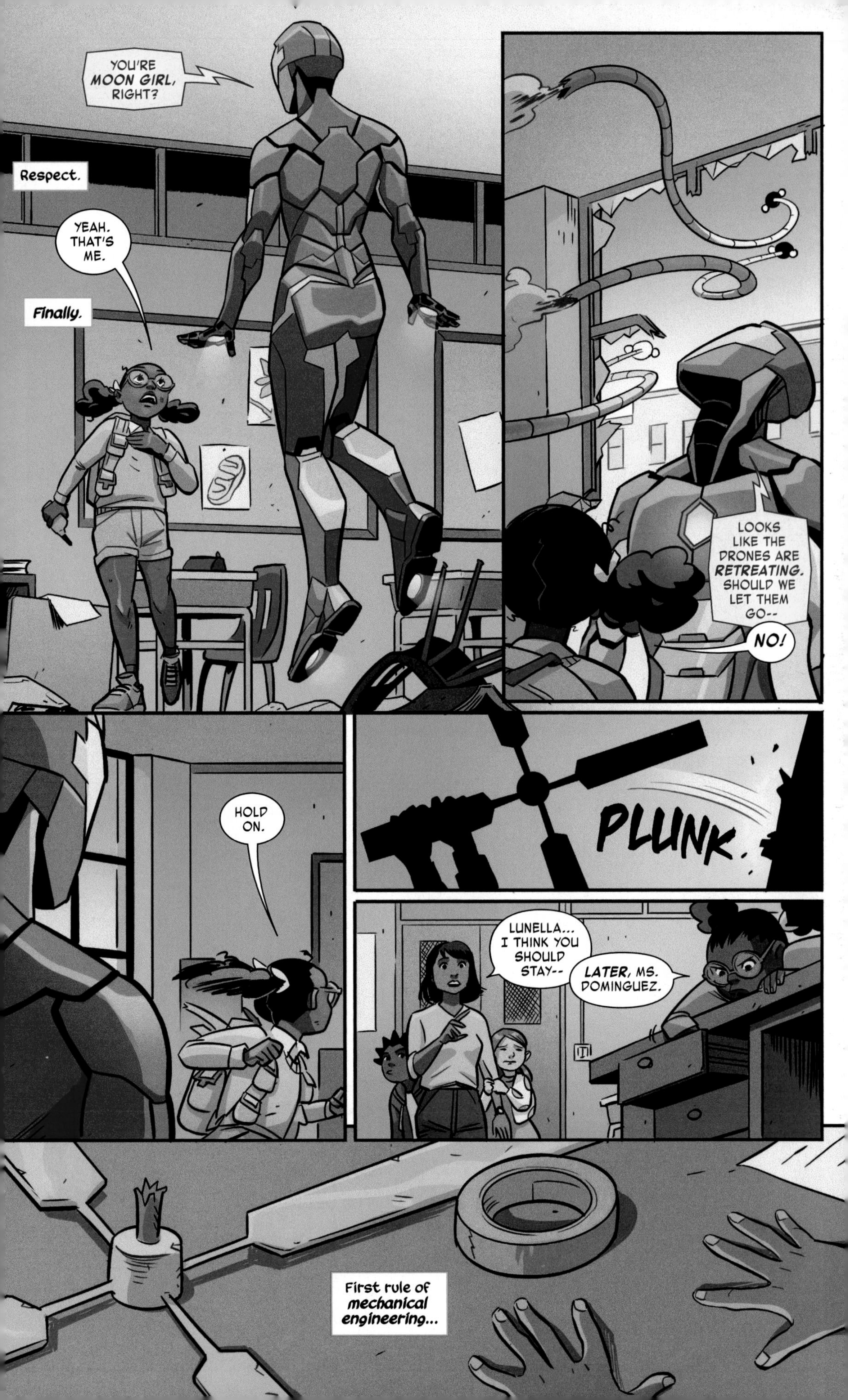

YOU'RE MOON GIRL, RIGHT?
Respect.
YEAH. THAT'S ME.
Finally.
LOOKS LIKE THE DRONES ARE RETREATING. SHOULD WE LET THEM GO--
NO!
HOLD ON.
PLUNK.
LUNELLA... I THINK YOU SHOULD STAY--
LATER, MS. DOMINGUEZ.
First rule of mechanical engineering...

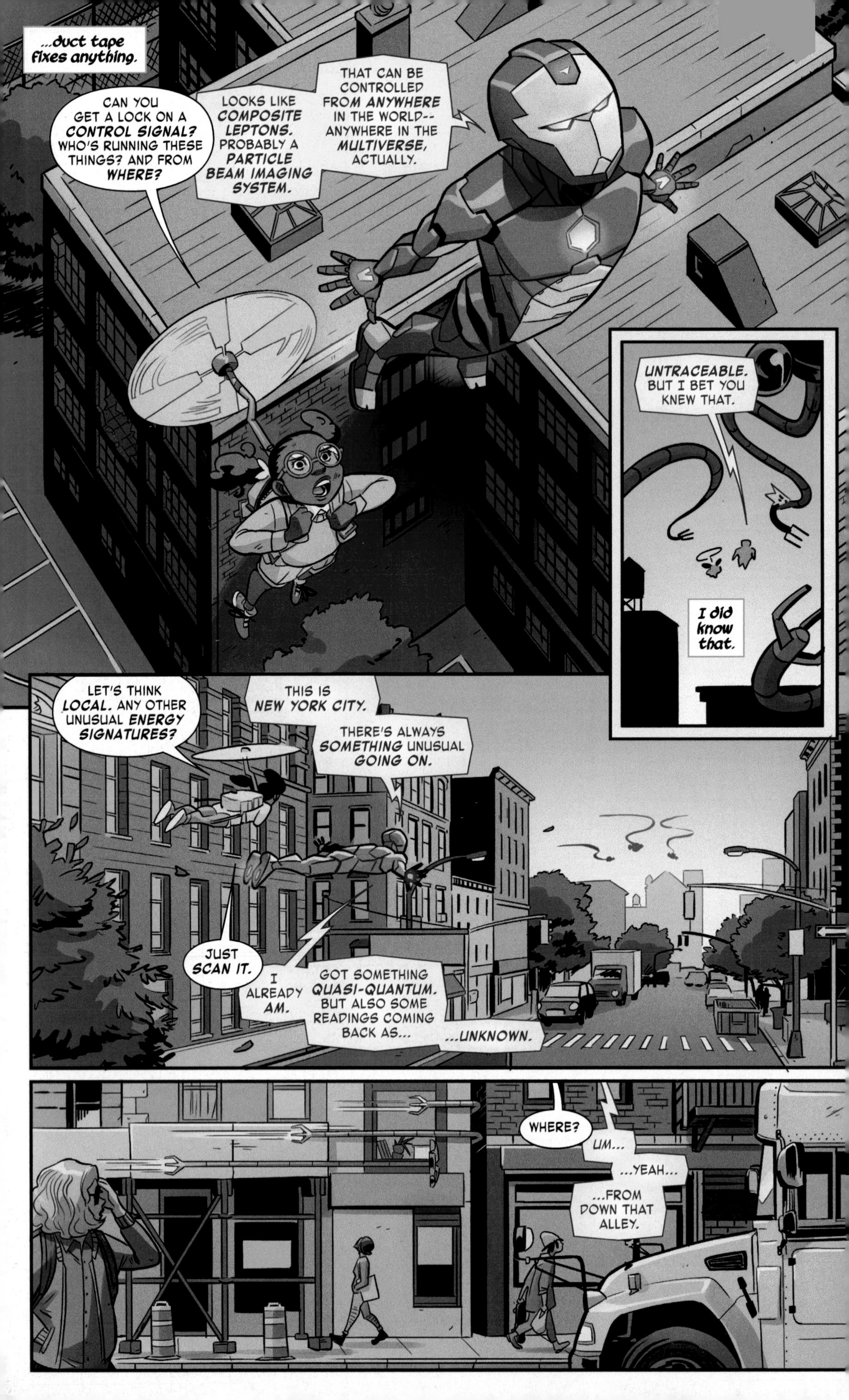
...duct tape fixes anything.
CAN YOU GET A LOCK ON A CONTROL SIGNAL? WHO'S RUNNING THESE THINGS? AND FROM WHERE?
LOOKS LIKE COMPOSITE LEPTONS. PROBABLY A PARTICLE BEAM IMAGING SYSTEM.
THAT CAN BE CONTROLLED FROM ANYWHERE IN THE WORLD-- ANYWHERE IN THE MULTIVERSE, ACTUALLY.
UNTRACEABLE. BUT I BET YOU KNEW THAT.
I did know that.
LET'S THINK LOCAL. ANY OTHER UNUSUAL ENERGY SIGNATURES?
THIS IS NEW YORK CITY.
THERE'S ALWAYS SOMETHING UNUSUAL GOING ON.
JUST SCAN IT.
I ALREADY AM.
GOT SOMETHING QUASI-QUANTUM. BUT ALSO SOME READINGS COMING BACK AS...
...UNKNOWN.
WHERE?
UM...
...YEAH...
...FROM DOWN THAT ALLEY.

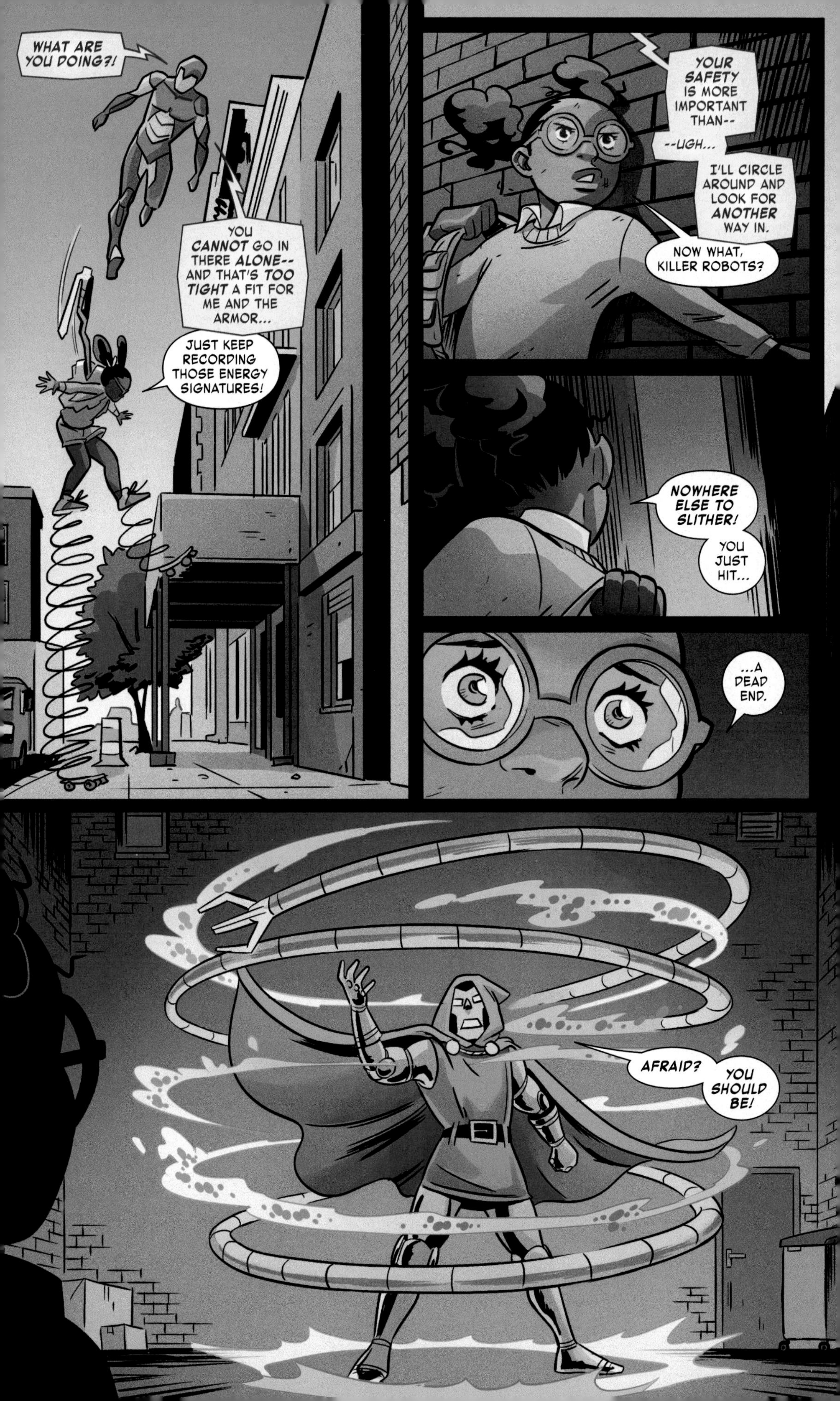
WHAT ARE YOU DOING?!
YOU CANNOT GO IN THERE ALONE-- AND THAT'S TOO TIGHT A FIT FOR ME AND THE ARMOR...
JUST KEEP RECORDING THOSE ENERGY SIGNATURES!
YOUR SAFETY IS MORE IMPORTANT THAN--
--UGH...
I'LL CIRCLE AROUND AND LOOK FOR ANOTHER WAY IN.
NOW WHAT, KILLER ROBOTS?
NOWHERE ELSE TO SLITHER!
YOU JUST HIT...
...A DEAD END.
AFRAID?
YOU SHOULD BE!

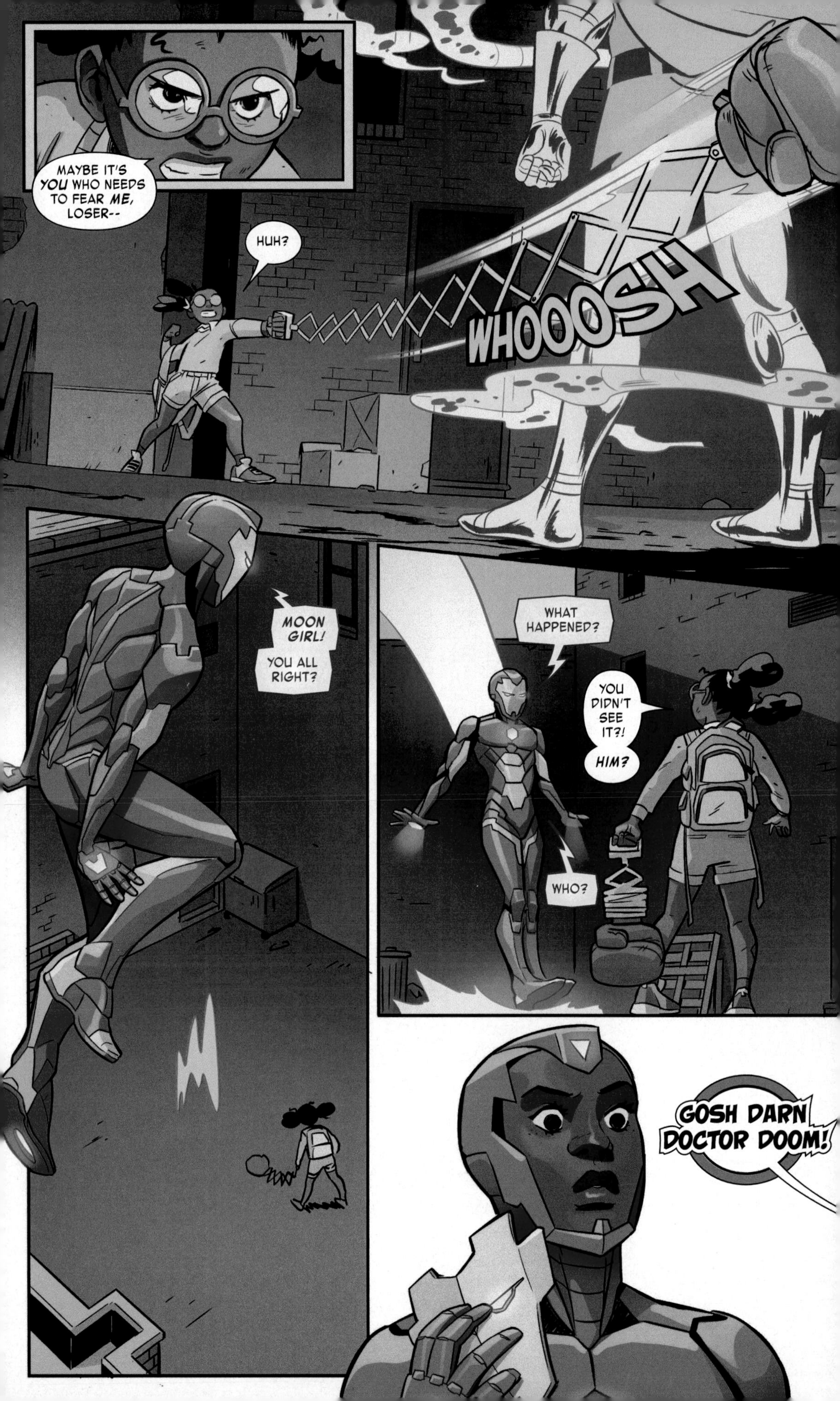

MAYBE IT'S YOU WHO NEEDS TO FEAR ME, LOSER--
HUH?
WHOOOSH
MOON GIRL!
YOU ALL RIGHT?
WHAT HAPPENED?
YOU DIDN'T SEE IT?!
HIM?
WHO?
GOSH DARN DOCTOR DOOM!

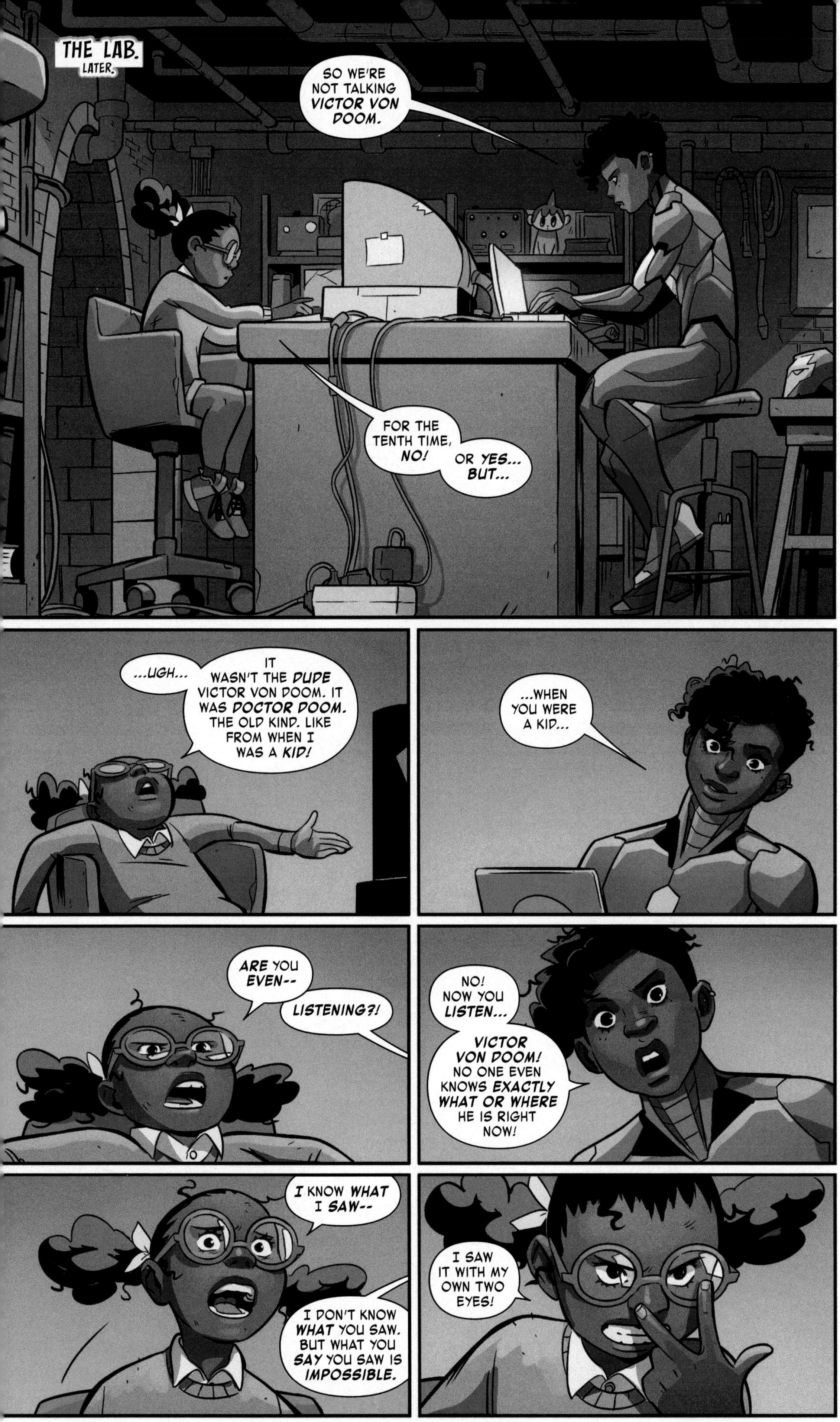
THE LAB. LATER.
SO WE'RE NOT TALKING VICTOR VON DOOM.
FOR THE TENTH TIME, NO!
OR YES... BUT...
...UGH...
IT WASN'T THE DUDE VICTOR VON DOOM. IT WAS DOCTOR DOOM. THE OLD KIND. LIKE FROM WHEN I WAS A KID!
...WHEN YOU WERE A KID...
ARE YOU EVEN--
LISTENING?!
NO! NOW YOU LISTEN...
VICTOR VON DOOM! NO ONE EVEN KNOWS EXACTLY WHAT OR WHERE HE IS RIGHT NOW!
I KNOW WHAT I SAW--
I DON'T KNOW WHAT YOU SAW. BUT WHAT YOU SAY YOU SAW IS IMPOSSIBLE.
I SAW IT WITH MY OWN TWO EYES!

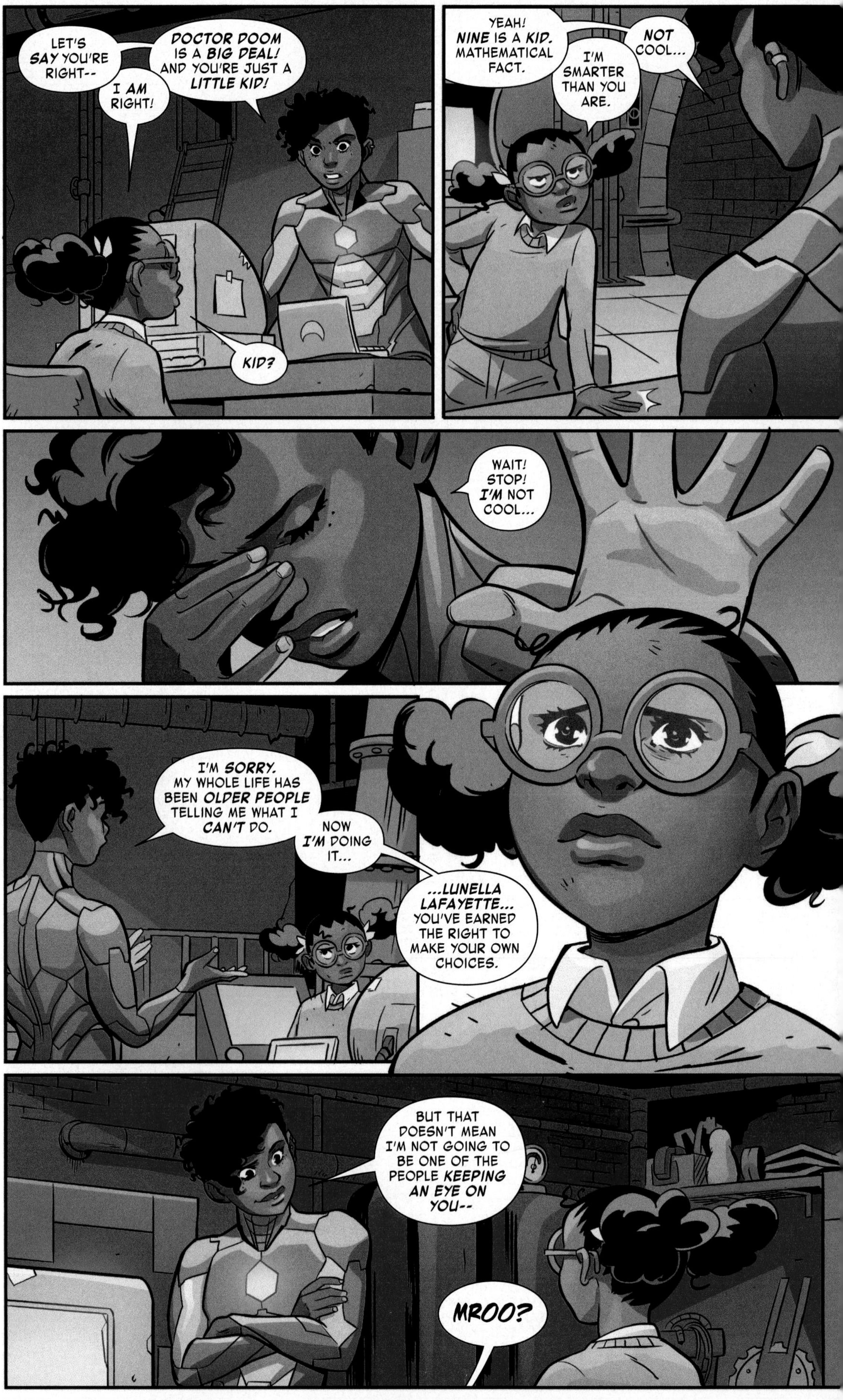
LET'S SAY YOU'RE RIGHT--
I AM RIGHT!
DOCTOR DOOM IS A BIG DEAL! AND YOU'RE JUST A LITTLE KID!
KID?
YEAH! NINE IS A KID. MATHEMATICAL FACT.
I'M SMARTER THAN YOU ARE.
NOT COOL...
WAIT! STOP! I'M NOT COOL...
I'M SORRY. MY WHOLE LIFE HAS BEEN OLDER PEOPLE TELLING ME WHAT I CAN'T DO.
NOW I'M DOING IT...
...LUNELLA LAFAYETTE... YOU'VE EARNED THE RIGHT TO MAKE YOUR OWN CHOICES.
BUT THAT DOESN'T MEAN I'M NOT GOING TO BE ONE OF THE PEOPLE KEEPING AN EYE ON YOU--
MROO?

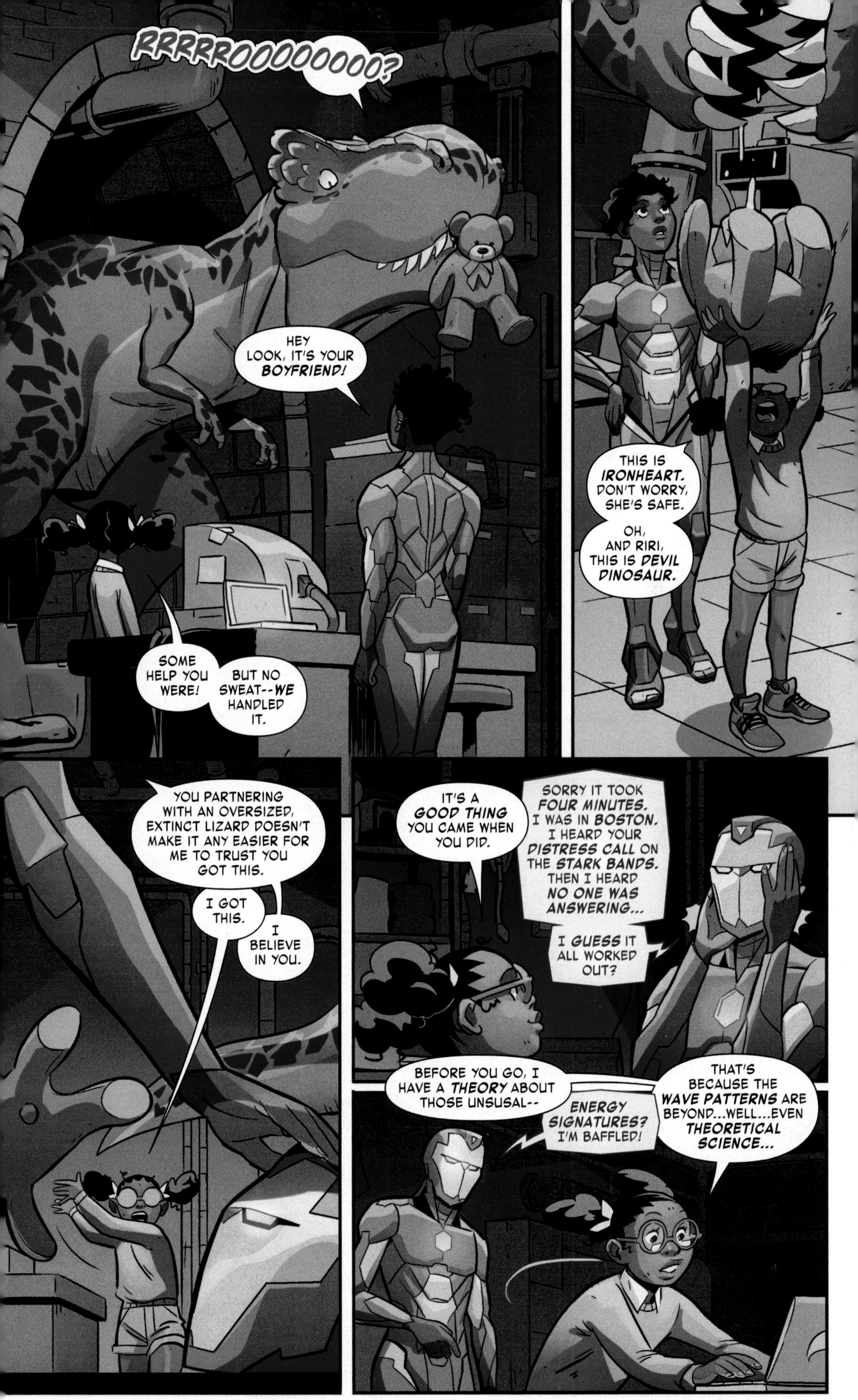
RRRRROOOOOOOO?
HEY LOOK, IT'S YOUR BOYFRIEND!
SOME HELP YOU WERE!
BUT NO SWEAT--WE HANDLED IT.
THIS IS IRONHEART. DON'T WORRY, SHE'S SAFE.
OH, AND RIRI, THIS IS DEVIL DINOSAUR.
YOU PARTNERING WITH AN OVERSIZED, EXTINCT LIZARD DOESN'T MAKE IT ANY EASIER FOR ME TO TRUST YOU GOT THIS.
I GOT THIS.
I BELIEVE IN YOU.
IT'S A GOOD THING YOU CAME WHEN YOU DID.
SORRY IT TOOK FOUR MINUTES. I WAS IN BOSTON. I HEARD YOUR DISTRESS CALL ON THE STARK BANDS. THEN I HEARD NO ONE WAS ANSWERING...
I GUESS IT ALL WORKED OUT?
BEFORE YOU GO, I HAVE A THEORY ABOUT THOSE UNUSAL--
ENERGY SIGNATURES? I'M BAFFLED!
THAT'S BECAUSE THE WAVE PATTERNS ARE BEYOND...WELL...EVEN THEORETICAL SCIENCE...

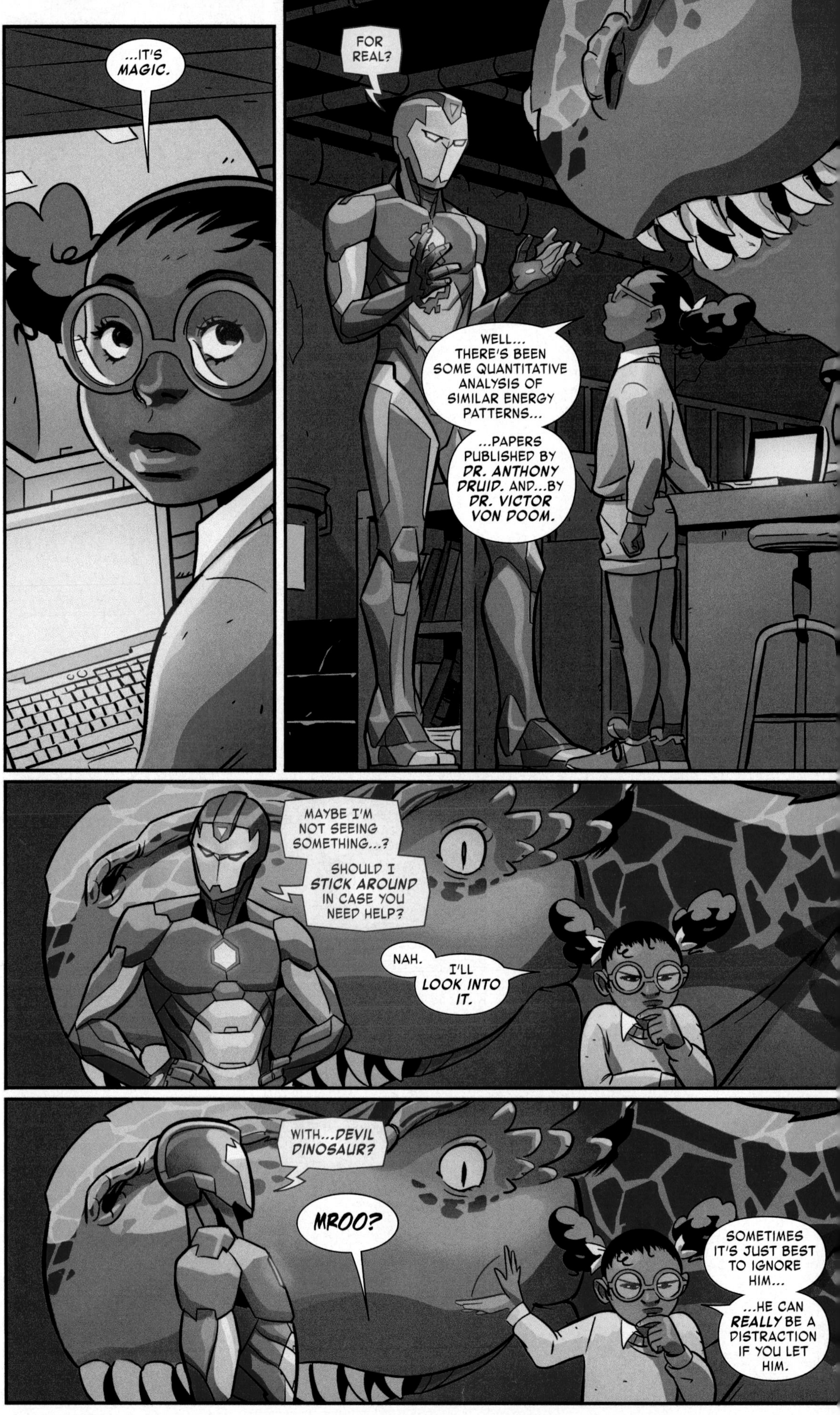

...IT'S MAGIC.
FOR REAL?
WELL... THERE'S BEEN SOME QUANTITATIVE ANALYSIS OF SIMILAR ENERGY PATTERNS...
...PAPERS PUBLISHED BY DR. ANTHONY DRUID. AND...BY DR. VICTOR VON DOOM.
MAYBE I'M NOT SEEING SOMETHING...?
SHOULD I STICK AROUND IN CASE YOU NEED HELP?
NAH.
I'LL LOOK INTO IT.
WITH...DEVIL DINOSAUR?
MROO?
SOMETIMES IT'S JUST BEST TO IGNORE HIM...
...HE CAN REALLY BE A DISTRACTION IF YOU LET HIM.

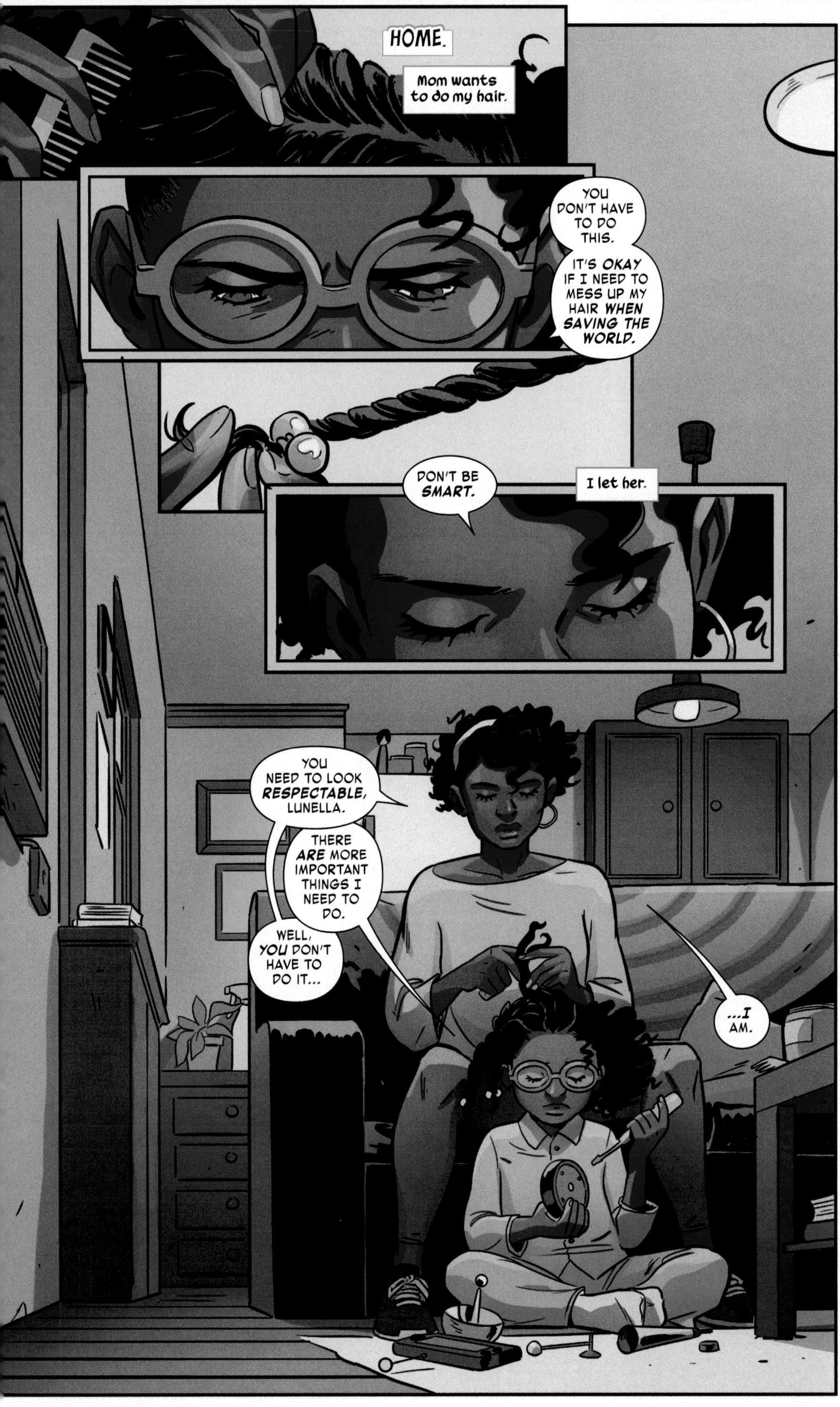
HOME.
Mom wants to do my hair.
YOU DON'T HAVE TO DO THIS.
IT'S OKAY IF I NEED TO MESS UP MY HAIR WHEN SAVING THE WORLD.
DON'T BE SMART.
I let her.
YOU NEED TO LOOK RESPECTABLE, LUNELLA.
THERE ARE MORE IMPORTANT THINGS I NEED TO DO.
WELL, YOU DON'T HAVE TO DO IT...
...I AM.

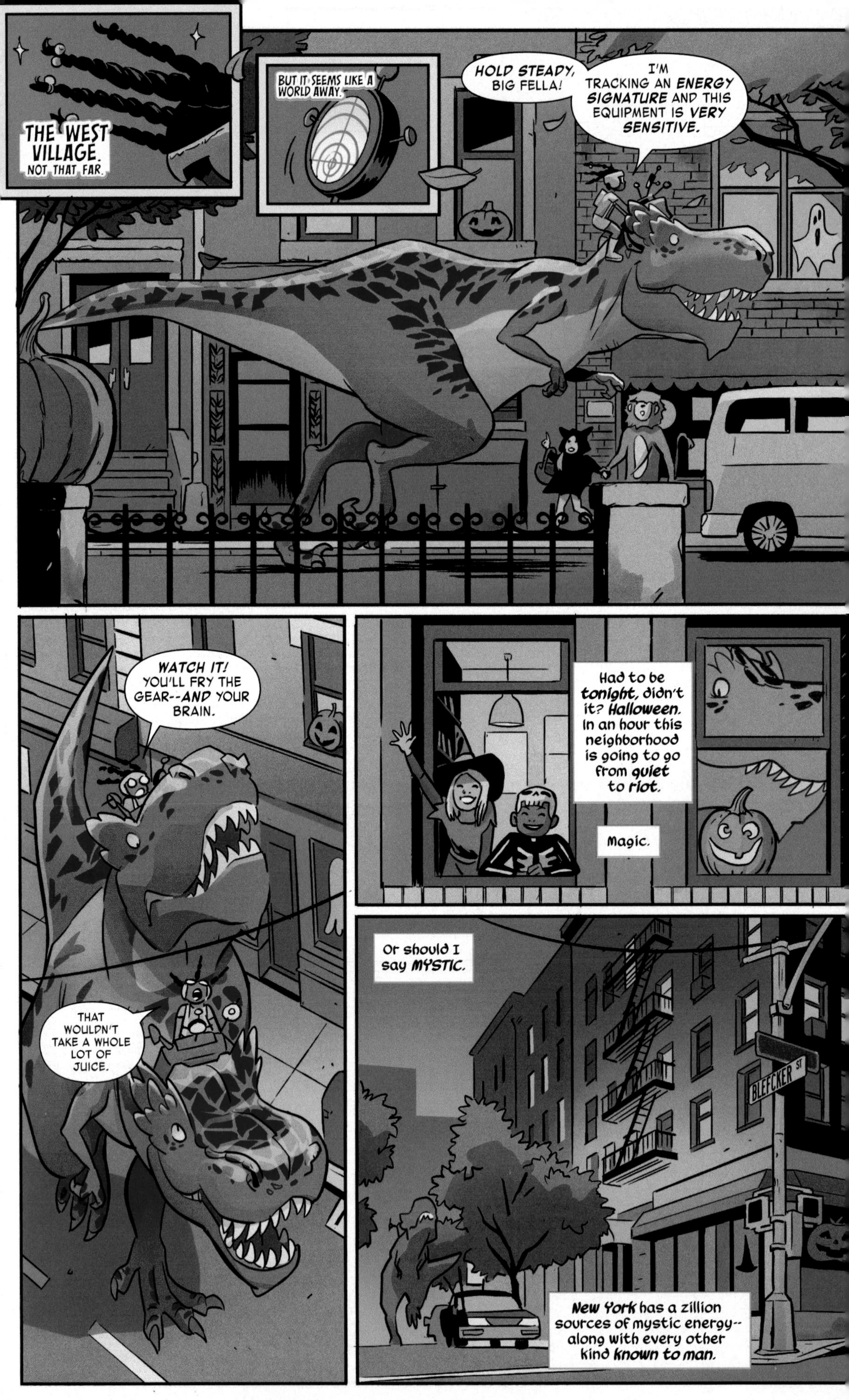
THE WEST VILLAGE. NOT THAT FAR.
BUT IT SEEMS LIKE A WORLD AWAY.
HOLD STEADY, BIG FELLA!
I'M TRACKING AN ENERGY SIGNATURE AND THIS EQUIPMENT IS VERY SENSITIVE.
WATCH IT! YOU'LL FRY THE GEAR--AND YOUR BRAIN.
THAT WOULDN'T TAKE A WHOLE LOT OF JUICE.
Had to be tonight, didn't it? Halloween. In an hour this neighborhood is going to go from quiet to riot.
Magic.
Or should I say MYSTIC.
BLEECKER ST
New York has a zillion sources of mystic energy--along with every other kind known to man.

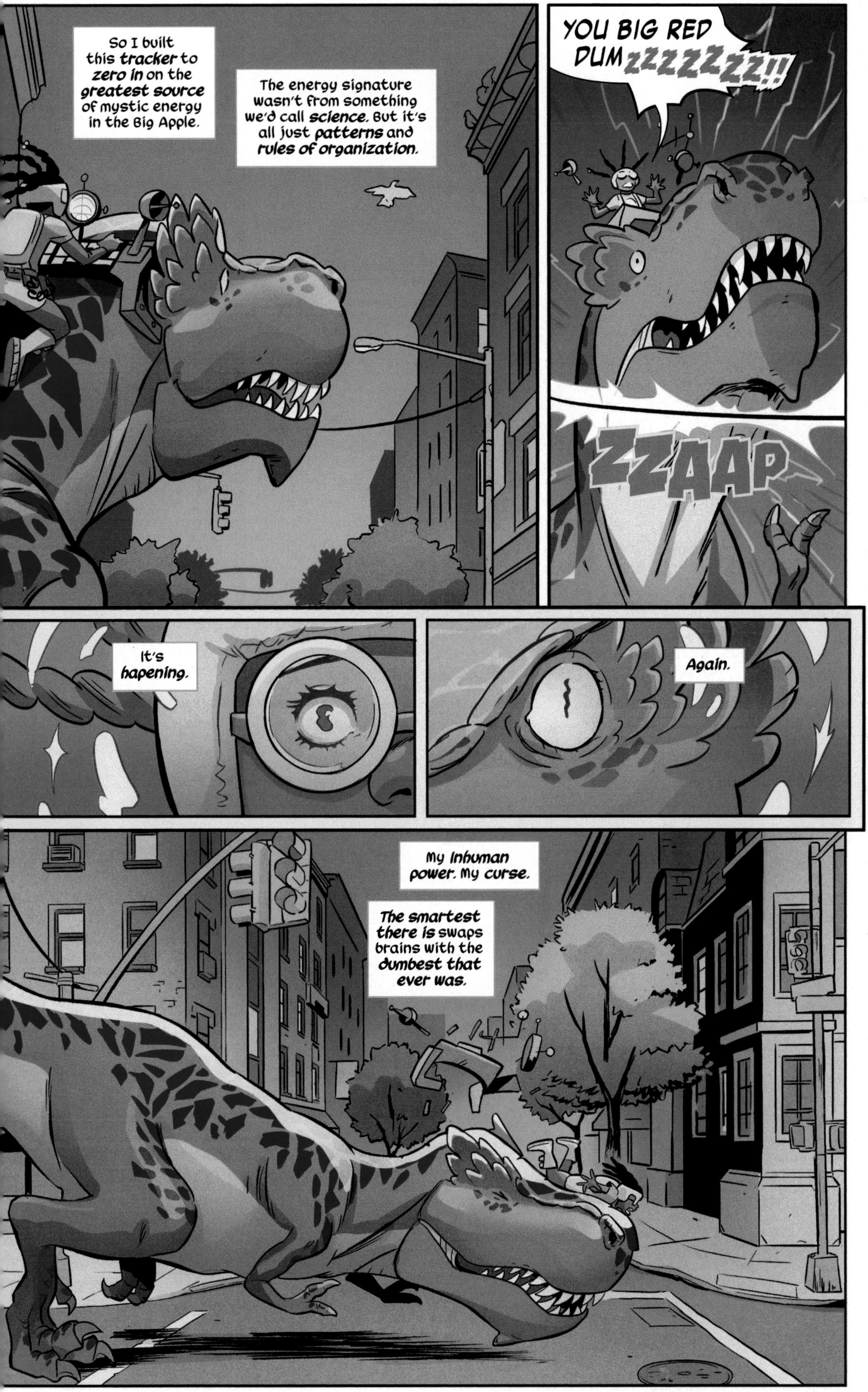
So I built this tracker to zero in on the greatest source of mystic energy in the Big Apple.
The energy signature wasn't from something we'd call science. But it's all just patterns and rules of organization.
YOU BIG RED DUMZZZZZZZ!!
ZZAAP
It's hapening.
Again.
My Inhuman power. My curse.
The smartest there is swaps brains with the dumbest that ever was.

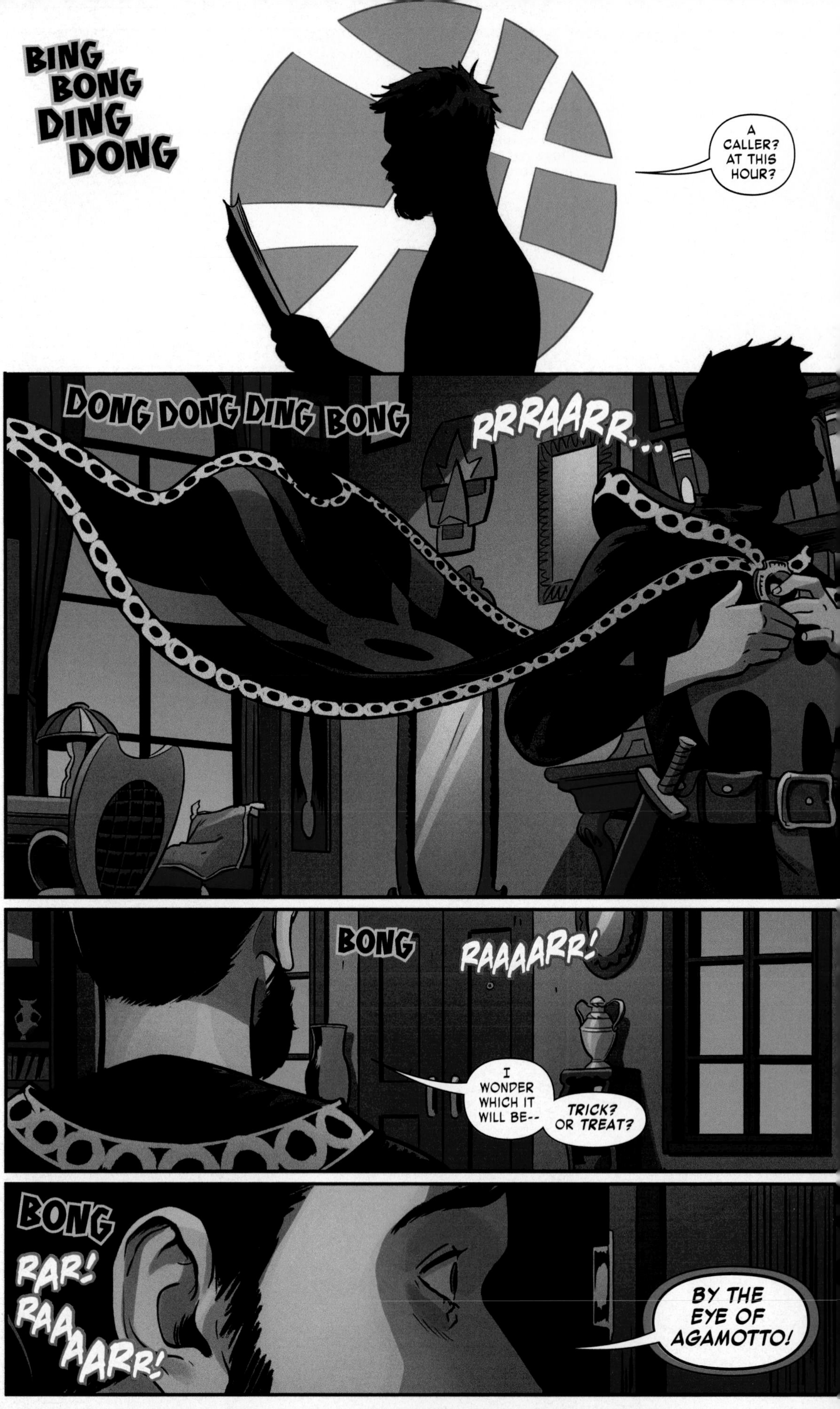
BING BONG DING DONG
A CALLER? AT THIS HOUR?
DONG DONG DING BONG
RRRAARR...
BONG
RAAAARR!
I WONDER WHICH IT WILL BE--
TRICK? OR TREAT?
BONG
RAR! RAAAARR!
BY THE EYE OF AGAMOTTO!

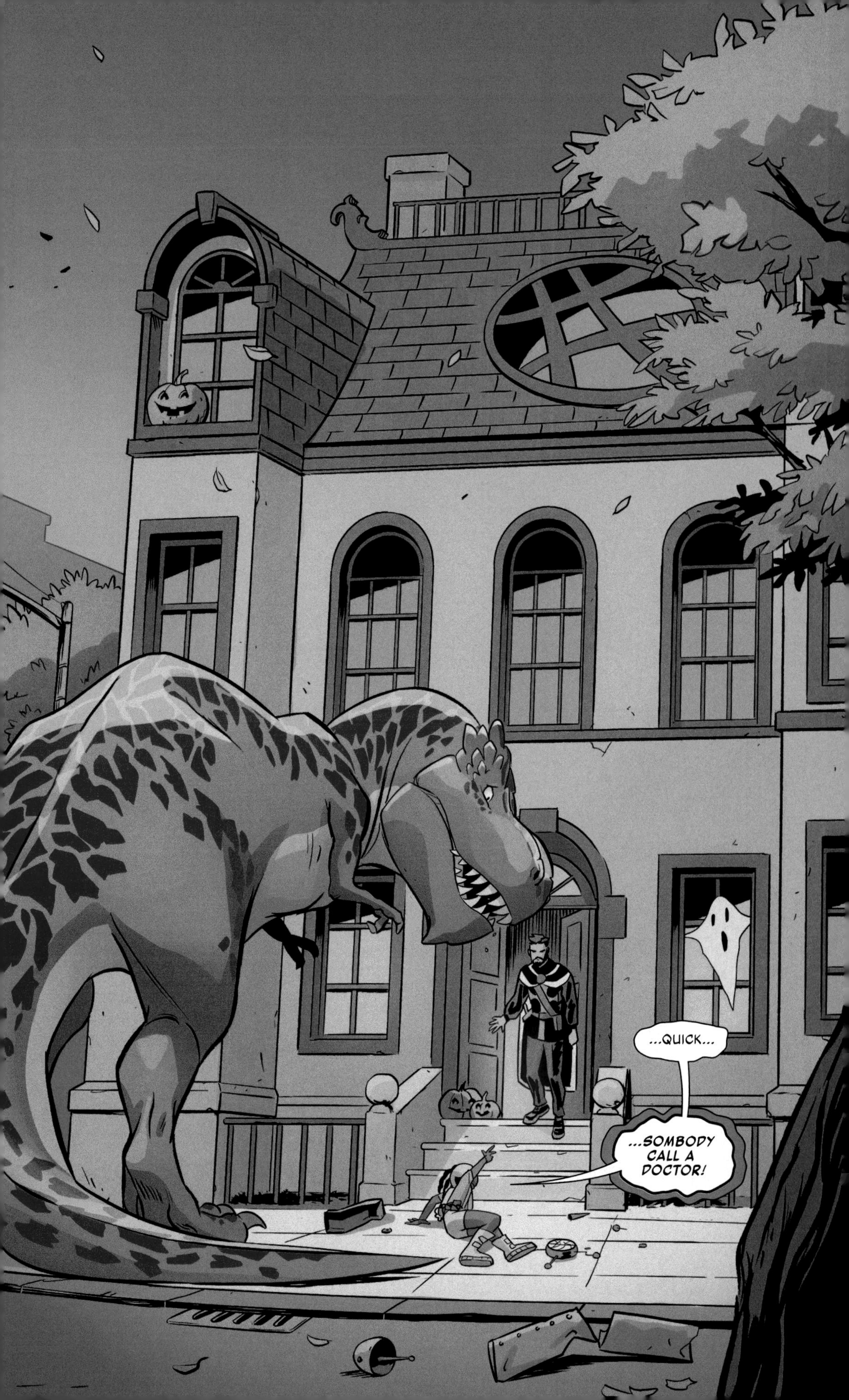
...QUICK...
...SOMBODY CALL A DOCTOR!

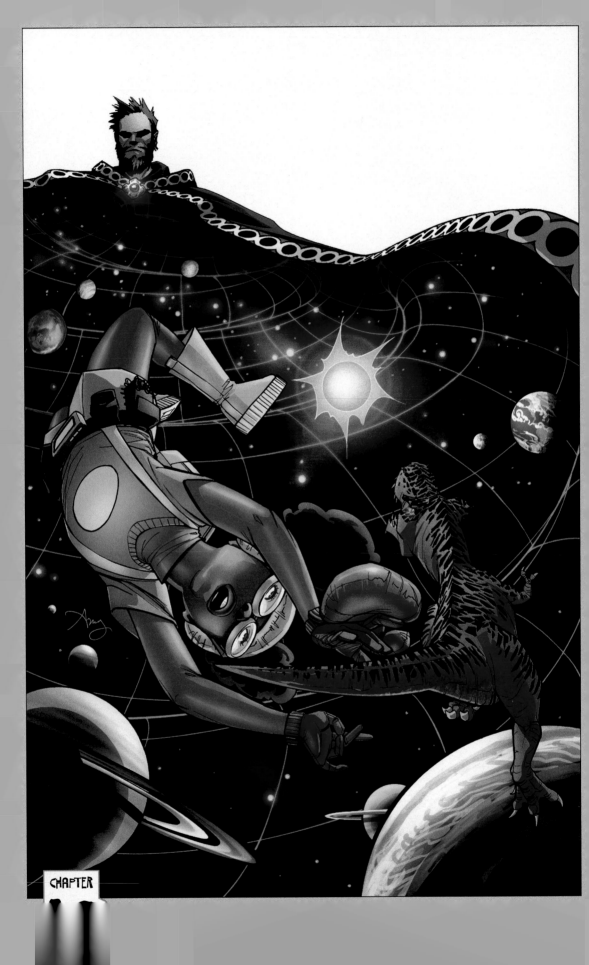

CHAPTER

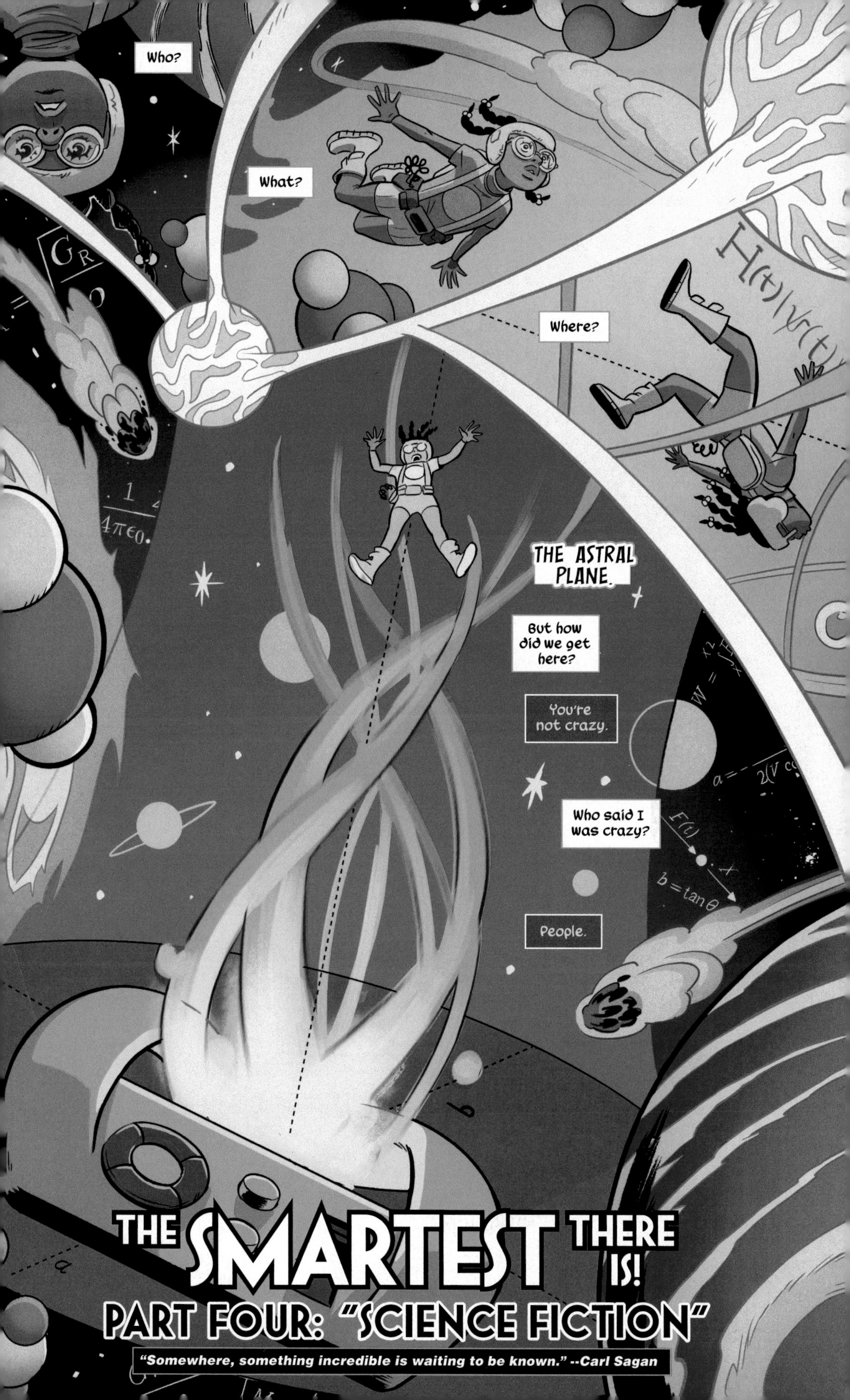

Who?
What?
Where?
THE ASTRAL PLANE.
But how did we get here?
You're not crazy.
Who said I was crazy?
People.
THE SMARTEST THERE IS!
PART FOUR: "SCIENCE FICTION"
"Somewhere, something incredible is waiting to be known." --Carl Sagan

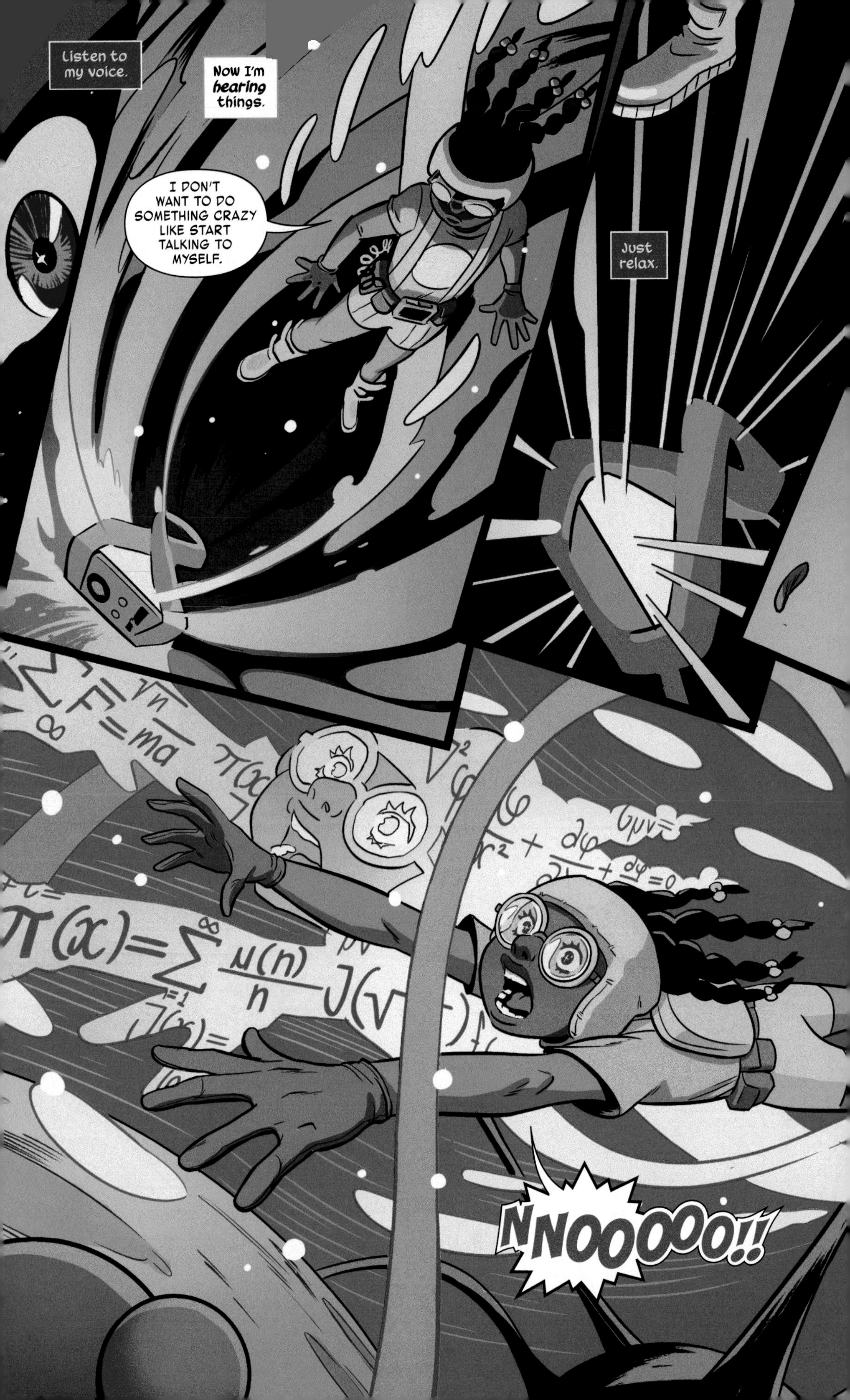
Listen to my voice.
Now I'm *hearing* things.
I DON'T WANT TO DO SOMETHING CRAZY LIKE START TALKING TO MYSELF.
Just relax.
NNOOOOOO!!

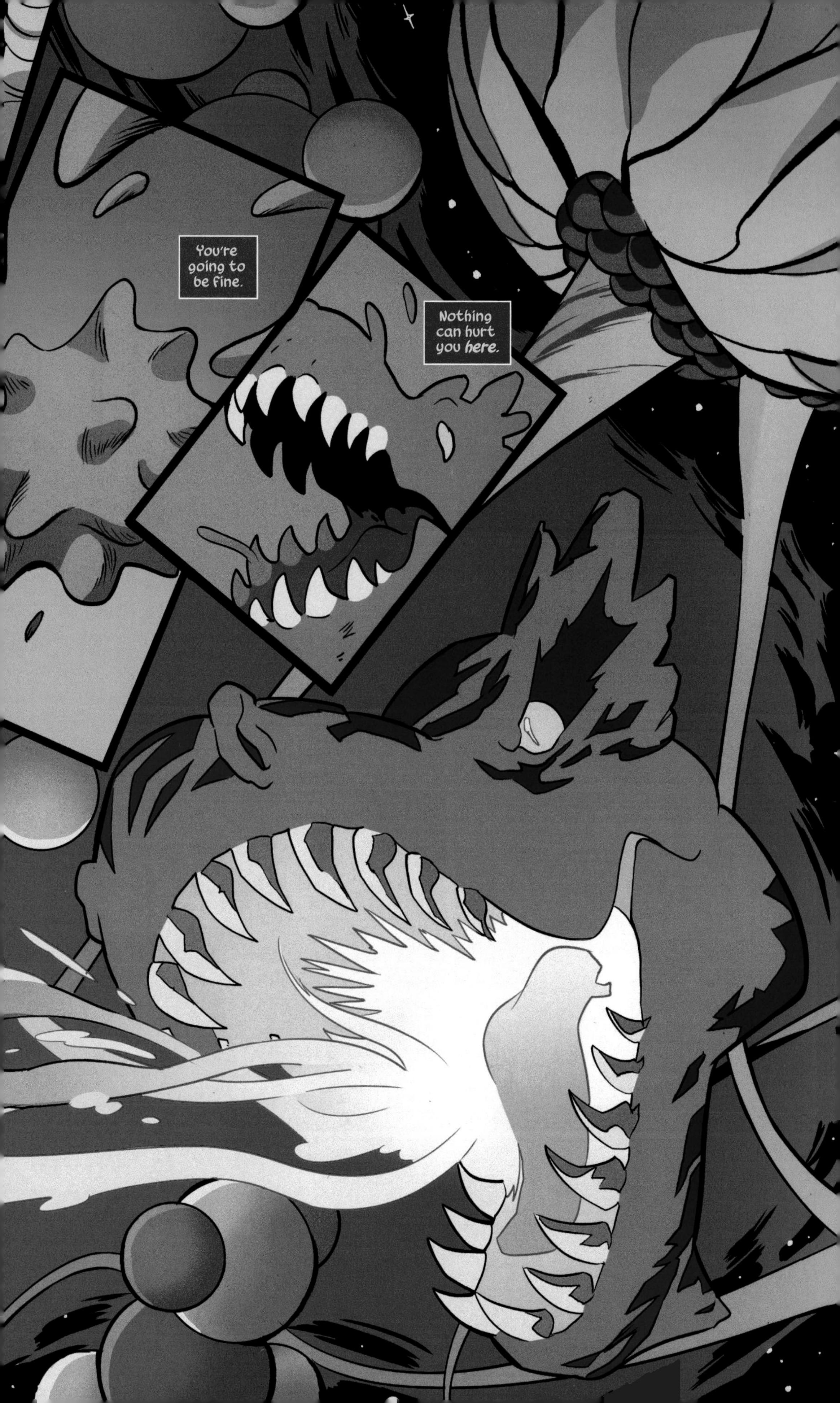
You're going to be fine.
Nothing can hurt you here.

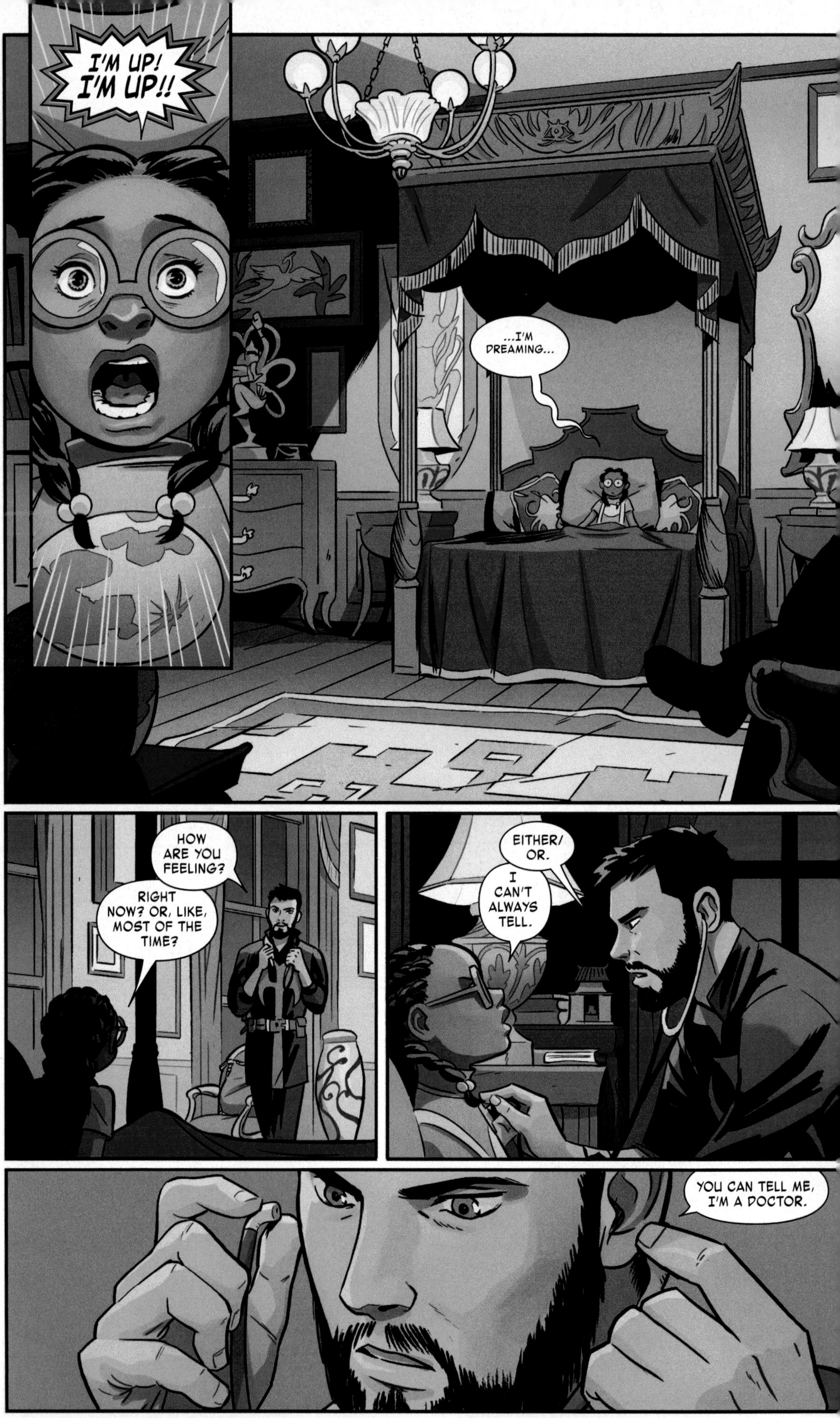
I'M UP! I'M UP!!
...I'M DREAMING...
HOW ARE YOU FEELING?
RIGHT NOW? OR, LIKE, MOST OF THE TIME?
EITHER/ OR.
I CAN'T ALWAYS TELL.
YOU CAN TELL ME, I'M A DOCTOR.

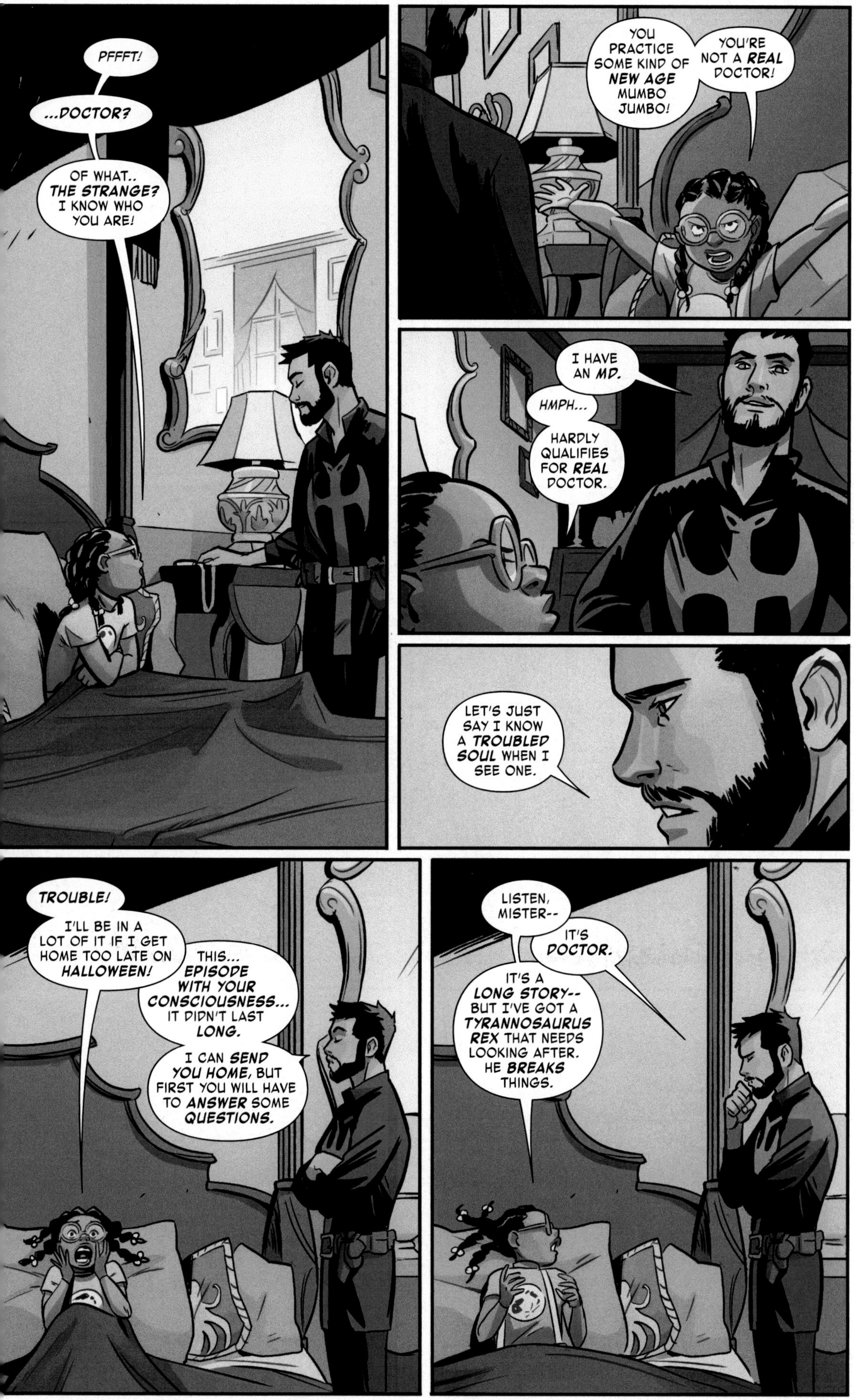
PFFFT!
...DOCTOR?
OF WHAT.. THE STRANGE? I KNOW WHO YOU ARE!
YOU PRACTICE SOME KIND OF NEW AGE MUMBO JUMBO!
YOU'RE NOT A REAL DOCTOR!
I HAVE AN MD.
HMPH...
HARDLY QUALIFIES FOR REAL DOCTOR.
LET'S JUST SAY I KNOW A TROUBLED SOUL WHEN I SEE ONE.
TROUBLE!
I'LL BE IN A LOT OF IT IF I GET HOME TOO LATE ON HALLOWEEN!
THIS... EPISODE WITH YOUR CONSCIOUSNESS... IT DIDN'T LAST LONG.
I CAN SEND YOU HOME, BUT FIRST YOU WILL HAVE TO ANSWER SOME QUESTIONS.
LISTEN, MISTER--
IT'S DOCTOR.
IT'S A LONG STORY-- BUT I'VE GOT A TYRANNOSAURUS REX THAT NEEDS LOOKING AFTER. HE BREAKS THINGS.

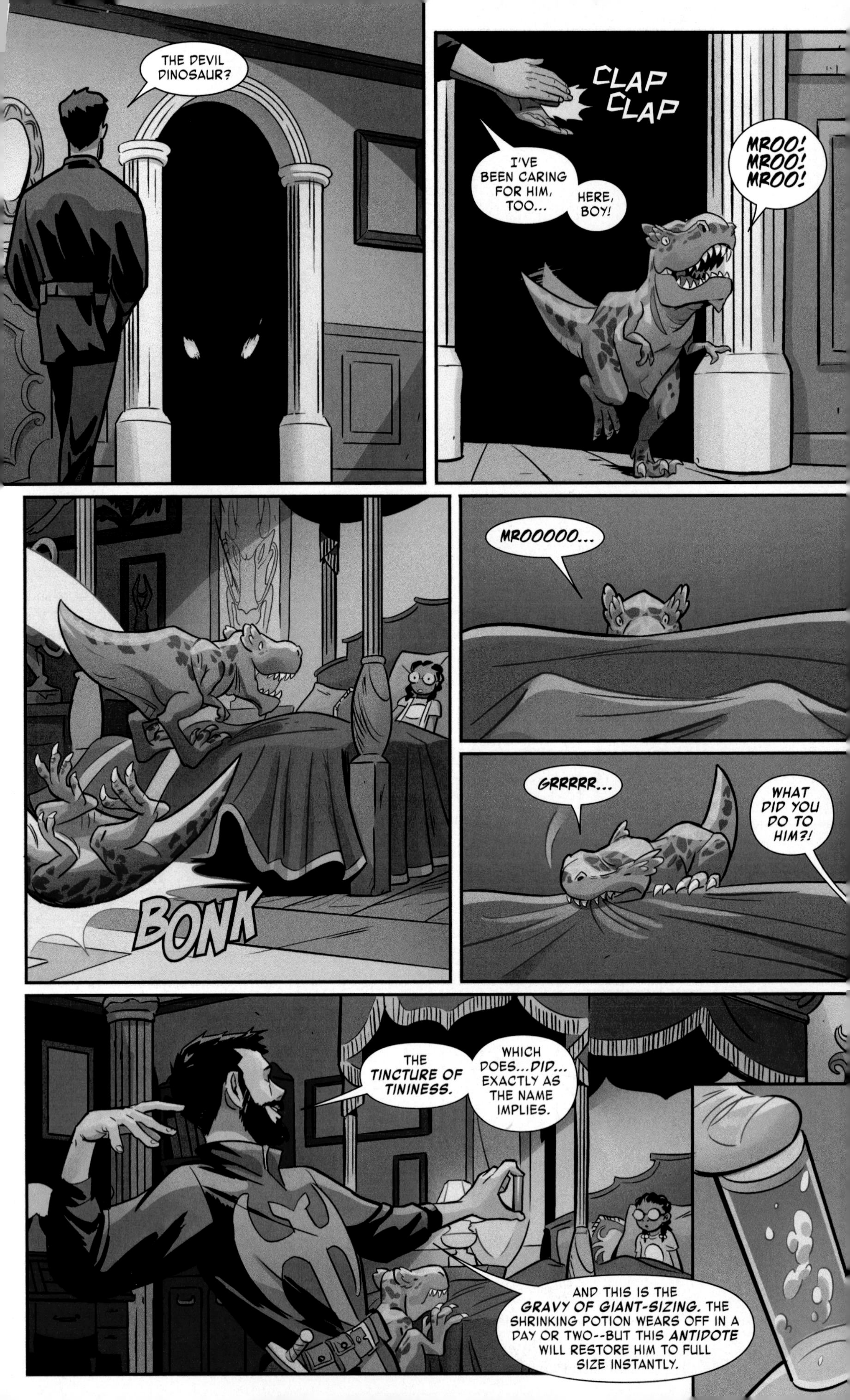
THE DEVIL DINOSAUR?
CLAP CLAP
I'VE BEEN CARING FOR HIM, TOO...
HERE, BOY!
MROO! MROO! MROO!
BONK
MROOOOO...
GRRRRR...
WHAT DID YOU DO TO HIM?!
THE TINCTURE OF TININESS.
WHICH DOES...DID... EXACTLY AS THE NAME IMPLIES.
AND THIS IS THE GRAVY OF GIANT-SIZING. THE SHRINKING POTION WEARS OFF IN A DAY OR TWO--BUT THIS ANTIDOTE WILL RESTORE HIM TO FULL SIZE INSTANTLY.

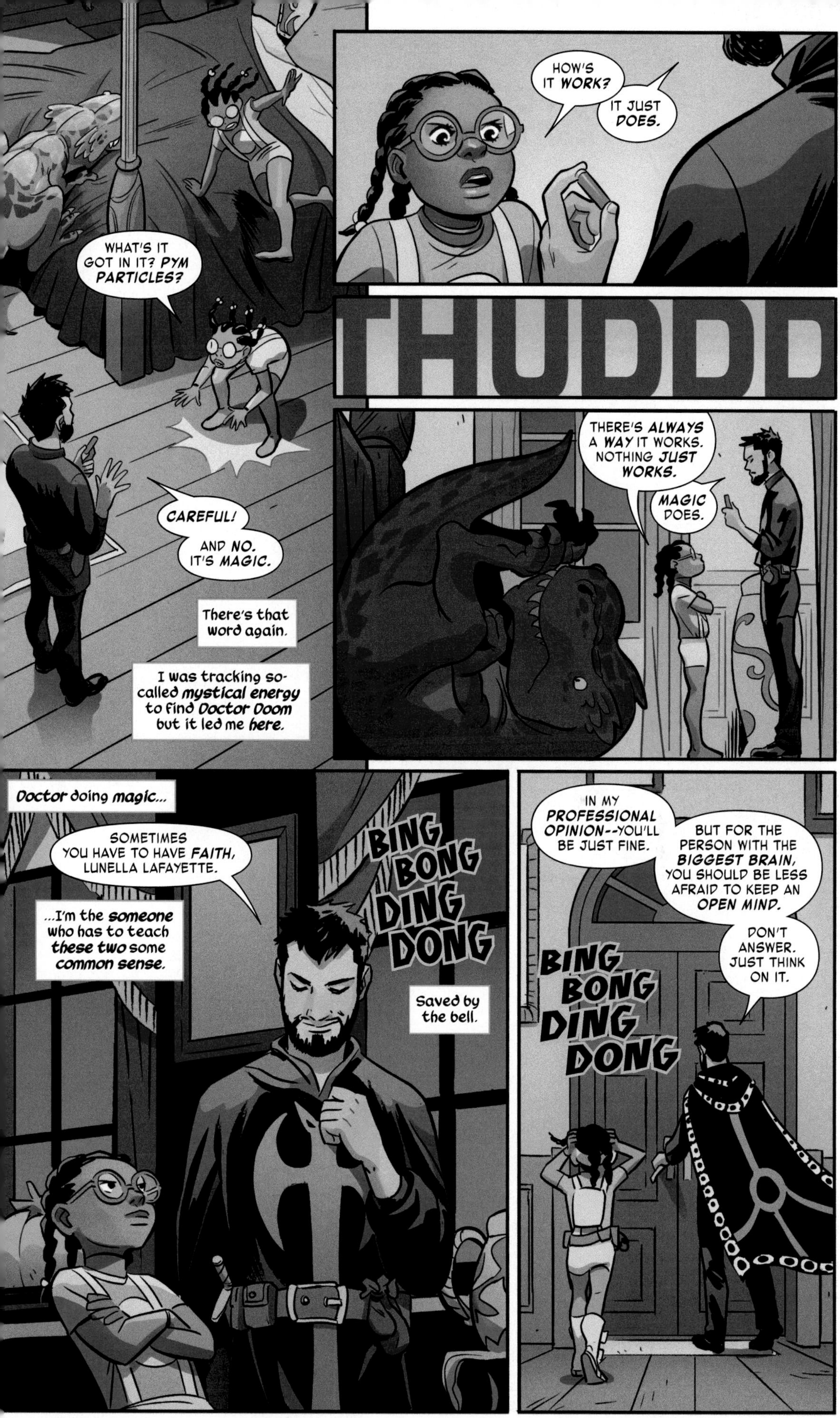
WHAT'S IT GOT IN IT? PYM PARTICLES?
HOW'S IT WORK?
IT JUST DOES.
THUDDD
CAREFUL!
AND NO. IT'S MAGIC.
There's that word again.
I was tracking so-called mystical energy to find Doctor Doom but it led me here.
THERE'S ALWAYS A WAY IT WORKS. NOTHING JUST WORKS.
MAGIC DOES.
Doctor doing magic...
SOMETIMES YOU HAVE TO HAVE FAITH, LUNELLA LAFAYETTE.
...I'm the someone who has to teach these two some common sense.
BING BONG DING DONG
Saved by the bell.
IN MY PROFESSIONAL OPINION--YOU'LL BE JUST FINE.
BUT FOR THE PERSON WITH THE BIGGEST BRAIN, YOU SHOULD BE LESS AFRAID TO KEEP AN OPEN MIND.
DON'T ANSWER. JUST THINK ON IT.
BING BONG DING DONG

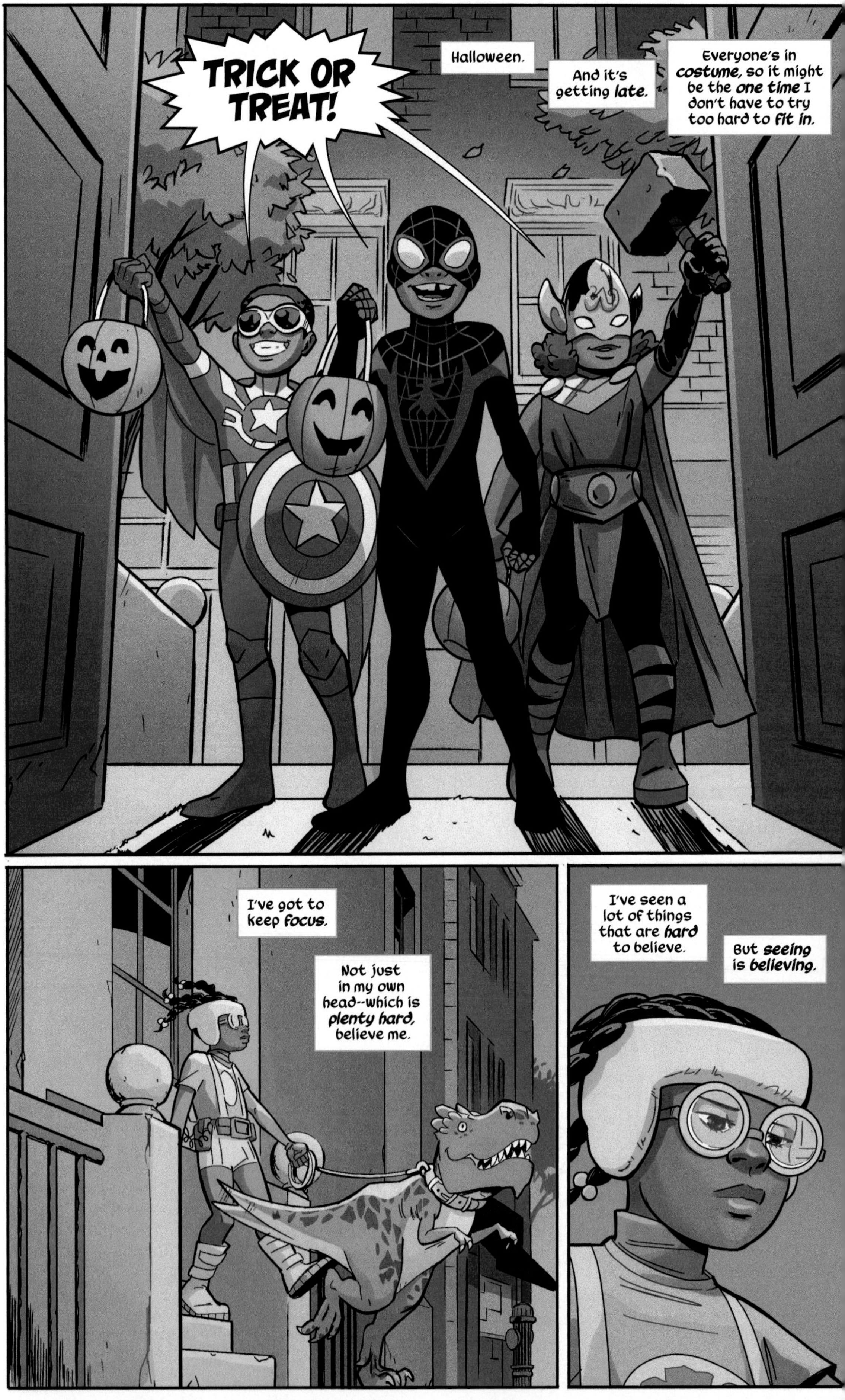
TRICK OR TREAT!
Halloween.
And it's getting late.
Everyone's in costume, so it might be the one time I don't have to try too hard to fit in.
I've got to keep focus.
Not just in my own head--which is plenty hard, believe me.
I've seen a lot of things that are hard to believe.
But seeing is believing.

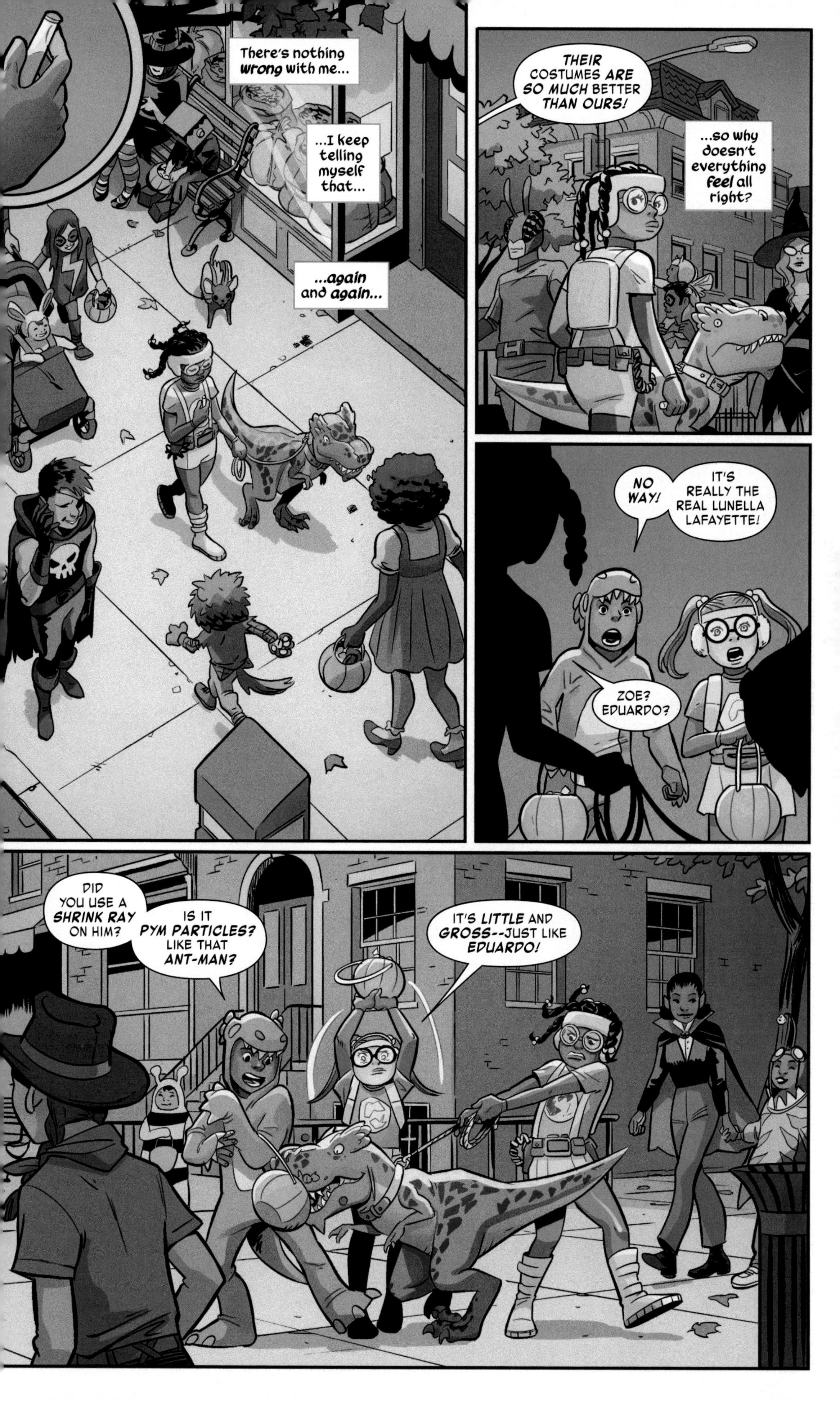

There's nothing **wrong** with me...
...I keep telling myself that...
...**again** and **again**...
THEIR COSTUMES **ARE SO MUCH** BETTER **THAN OURS!**
...so why doesn't everything **feel** all right?
NO WAY!
IT'S REALLY THE REAL LUNELLA LAFAYETTE!
ZOE? EDUARDO?
DID YOU USE A **SHRINK RAY** ON HIM?
IS IT **PYM PARTICLES?** LIKE THAT **ANT-MAN?**
IT'S **LITTLE** AND **GROSS**--JUST LIKE **EDUARDO!**

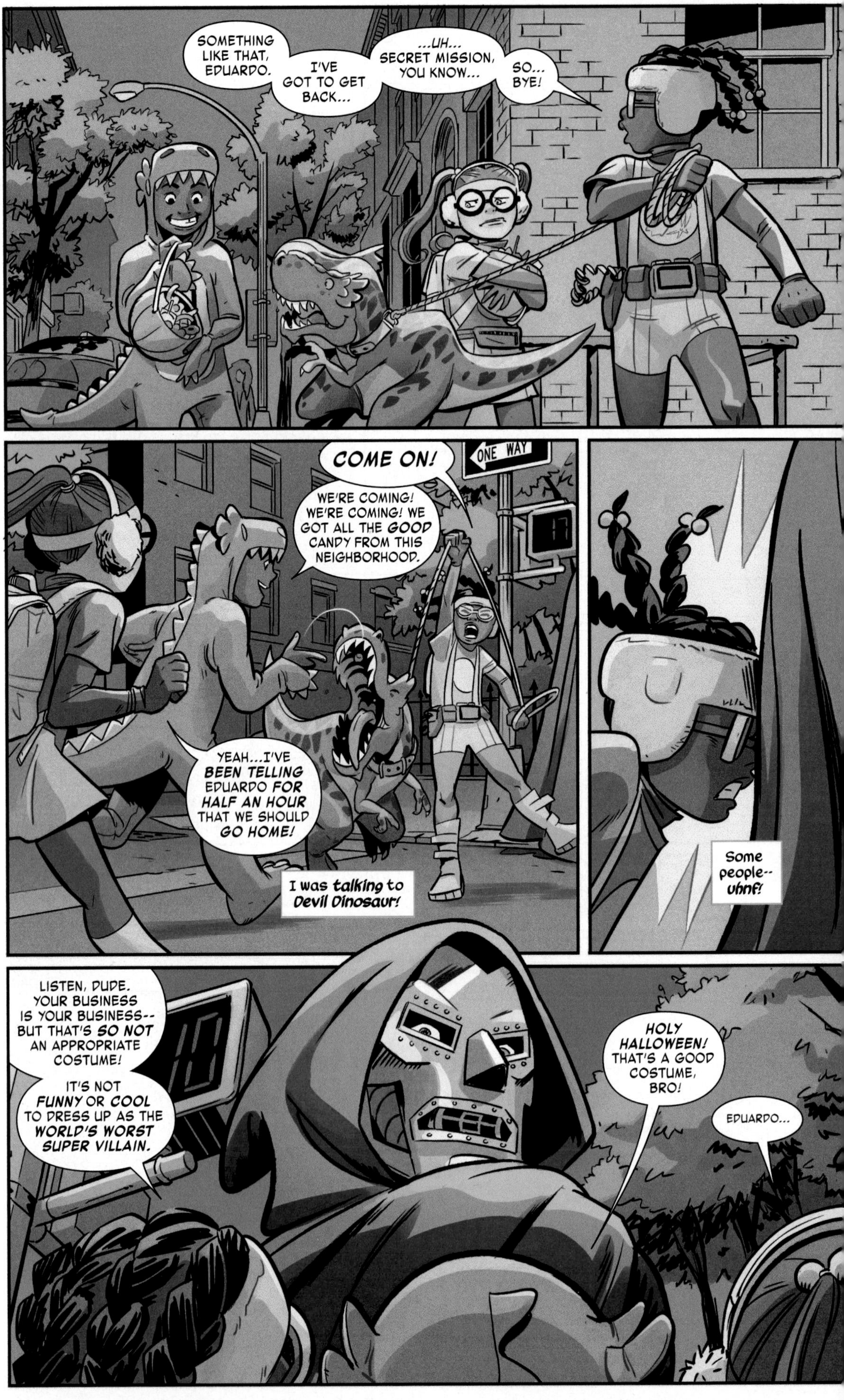

SOMETHING LIKE THAT, EDUARDO.
I'VE GOT TO GET BACK...
...UH... SECRET MISSION, YOU KNOW...
SO... BYE!
COME ON!
ONE WAY
WE'RE COMING! WE'RE COMING! WE GOT ALL THE GOOD CANDY FROM THIS NEIGHBORHOOD.
YEAH...I'VE BEEN TELLING EDUARDO FOR HALF AN HOUR THAT WE SHOULD GO HOME!
I was talking to Devil Dinosaur!
Some people--uhnf!
LISTEN, DUDE. YOUR BUSINESS IS YOUR BUSINESS--BUT THAT'S SO NOT AN APPROPRIATE COSTUME!
IT'S NOT FUNNY OR COOL TO DRESS UP AS THE WORLD'S WORST SUPER VILLAIN.
HOLY HALLOWEEN! THAT'S A GOOD COSTUME, BRO!
EDUARDO...

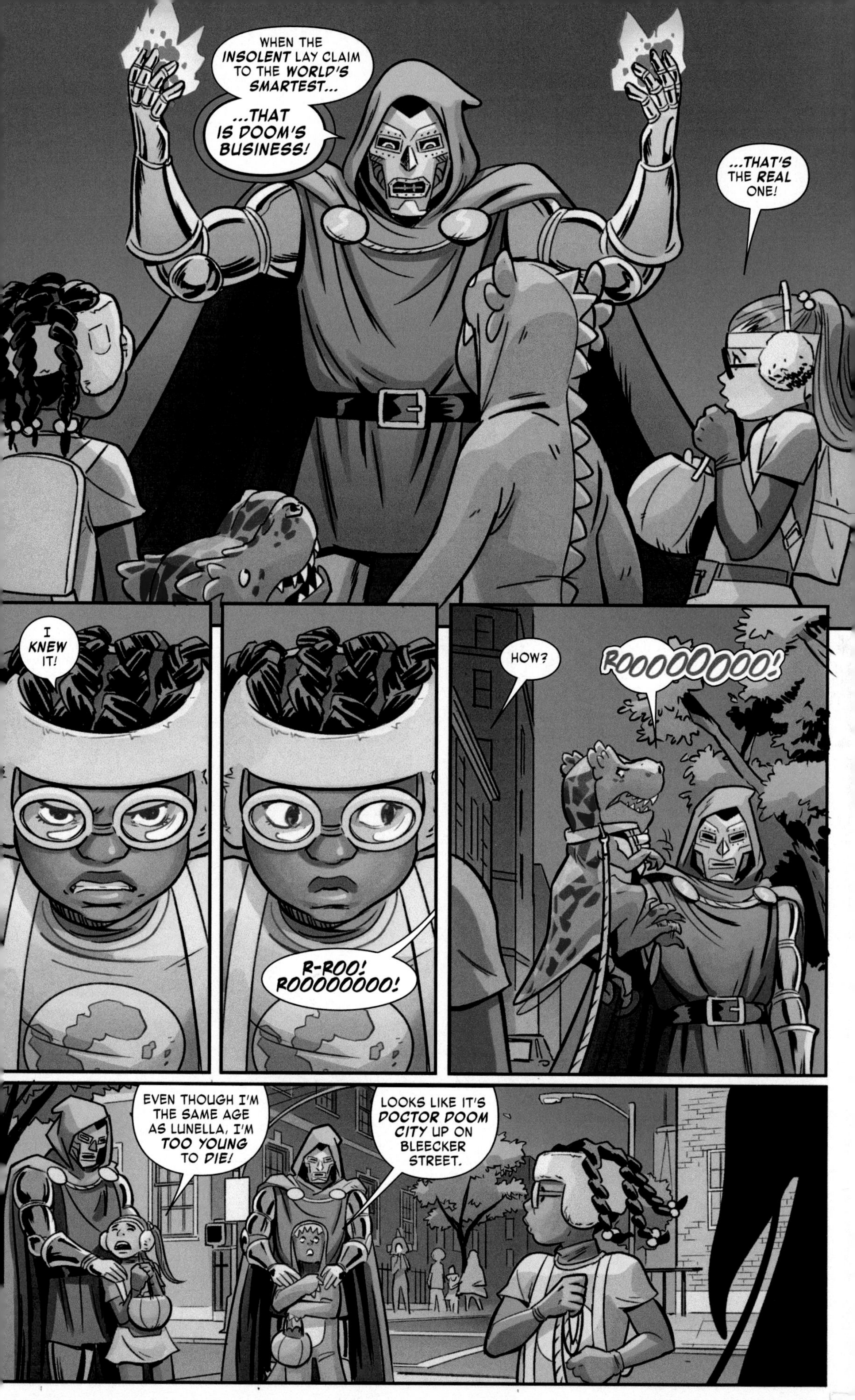

WHEN THE INSOLENT LAY CLAIM TO THE WORLD'S SMARTEST...
...THAT IS DOOM'S BUSINESS!
...THAT'S THE REAL ONE!
I KNEW IT!
R-ROO! ROOOOOOOO!
HOW?
ROOOOOOOO!
EVEN THOUGH I'M THE SAME AGE AS LUNELLA, I'M TOO YOUNG TO DIE!
LOOKS LIKE IT'S DOCTOR DOOM CITY UP ON BLEECKER STREET.

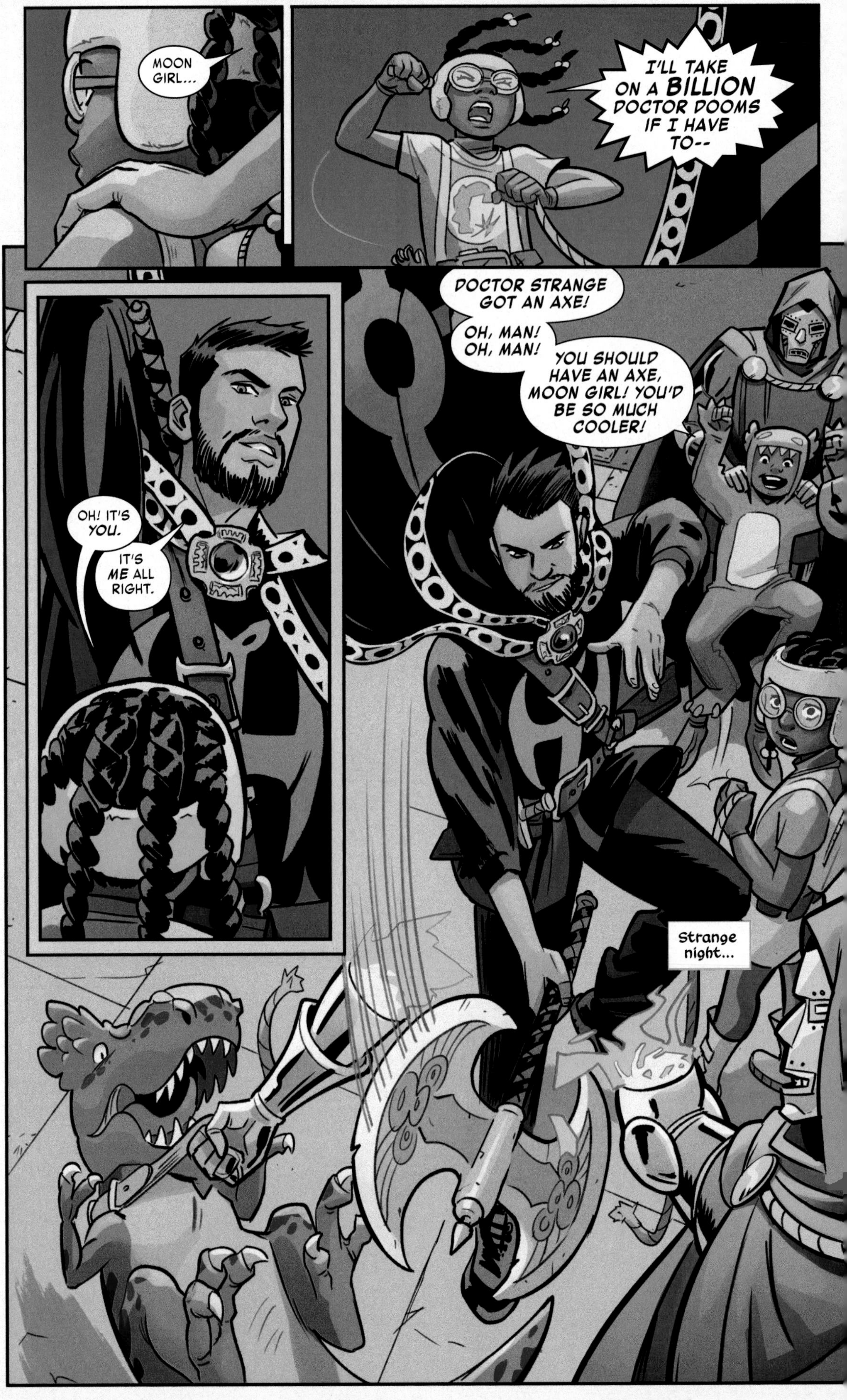
MOON GIRL...
I'LL TAKE ON A BILLION DOCTOR DOOMS IF I HAVE TO--
OH! IT'S YOU.
IT'S ME ALL RIGHT.
DOCTOR STRANGE GOT AN AXE!
OH, MAN! OH, MAN!
YOU SHOULD HAVE AN AXE, MOON GIRL! YOU'D BE SO MUCH COOLER!
Strange night...

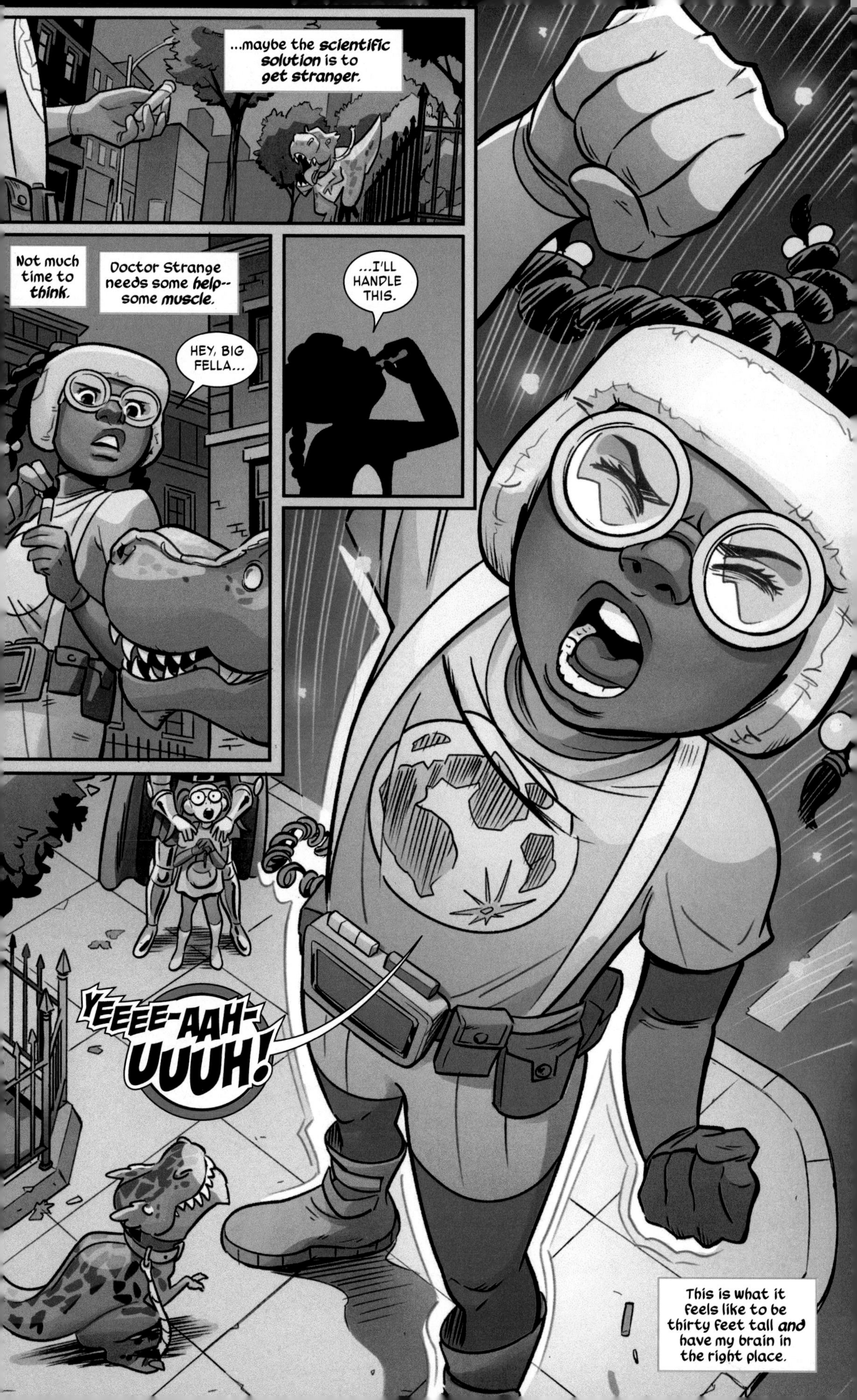

...maybe the **scientific solution** is to **get stranger.**
Not much time to **think.**
Doctor Strange needs some **help**-- some **muscle.**
HEY, BIG FELLA...
...I'LL HANDLE THIS.
YEEEE-AAH-UUUH!
This is what it feels like to be thirty feet tall **and** have my brain in the right place.

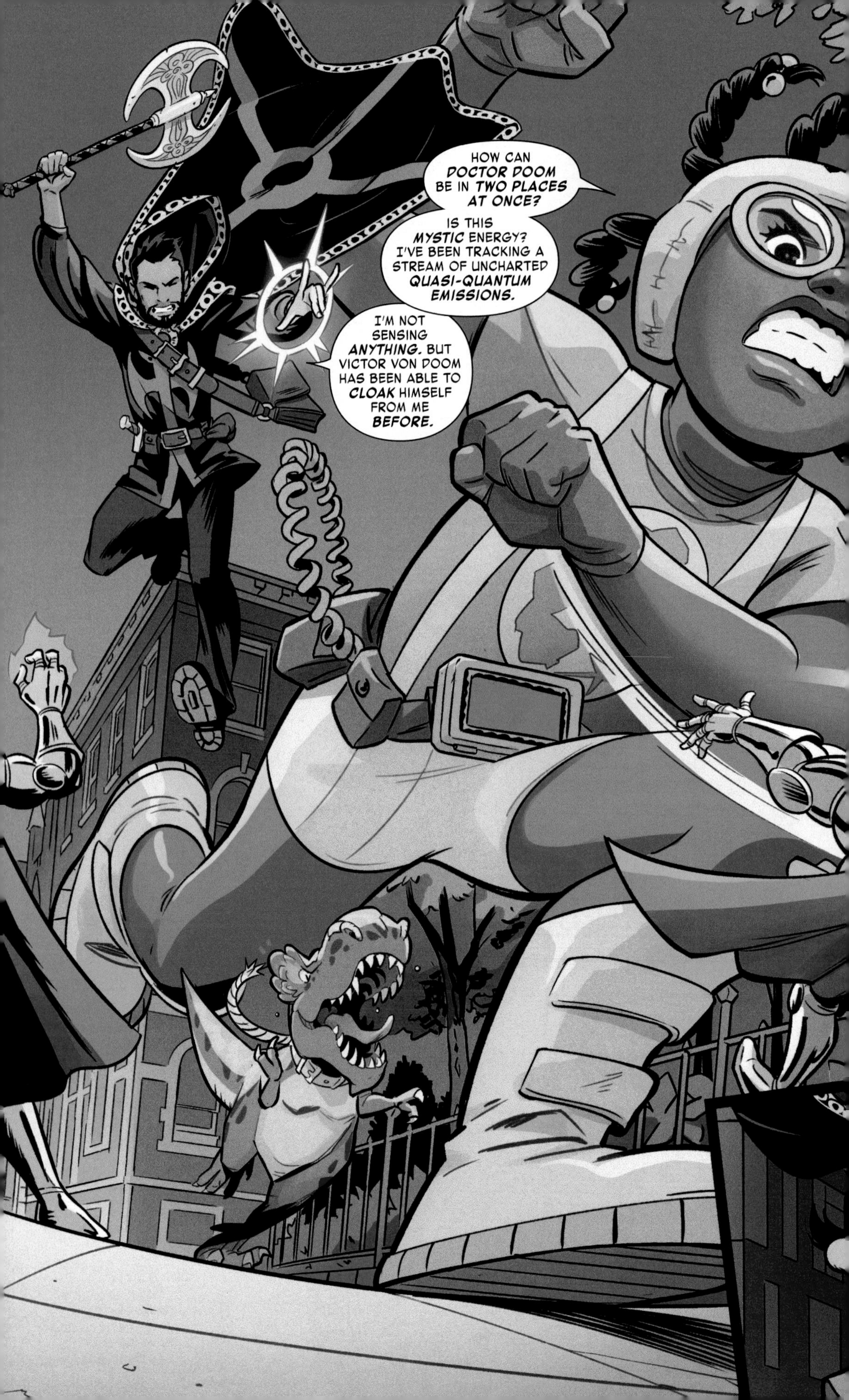
HOW CAN DOCTOR DOOM BE IN TWO PLACES AT ONCE?
IS THIS MYSTIC ENERGY? I'VE BEEN TRACKING A STREAM OF UNCHARTED QUASI-QUANTUM EMISSIONS.
I'M NOT SENSING ANYTHING. BUT VICTOR VON DOOM HAS BEEN ABLE TO CLOAK HIMSELF FROM ME BEFORE.

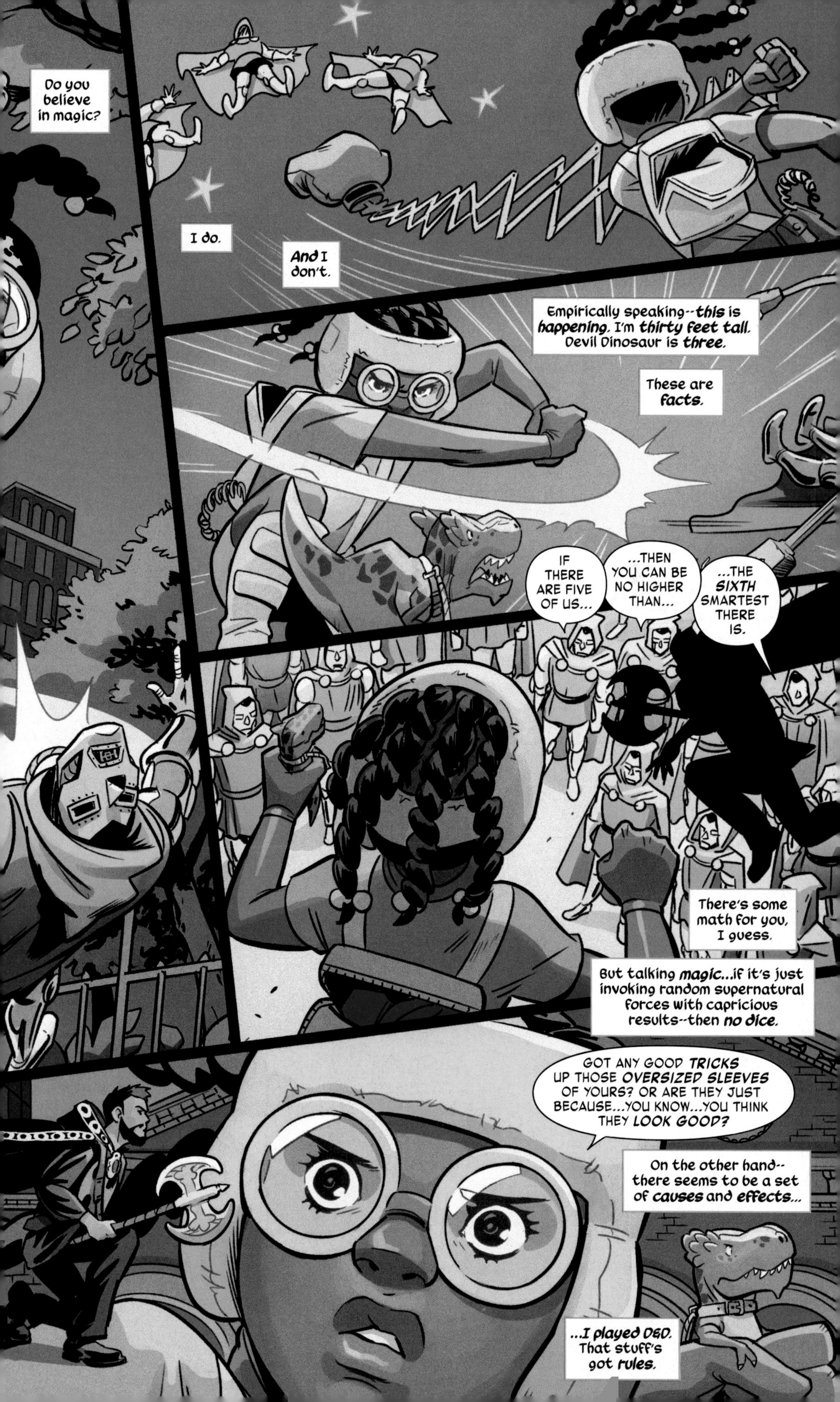

Do you believe in magic?
I do.
And I don't.
Empirically speaking--this is happening. I'm thirty feet tall. Devil Dinosaur is three.
These are facts.
IF THERE ARE FIVE OF US...
...THEN YOU CAN BE NO HIGHER THAN...
...THE SIXTH SMARTEST THERE IS.
There's some math for you, I guess.
But talking magic...if it's just invoking random supernatural forces with capricious results--then no dice.
GOT ANY GOOD TRICKS UP THOSE OVERSIZED SLEEVES OF YOURS? OR ARE THEY JUST BECAUSE...YOU KNOW...YOU THINK THEY LOOK GOOD?
On the other hand--there seems to be a set of causes and effects...
...I played D&D. That stuff's got rules.

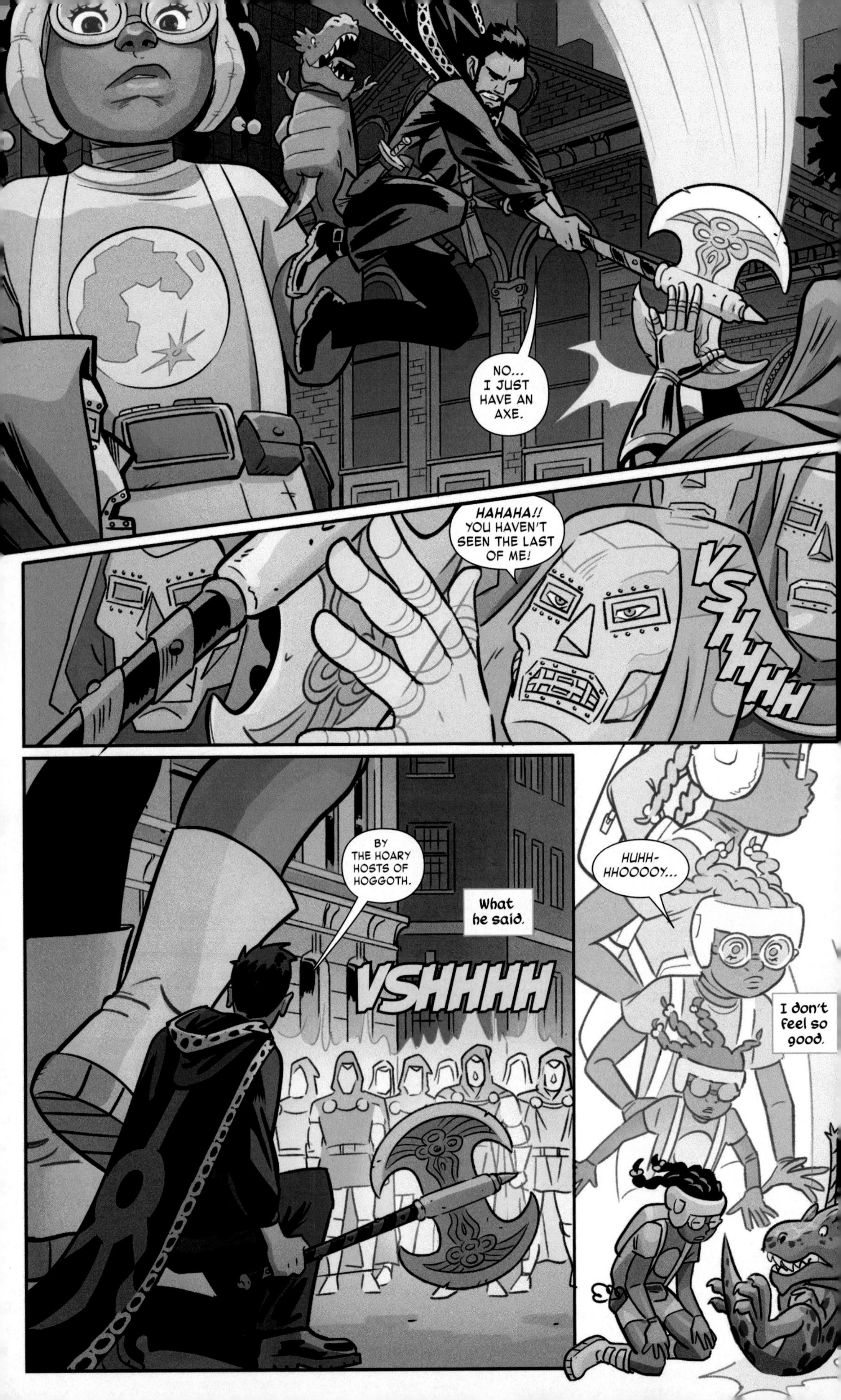

NO... I JUST HAVE AN AXE.
HAHAHA!! YOU HAVEN'T SEEN THE LAST OF ME!
VSHHHHH
BY THE HOARY HOSTS OF HOGGOTH.
What he said.
VSHHHH
HUHH-HHOOOOY...
I don't feel so good.

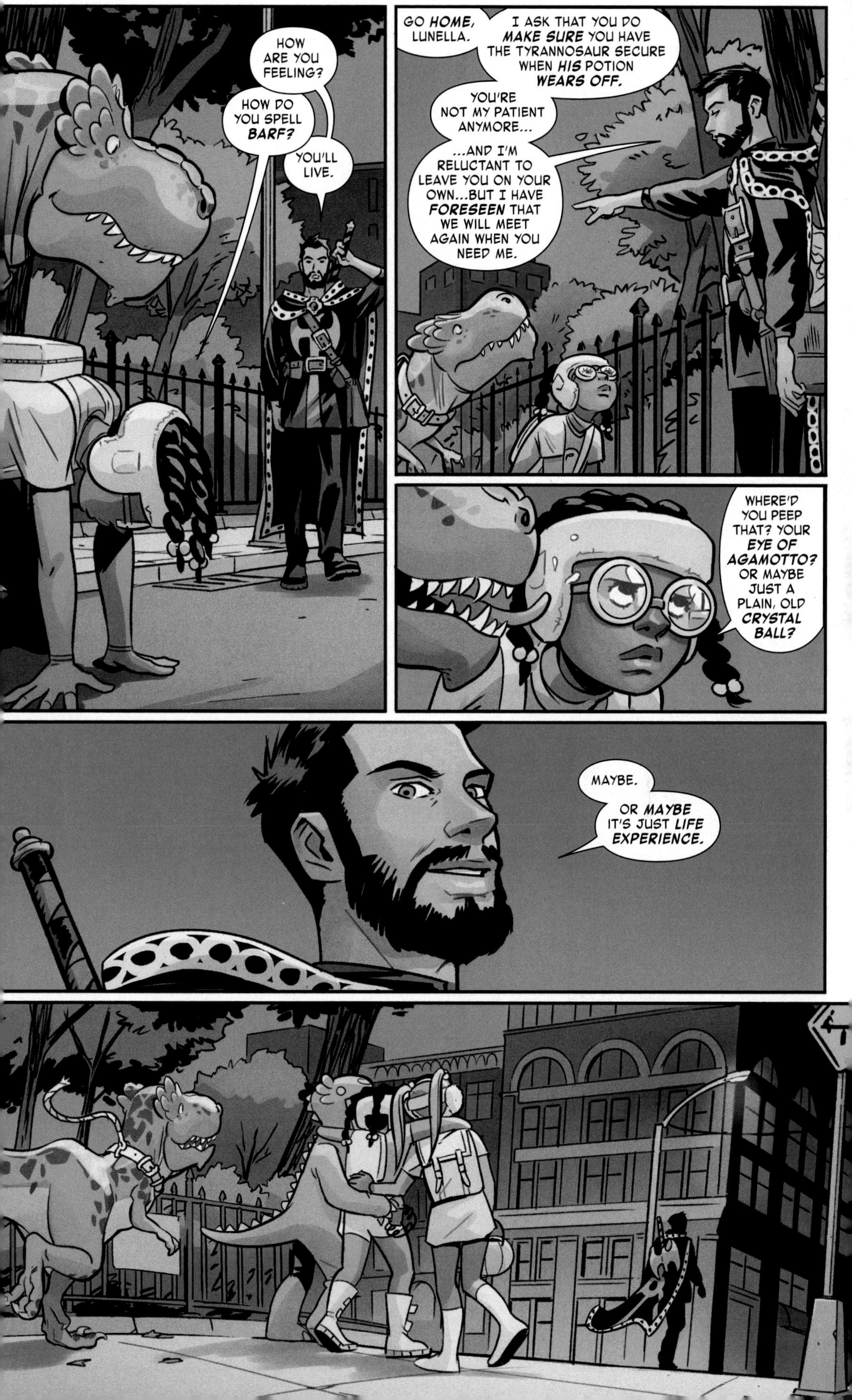

HOW ARE YOU FEELING?
HOW DO YOU SPELL **BARF?**
YOU'LL LIVE.
GO **HOME,** LUNELLA.
I ASK THAT YOU DO **MAKE SURE** YOU HAVE THE TYRANNOSAUR SECURE WHEN **HIS** POTION **WEARS OFF.**
YOU'RE NOT MY PATIENT ANYMORE...
...AND I'M RELUCTANT TO LEAVE YOU ON YOUR OWN...BUT I HAVE **FORESEEN** THAT WE WILL MEET AGAIN WHEN YOU NEED ME.
WHERE'D YOU PEEP THAT? YOUR **EYE OF AGAMOTTO?** OR MAYBE JUST A PLAIN, OLD **CRYSTAL BALL?**
MAYBE.
OR **MAYBE** IT'S JUST **LIFE EXPERIENCE.**

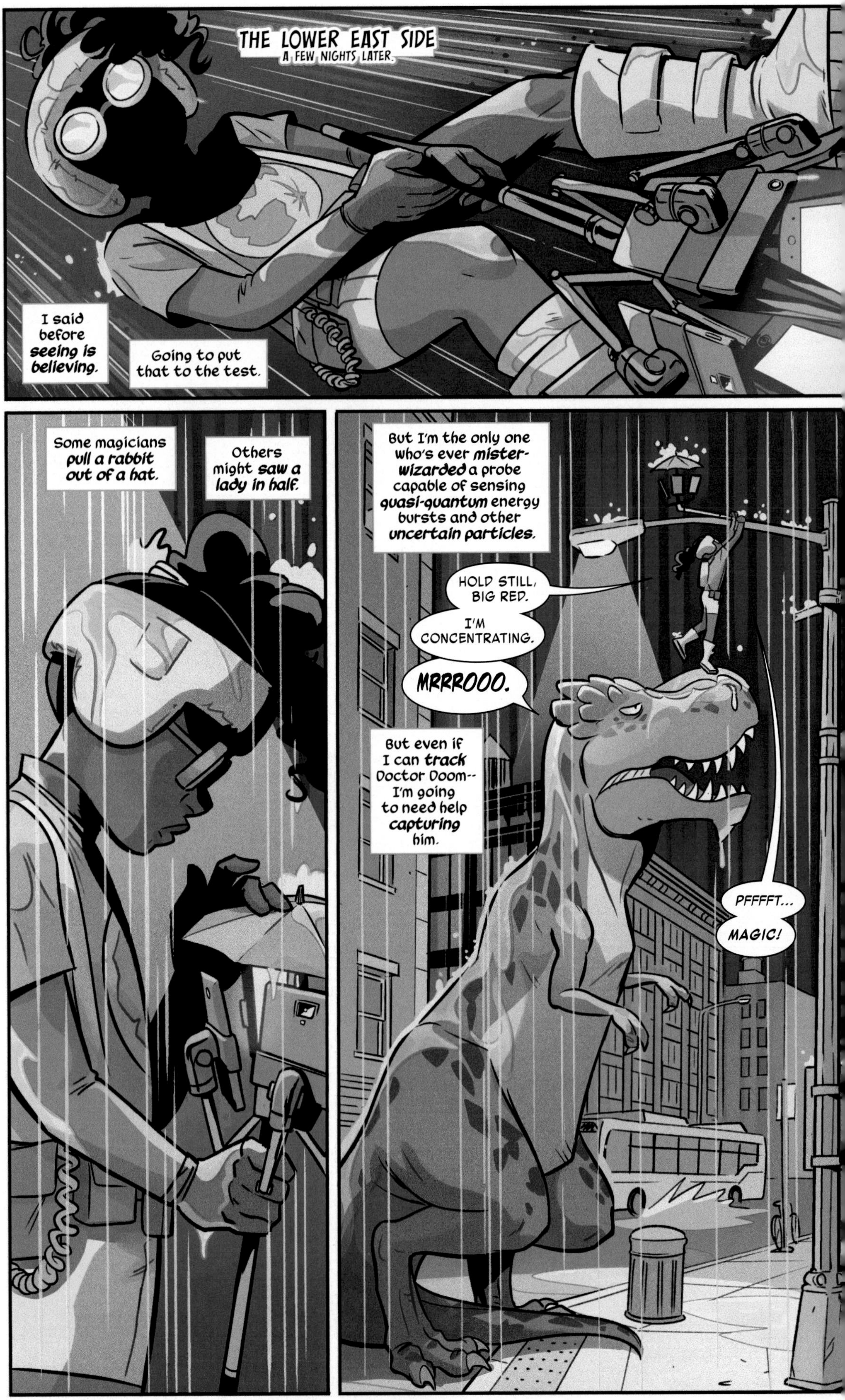
THE LOWER EAST SIDE
A FEW NIGHTS LATER.
I said before seeing is believing.
Going to put that to the test.
Some magicians pull a rabbit out of a hat.
Others might saw a lady in half.
But I'm the only one who's ever mister-wizarded a probe capable of sensing quasi-quantum energy bursts and other uncertain particles.
HOLD STILL, BIG RED.
I'M CONCENTRATING.
MRRROOO.
But even if I can track Doctor Doom-- I'm going to need help capturing him.
PFFFFT...
MAGIC!

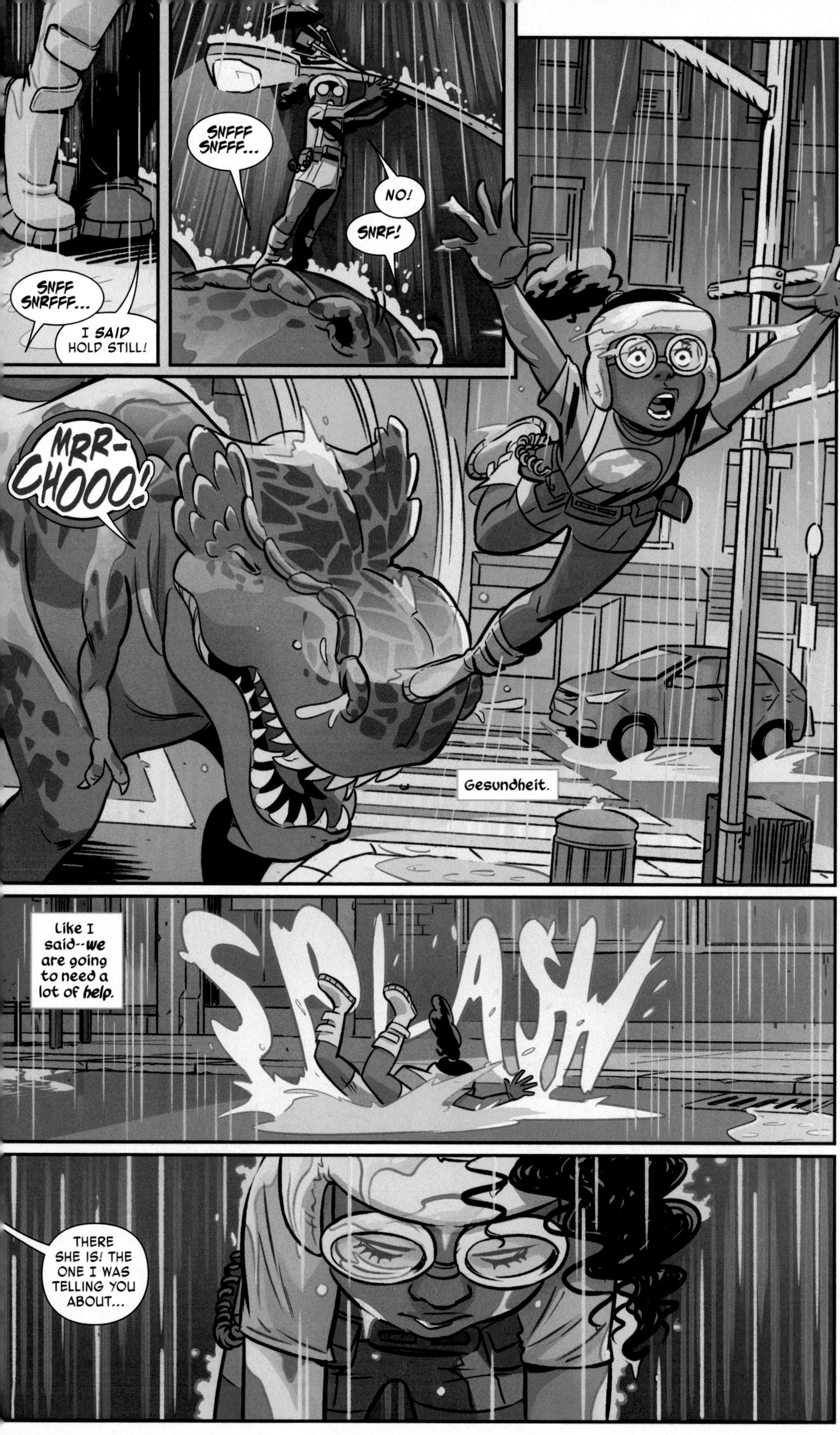
SNFFF SNFFF...
NO!
SNRF!
SNFF SNRFFF...
I SAID HOLD STILL!
MRR-CHOOO!
Gesundheit.
Like I said--we are going to need a lot of help.
SPLASH
THERE SHE IS! THE ONE I WAS TELLING YOU ABOUT...

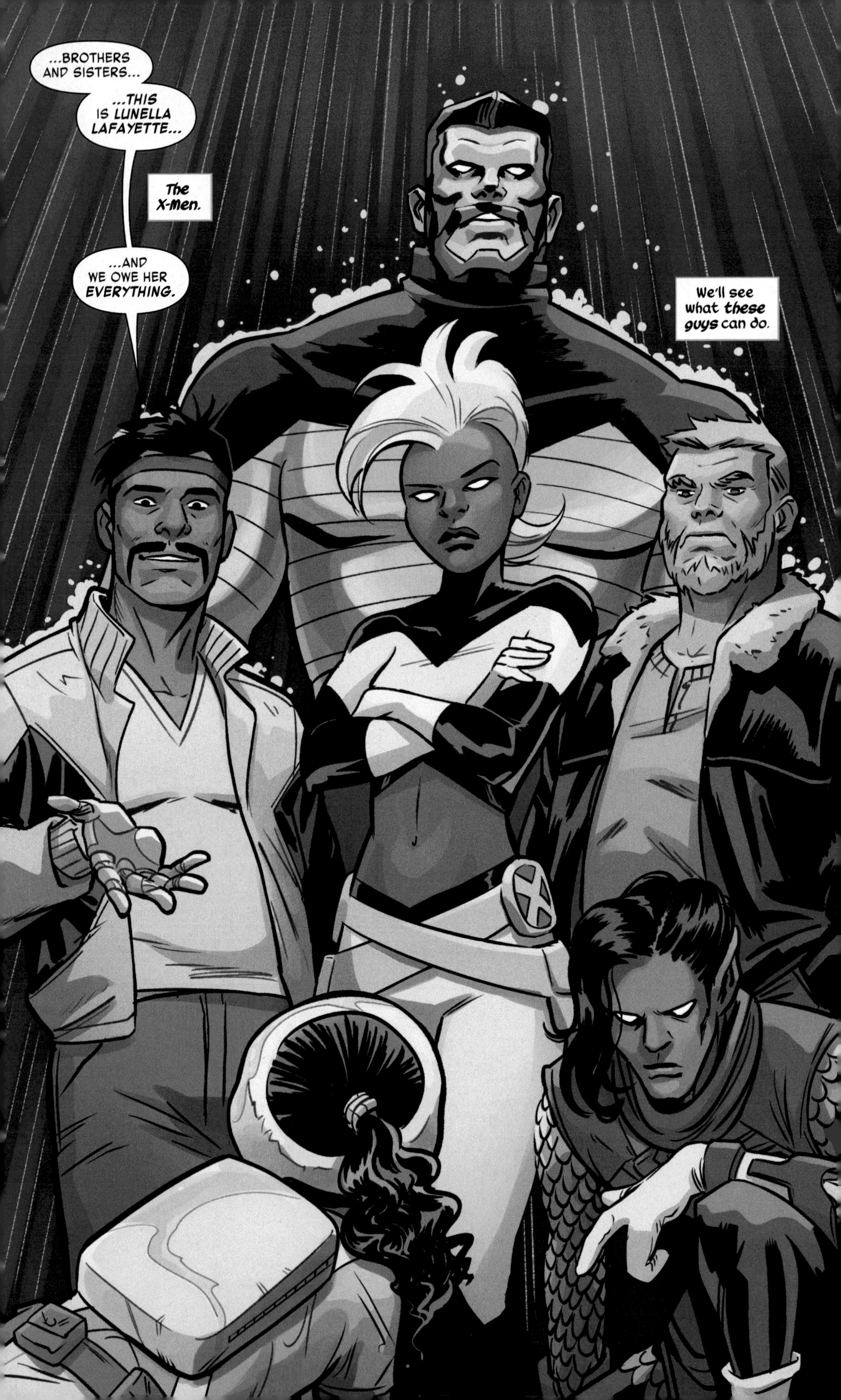
...BROTHERS AND SISTERS...
...THIS IS LUNELLA LAFAYETTE...
The X-Men.
...AND WE OWE HER EVERYTHING.
We'll see what these guys can do.

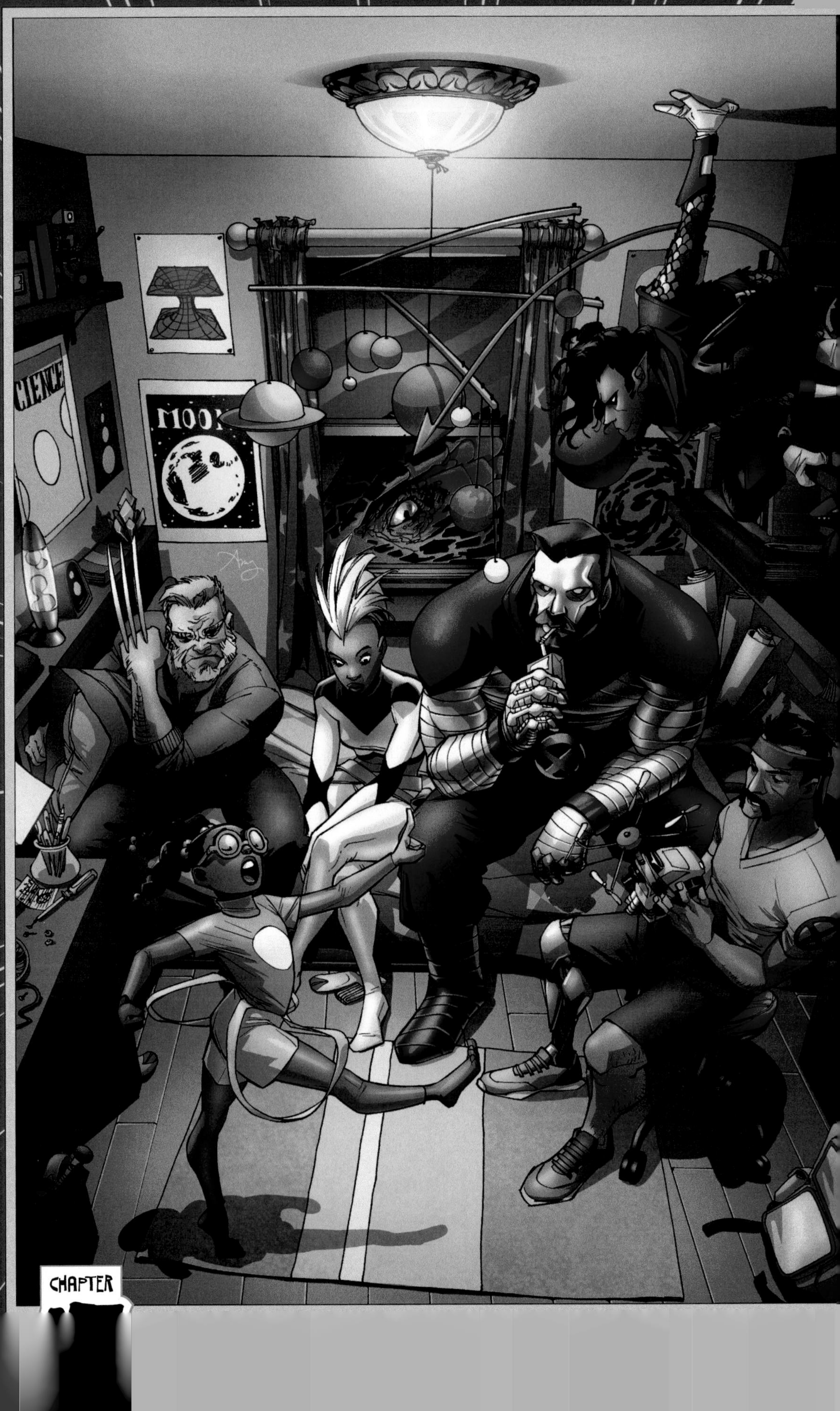
CIENCE
MOON
CHAPTER

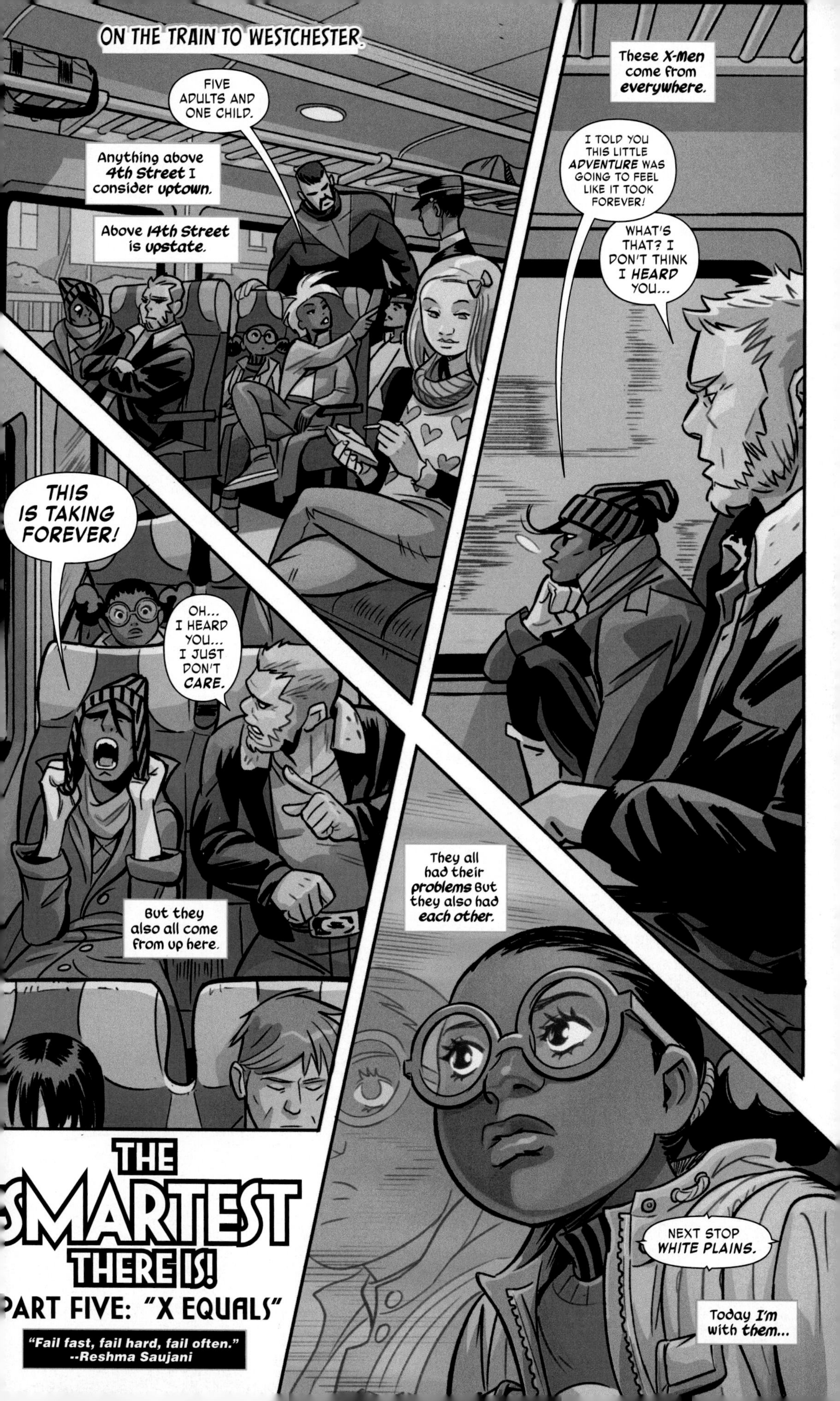

ON THE TRAIN TO WESTCHESTER.
FIVE ADULTS AND ONE CHILD.
Anything above 4th Street I consider uptown.
Above 14th Street is upstate.
These X-Men come from everywhere.
I TOLD YOU THIS LITTLE ADVENTURE WAS GOING TO FEEL LIKE IT TOOK FOREVER!
WHAT'S THAT? I DON'T THINK I HEARD YOU...
THIS IS TAKING FOREVER!
OH... I HEARD YOU... I JUST DON'T CARE.
But they also all come from up here.
They all had their problems but they also had each other.
NEXT STOP WHITE PLAINS.
Today I'm with them...
THE SMARTEST THERE IS!
PART FIVE: "X EQUALS"
"Fail fast, fail hard, fail often."
--Reshma Saujani

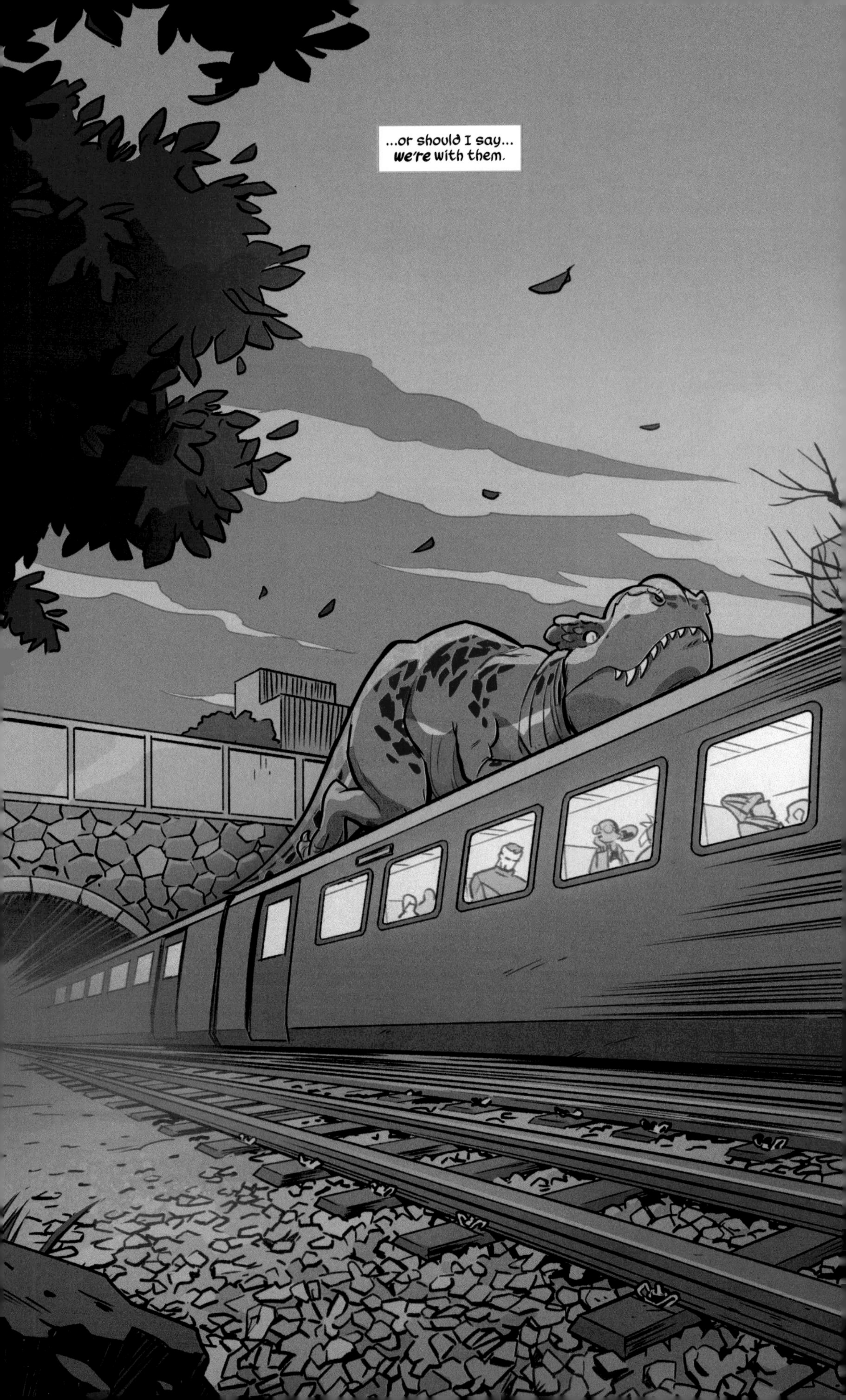
...or should I say...
we're with them.

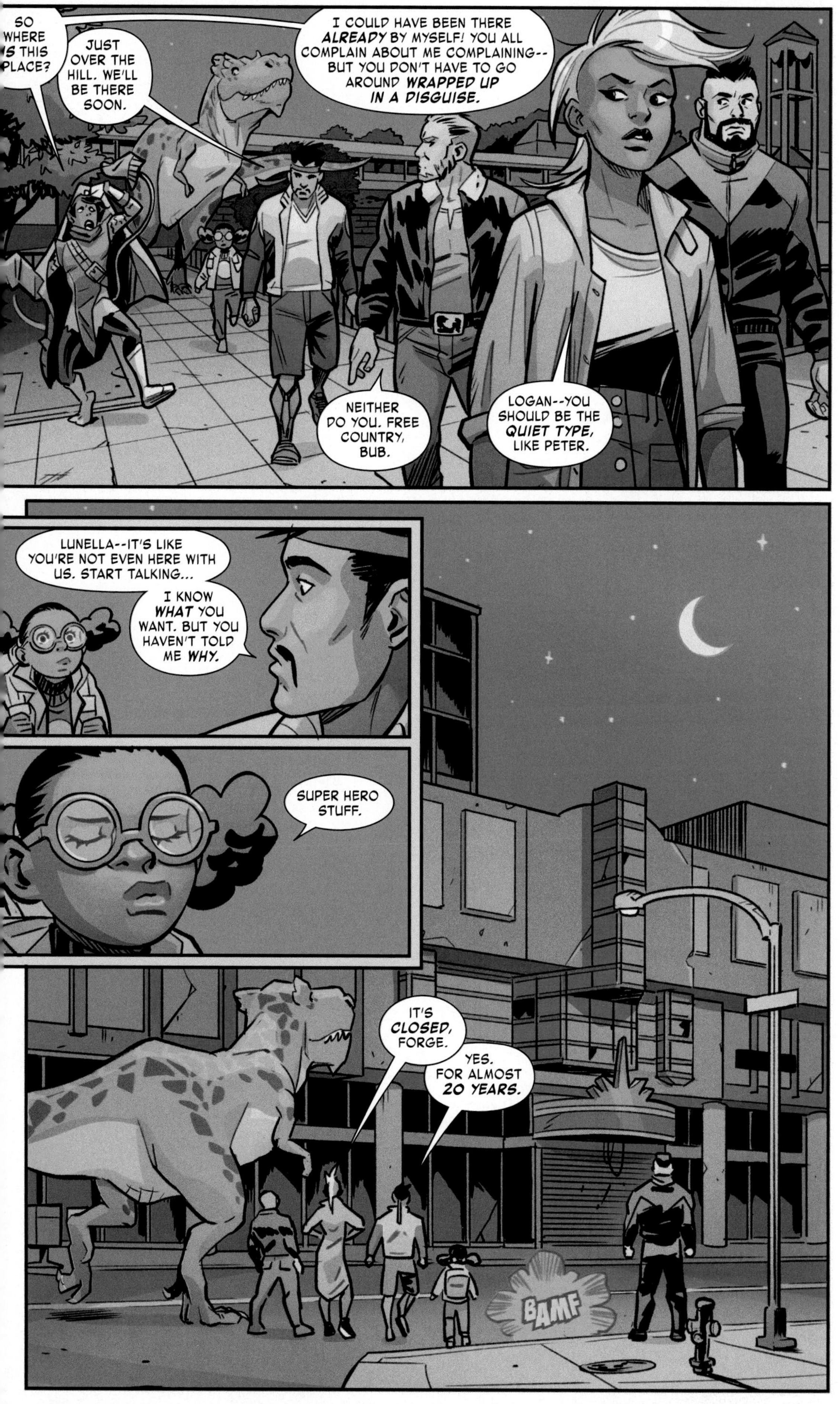

SO WHERE IS THIS PLACE?
JUST OVER THE HILL. WE'LL BE THERE SOON.
I COULD HAVE BEEN THERE ALREADY BY MYSELF! YOU ALL COMPLAIN ABOUT ME COMPLAINING-- BUT YOU DON'T HAVE TO GO AROUND WRAPPED UP IN A DISGUISE.
NEITHER DO YOU. FREE COUNTRY, BUB.
LOGAN--YOU SHOULD BE THE QUIET TYPE, LIKE PETER.
LUNELLA--IT'S LIKE YOU'RE NOT EVEN HERE WITH US. START TALKING...
I KNOW WHAT YOU WANT. BUT YOU HAVEN'T TOLD ME WHY.
SUPER HERO STUFF.
IT'S CLOSED, FORGE.
YES. FOR ALMOST 20 YEARS.
BAMF

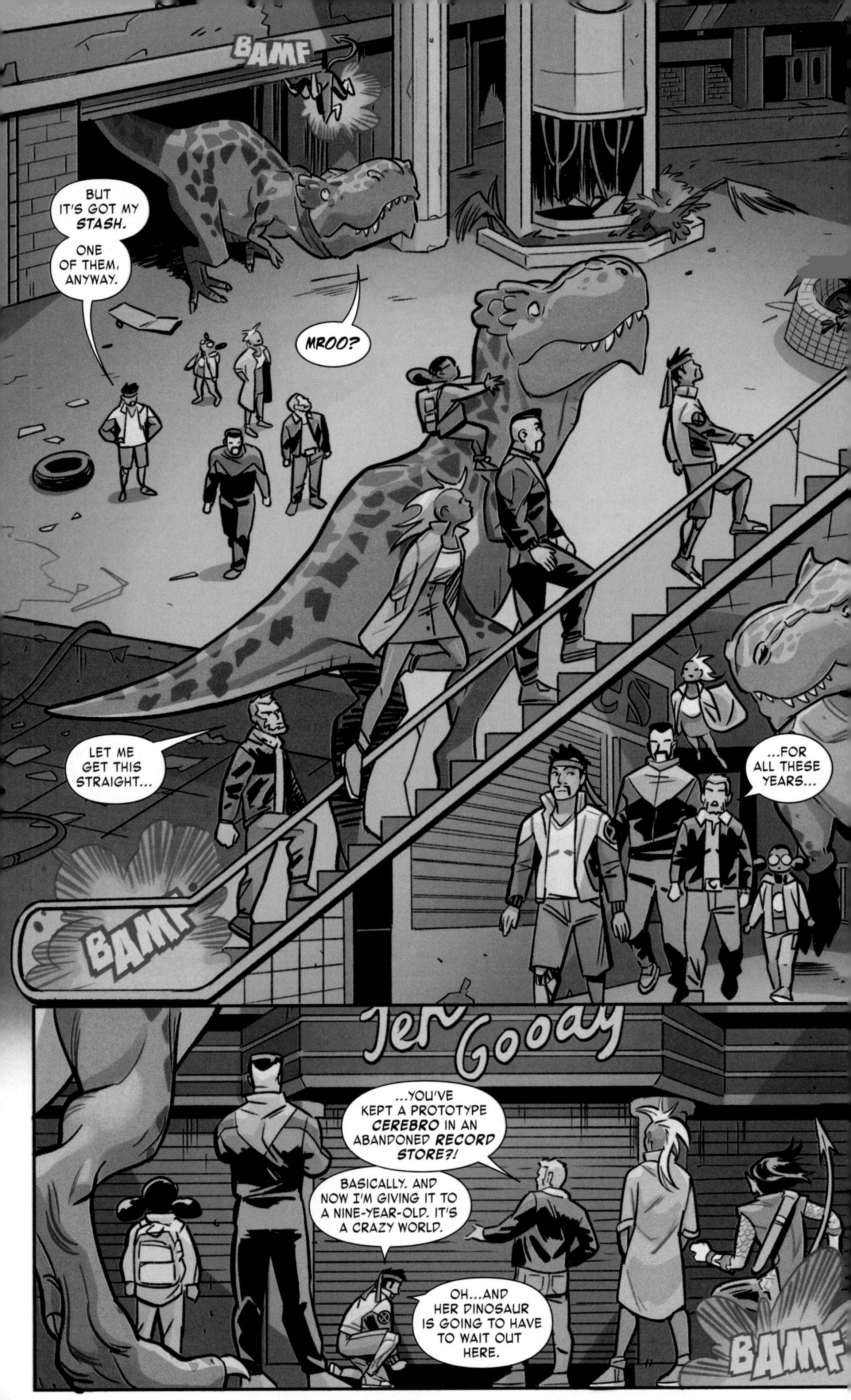
BAMF
BUT IT'S GOT MY STASH.
ONE OF THEM, ANYWAY.
MROO?
LET ME GET THIS STRAIGHT...
BAMF
...FOR ALL THESE YEARS...
...YOU'VE KEPT A PROTOTYPE CEREBRO IN AN ABANDONED RECORD STORE?!
BASICALLY. AND NOW I'M GIVING IT TO A NINE-YEAR-OLD. IT'S A CRAZY WORLD.
OH...AND HER DINOSAUR IS GOING TO HAVE TO WAIT OUT HERE.
BAMF

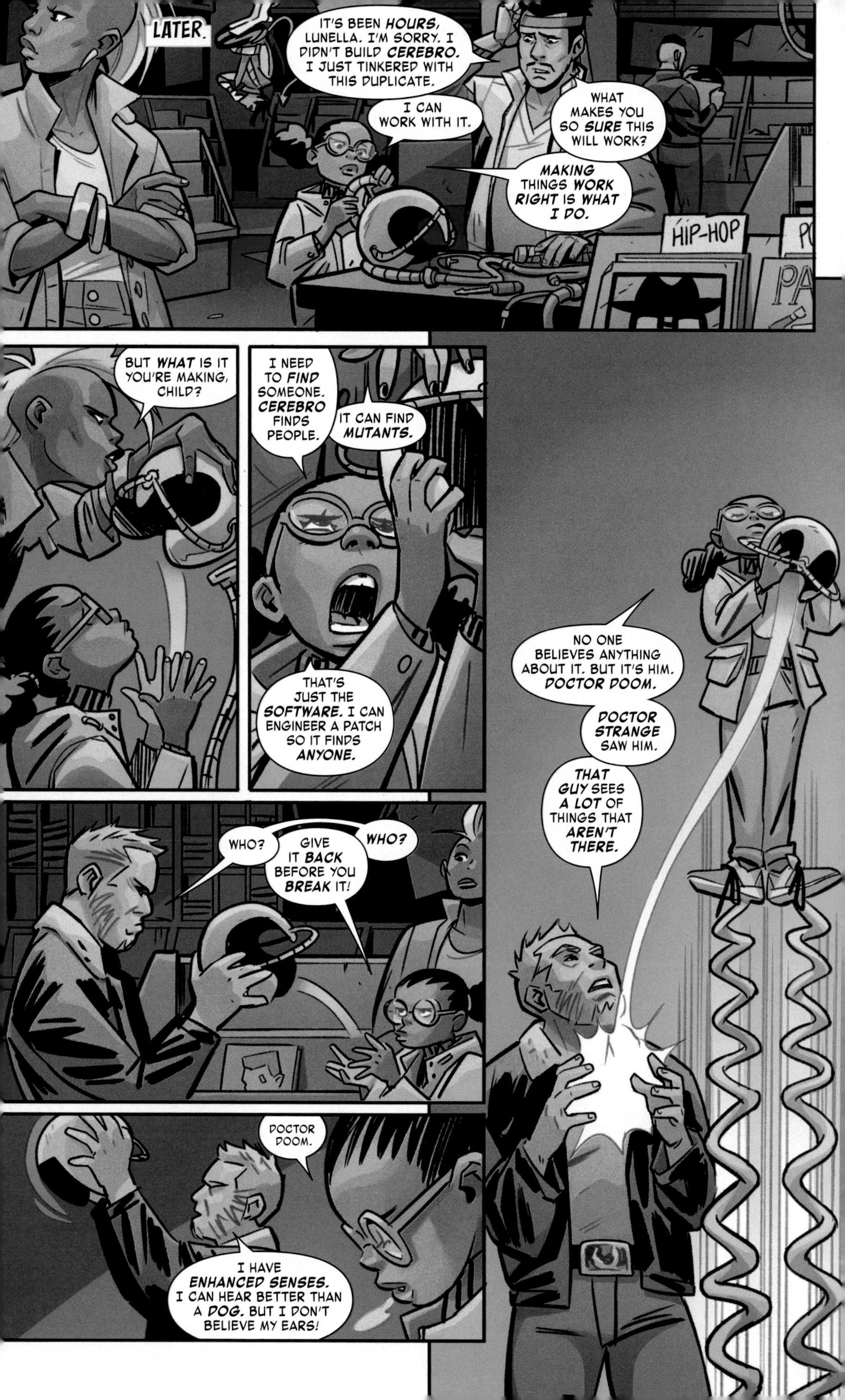
LATER.
IT'S BEEN HOURS, LUNELLA. I'M SORRY. I DIDN'T BUILD CEREBRO. I JUST TINKERED WITH THIS DUPLICATE.
I CAN WORK WITH IT.
WHAT MAKES YOU SO SURE THIS WILL WORK?
MAKING THINGS WORK RIGHT IS WHAT I DO.
HIP-HOP
BUT WHAT IS IT YOU'RE MAKING, CHILD?
I NEED TO FIND SOMEONE. CEREBRO FINDS PEOPLE.
IT CAN FIND MUTANTS.
THAT'S JUST THE SOFTWARE. I CAN ENGINEER A PATCH SO IT FINDS ANYONE.
WHO?
WHO?
GIVE IT BACK BEFORE YOU BREAK IT!
DOCTOR DOOM.
I HAVE ENHANCED SENSES. I CAN HEAR BETTER THAN A DOG. BUT I DON'T BELIEVE MY EARS!
NO ONE BELIEVES ANYTHING ABOUT IT. BUT IT'S HIM. DOCTOR DOOM.
DOCTOR STRANGE SAW HIM.
THAT GUY SEES A LOT OF THINGS THAT AREN'T THERE.

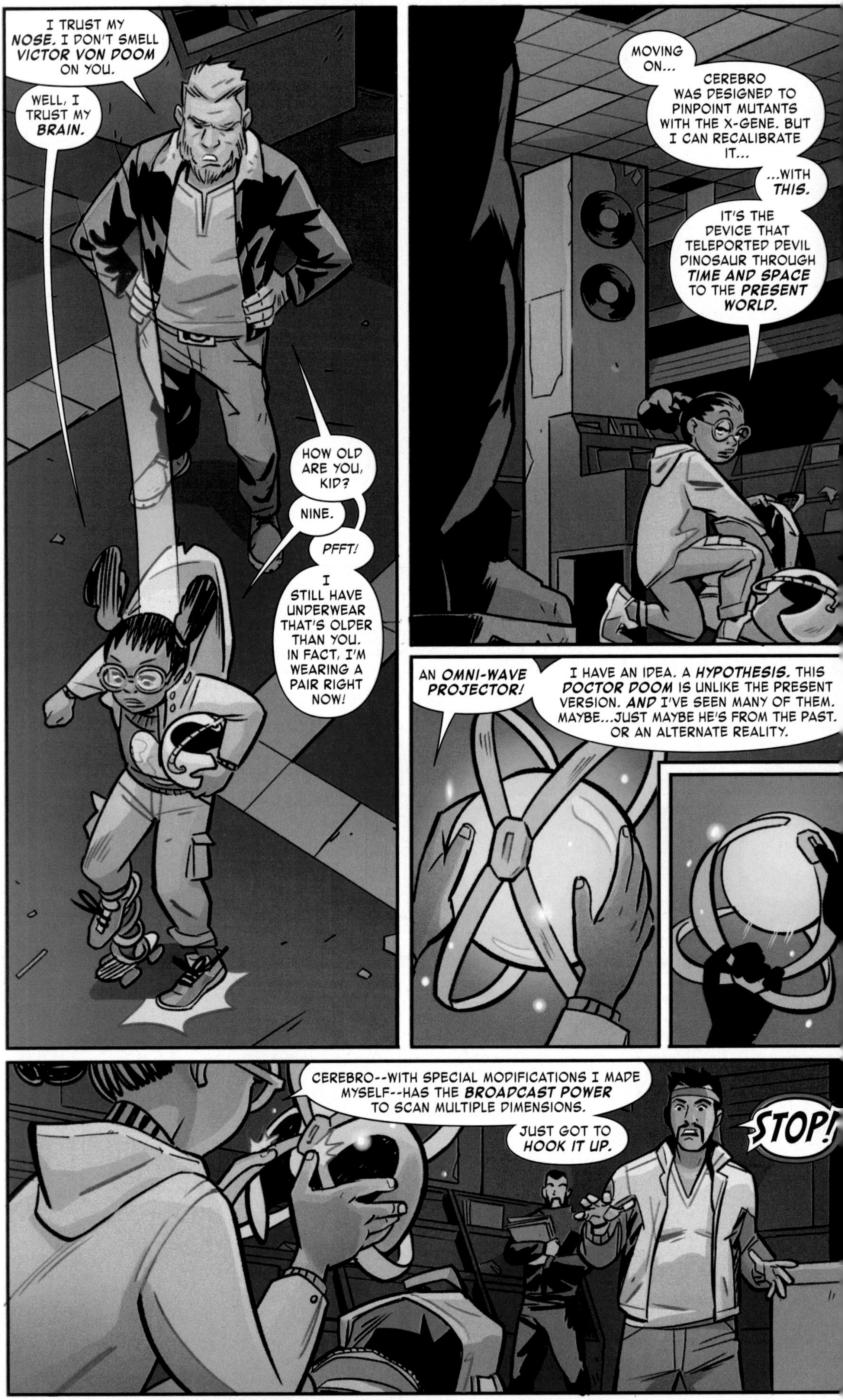
I TRUST MY NOSE. I DON'T SMELL VICTOR VON DOOM ON YOU.
WELL, I TRUST MY BRAIN.
HOW OLD ARE YOU, KID?
NINE.
PFFT!
I STILL HAVE UNDERWEAR THAT'S OLDER THAN YOU. IN FACT, I'M WEARING A PAIR RIGHT NOW!
MOVING ON...
CEREBRO WAS DESIGNED TO PINPOINT MUTANTS WITH THE X-GENE. BUT I CAN RECALIBRATE IT...
...WITH THIS.
IT'S THE DEVICE THAT TELEPORTED DEVIL DINOSAUR THROUGH TIME AND SPACE TO THE PRESENT WORLD.
AN OMNI-WAVE PROJECTOR!
I HAVE AN IDEA. A HYPOTHESIS. THIS DOCTOR DOOM IS UNLIKE THE PRESENT VERSION. AND I'VE SEEN MANY OF THEM. MAYBE...JUST MAYBE HE'S FROM THE PAST. OR AN ALTERNATE REALITY.
CEREBRO--WITH SPECIAL MODIFICATIONS I MADE MYSELF--HAS THE BROADCAST POWER TO SCAN MULTIPLE DIMENSIONS.
JUST GOT TO HOOK IT UP.
STOP!

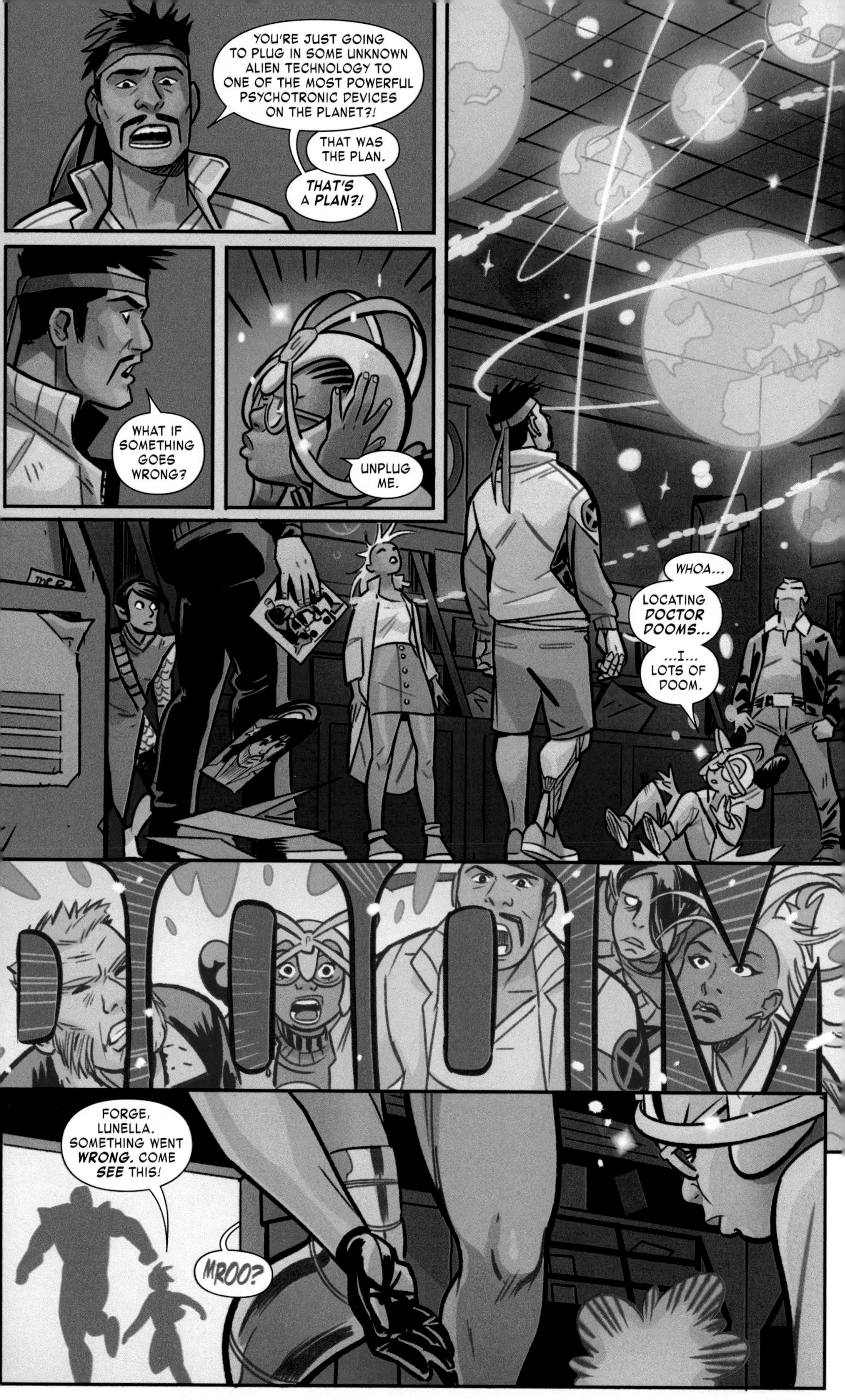
YOU'RE JUST GOING TO PLUG IN SOME UNKNOWN ALIEN TECHNOLOGY TO ONE OF THE MOST POWERFUL PSYCHOTRONIC DEVICES ON THE PLANET?!
THAT WAS THE PLAN.
THAT'S A PLAN?!
WHAT IF SOMETHING GOES WRONG?
UNPLUG ME.
WHOA...
LOCATING DOCTOR DOOMS...
...I... LOTS OF DOOM.
FORGE, LUNELLA. SOMETHING WENT WRONG. COME SEE THIS!
MROO?

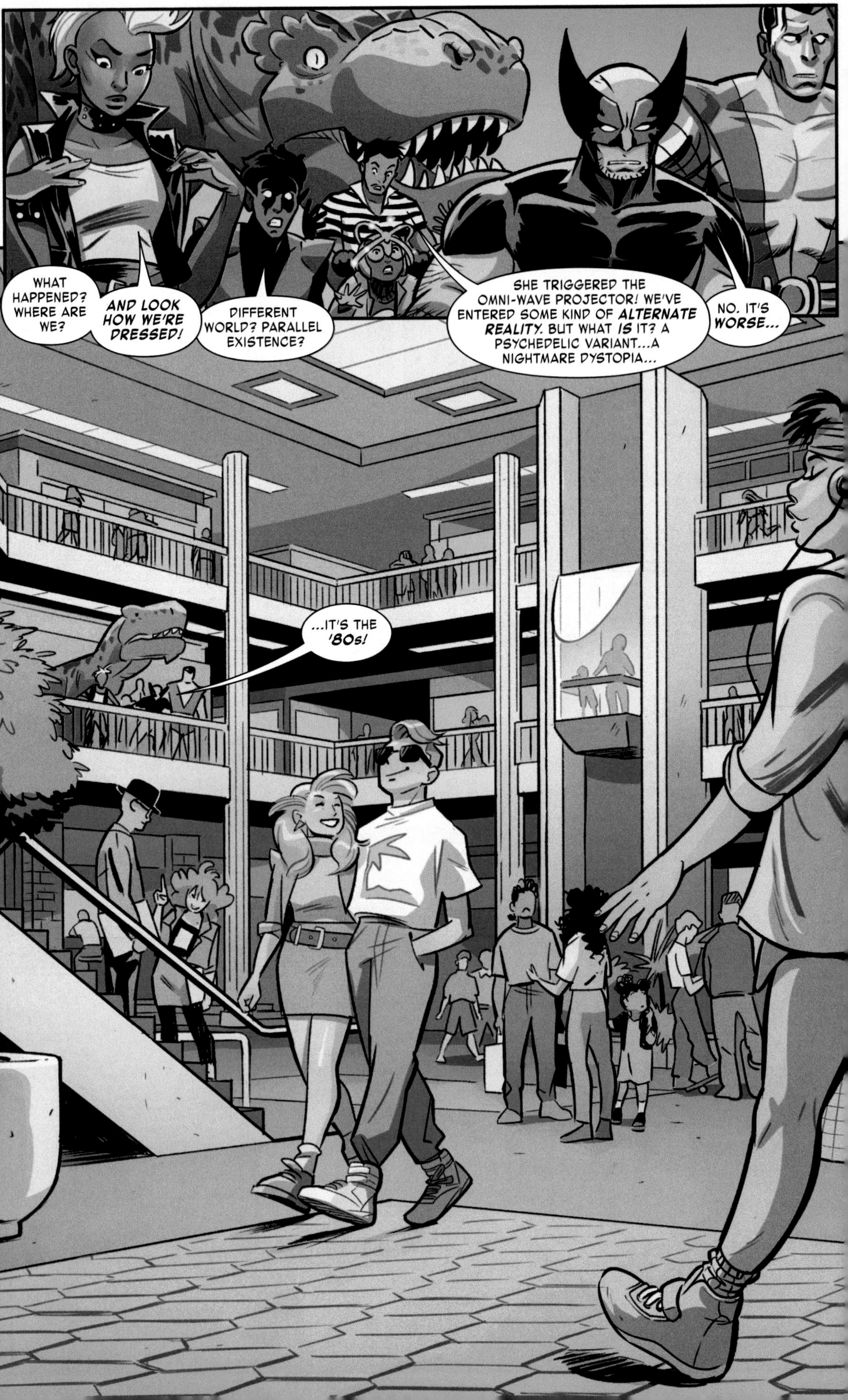

WHAT HAPPENED? WHERE ARE WE?
AND LOOK HOW WE'RE DRESSED!
DIFFERENT WORLD? PARALLEL EXISTENCE?
SHE TRIGGERED THE OMNI-WAVE PROJECTOR! WE'VE ENTERED SOME KIND OF ALTERNATE REALITY. BUT WHAT IS IT? A PSYCHEDELIC VARIANT...A NIGHTMARE DYSTOPIA...
NO. IT'S WORSE...
...IT'S THE '80s!

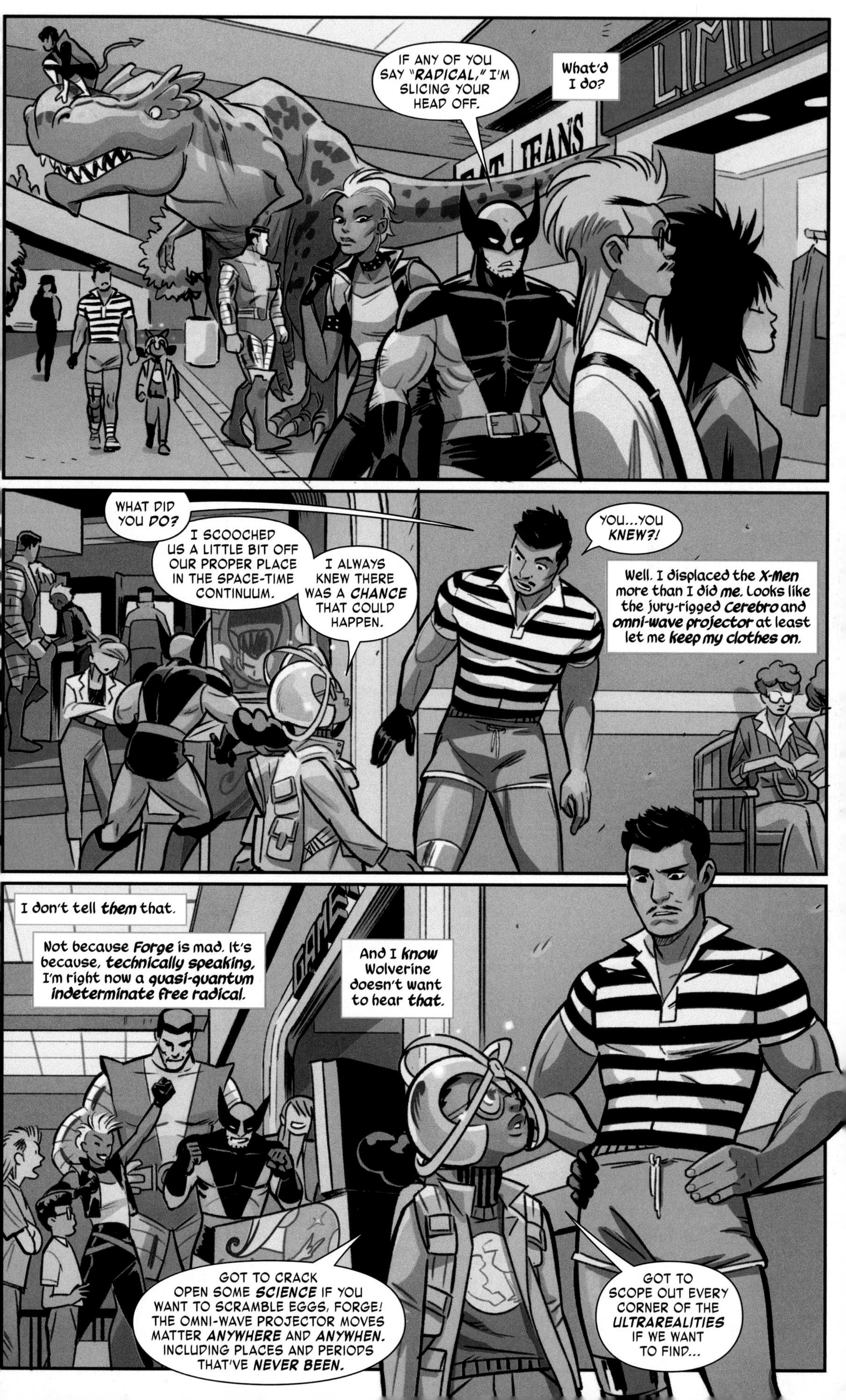
IF ANY OF YOU SAY "RADICAL," I'M SLICING YOUR HEAD OFF.
What'd I do?
LIMIT
JEANS
WHAT DID YOU DO?
I SCOOCHED US A LITTLE BIT OFF OUR PROPER PLACE IN THE SPACE-TIME CONTINUUM.
I ALWAYS KNEW THERE WAS A CHANCE THAT COULD HAPPEN.
YOU...YOU KNEW?!
Well. I displaced the X-Men more than I did me. Looks like the jury-rigged Cerebro and omni-wave projector at least let me keep my clothes on.
I don't tell them that.
Not because Forge is mad. It's because, technically speaking, I'm right now a quasi-quantum indeterminate free radical.
And I know Wolverine doesn't want to hear that.
GOT TO CRACK OPEN SOME SCIENCE IF YOU WANT TO SCRAMBLE EGGS, FORGE! THE OMNI-WAVE PROJECTOR MOVES MATTER ANYWHERE AND ANYWHEN. INCLUDING PLACES AND PERIODS THAT'VE NEVER BEEN.
GOT TO SCOPE OUT EVERY CORNER OF THE ULTRAREALITIES IF WE WANT TO FIND...

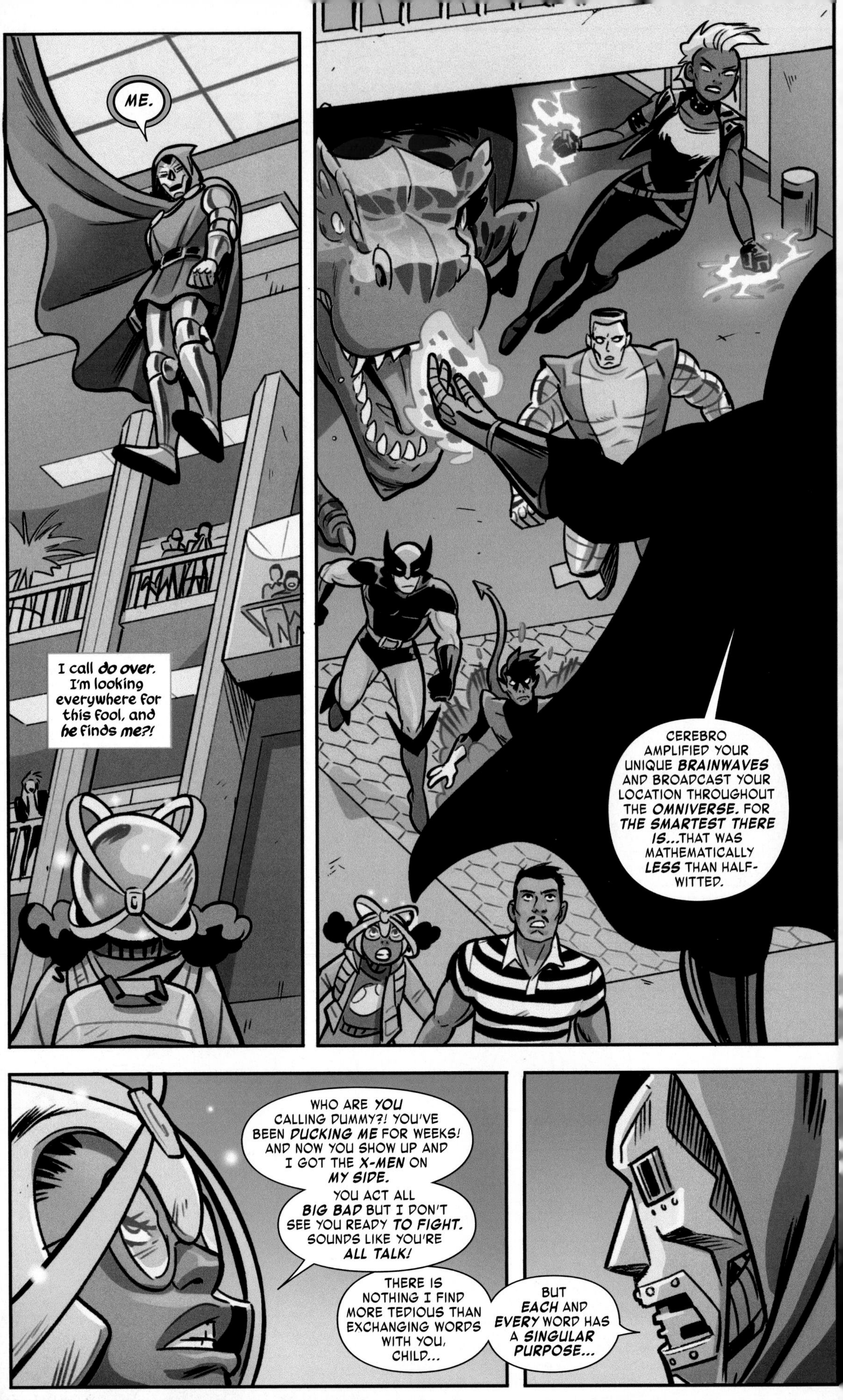
ME.
I call do over. I'm looking everywhere for this fool, and he finds me?!
CEREBRO AMPLIFIED YOUR UNIQUE BRAINWAVES AND BROADCAST YOUR LOCATION THROUGHOUT THE OMNIVERSE. FOR THE SMARTEST THERE IS...THAT WAS MATHEMATICALLY LESS THAN HALF-WITTED.
WHO ARE YOU CALLING DUMMY?! YOU'VE BEEN DUCKING ME FOR WEEKS! AND NOW YOU SHOW UP AND I GOT THE X-MEN ON MY SIDE.
YOU ACT ALL BIG BAD BUT I DON'T SEE YOU READY TO FIGHT. SOUNDS LIKE YOU'RE ALL TALK!
THERE IS NOTHING I FIND MORE TEDIOUS THAN EXCHANGING WORDS WITH YOU, CHILD...
BUT EACH AND EVERY WORD HAS A SINGULAR PURPOSE...

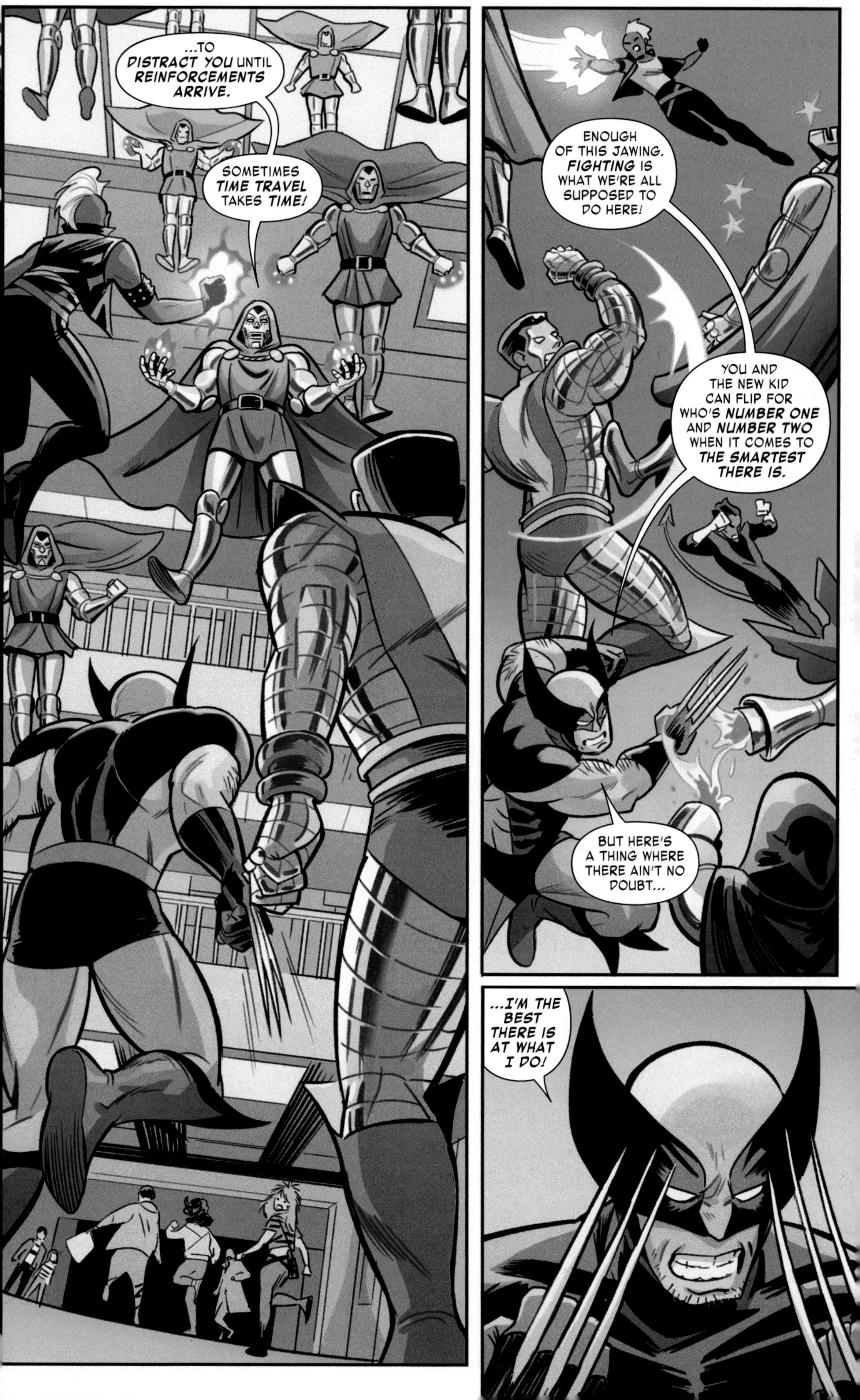
...TO DISTRACT YOU UNTIL REINFORCEMENTS ARRIVE.
SOMETIMES TIME TRAVEL TAKES TIME!
ENOUGH OF THIS JAWING. FIGHTING IS WHAT WE'RE ALL SUPPOSED TO DO HERE!
YOU AND THE NEW KID CAN FLIP FOR WHO'S NUMBER ONE AND NUMBER TWO WHEN IT COMES TO THE SMARTEST THERE IS.
BUT HERE'S A THING WHERE THERE AIN'T NO DOUBT...
...I'M THE BEST THERE IS AT WHAT I DO!

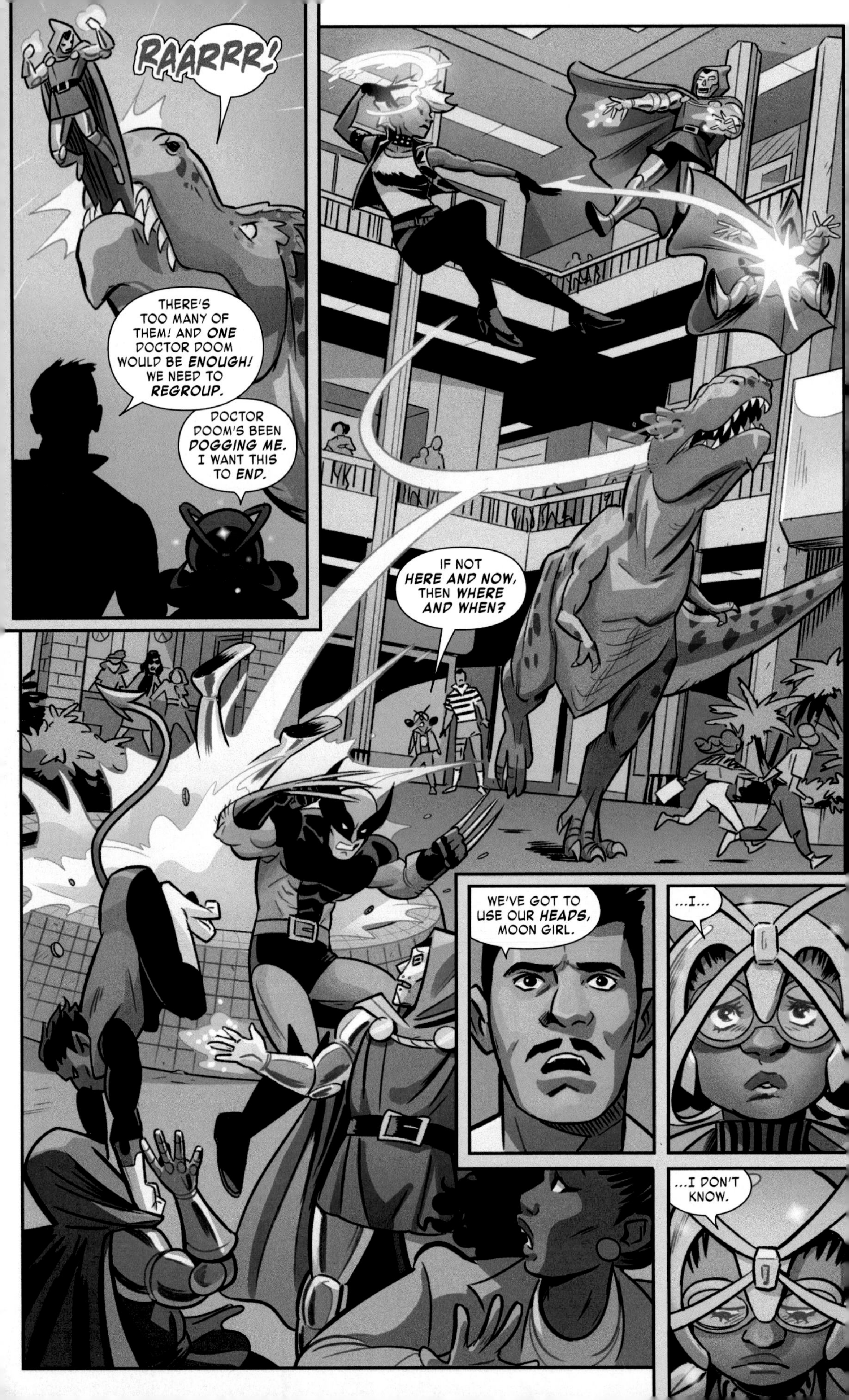
RAARRR!
THERE'S TOO MANY OF THEM! AND ONE DOCTOR DOOM WOULD BE ENOUGH! WE NEED TO REGROUP.
DOCTOR DOOM'S BEEN DOGGING ME. I WANT THIS TO END.
IF NOT HERE AND NOW, THEN WHERE AND WHEN?
WE'VE GOT TO USE OUR HEADS, MOON GIRL.
...I...
...I DON'T KNOW.

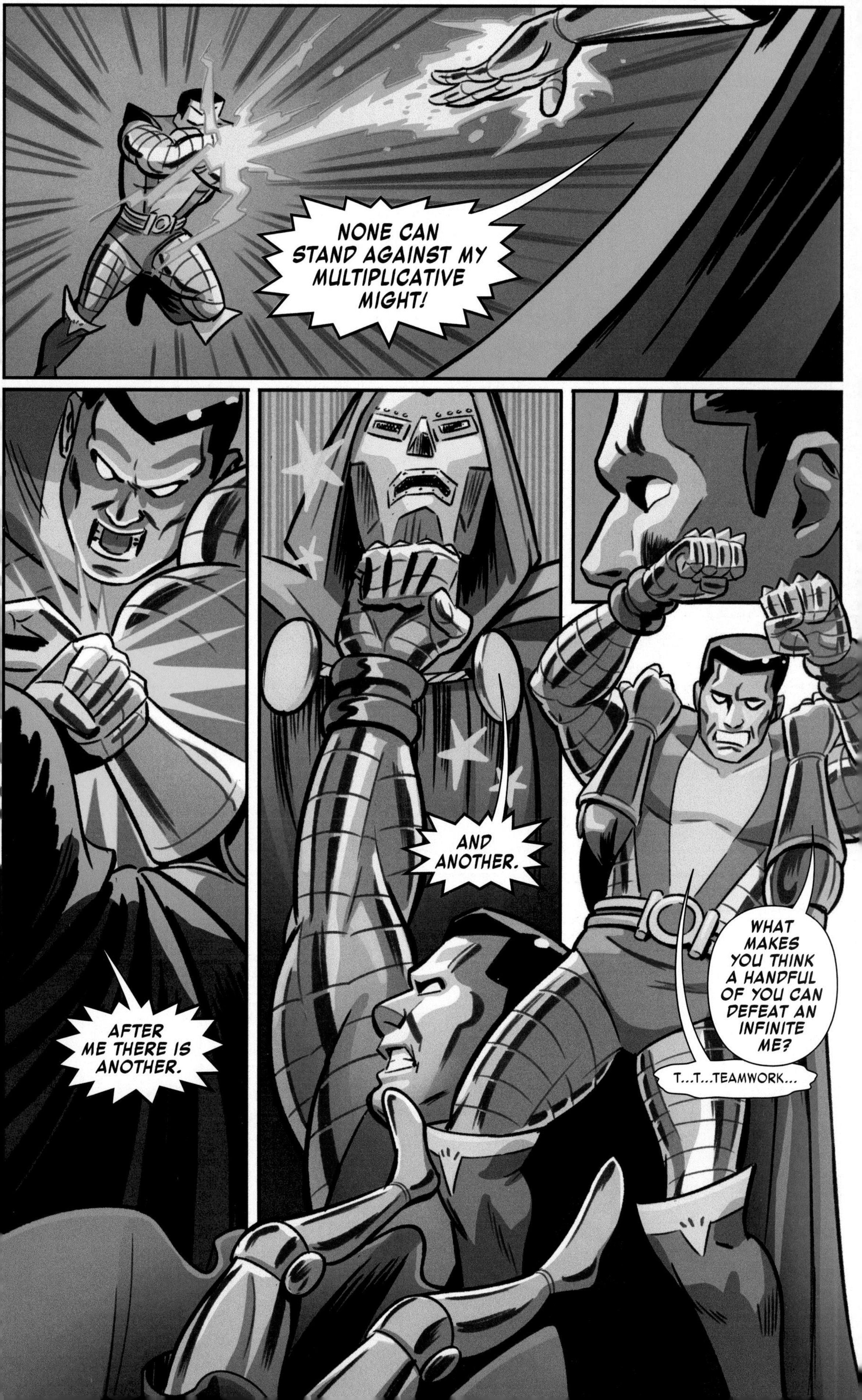
NONE CAN STAND AGAINST MY MULTIPLICATIVE MIGHT!
AFTER ME THERE IS ANOTHER.
AND ANOTHER.
WHAT MAKES YOU THINK A HANDFUL OF YOU CAN DEFEAT AN INFINITE ME?
T...T...TEAMWORK...

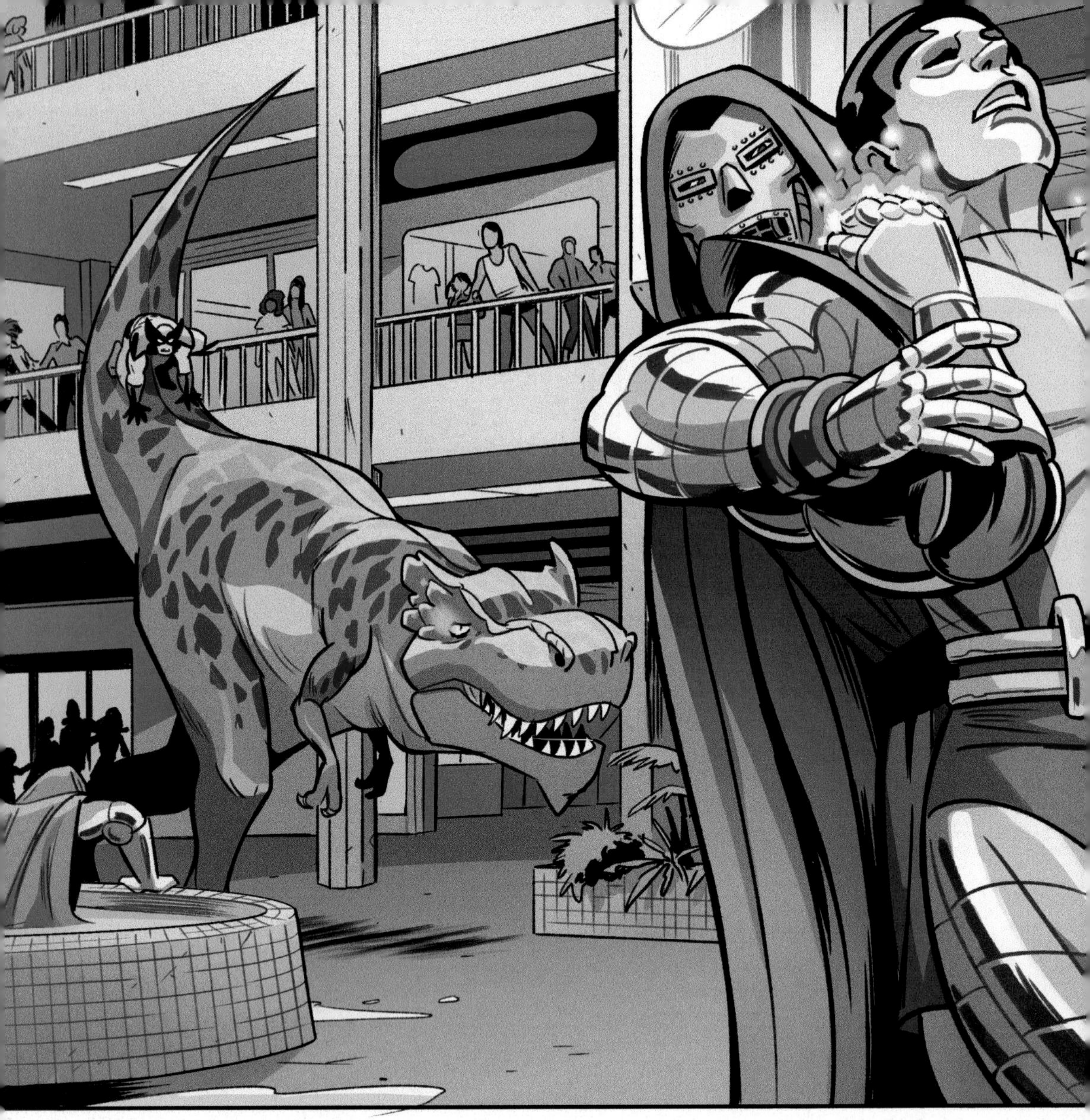

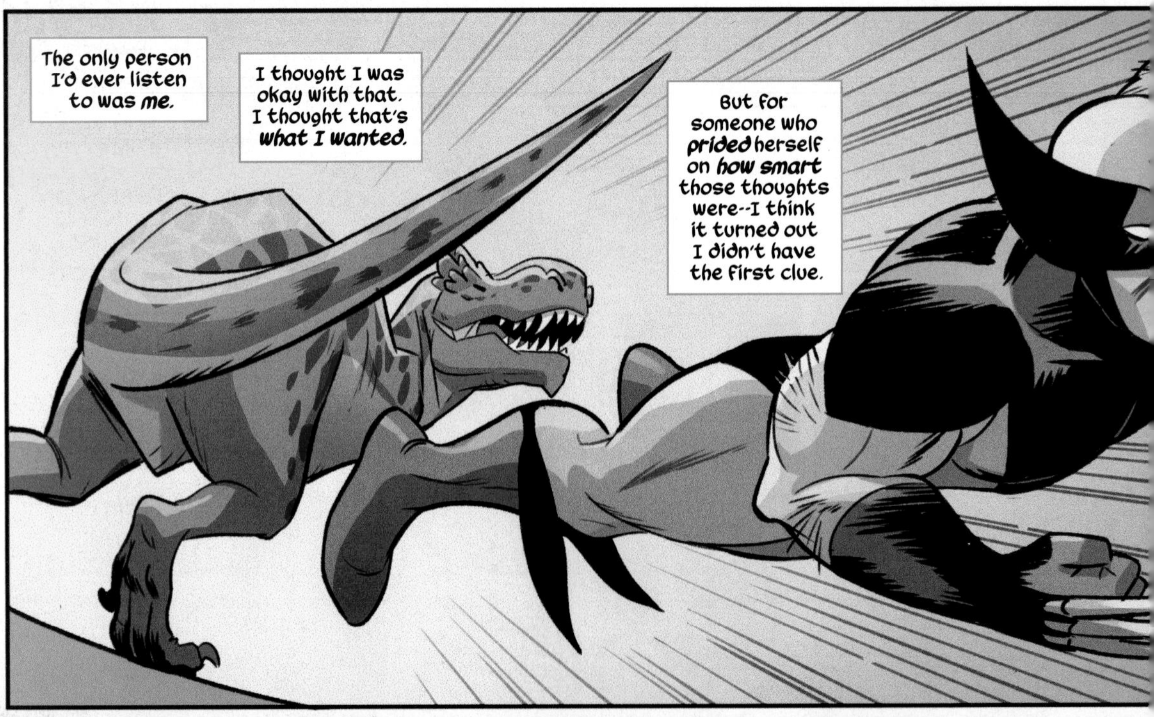
The only person I'd ever listen to was *me.*
I thought I was okay with that. I thought that's *what I wanted.*
But for someone who *prided* herself on *how smart* those thoughts were--I think it turned out I didn't have the first clue.

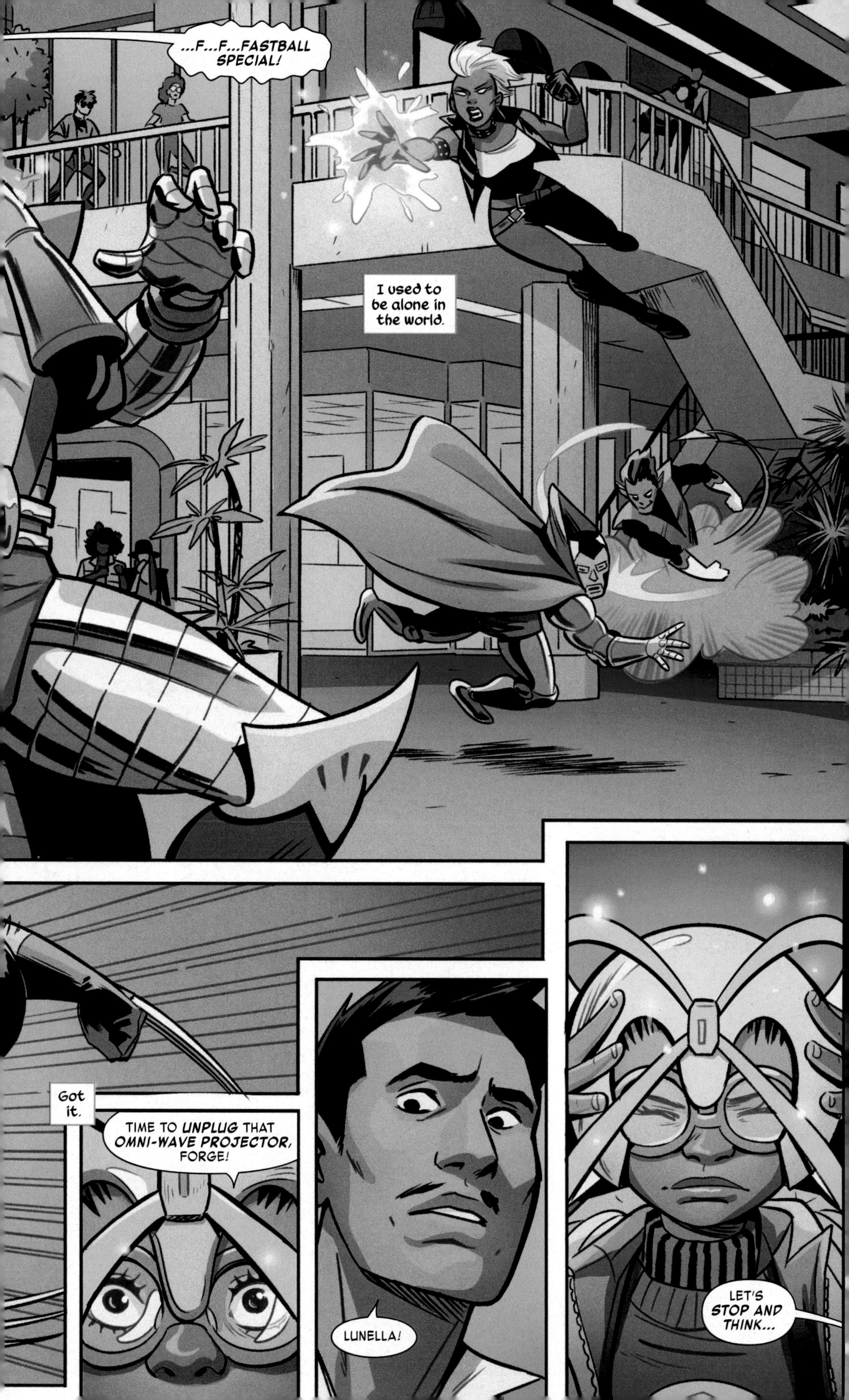
...F...F...FASTBALL SPECIAL!
I used to be alone in the world.
Got it.
TIME TO UNPLUG THAT OMNI-WAVE PROJECTOR, FORGE!
LUNELLA!
LET'S STOP AND THINK...

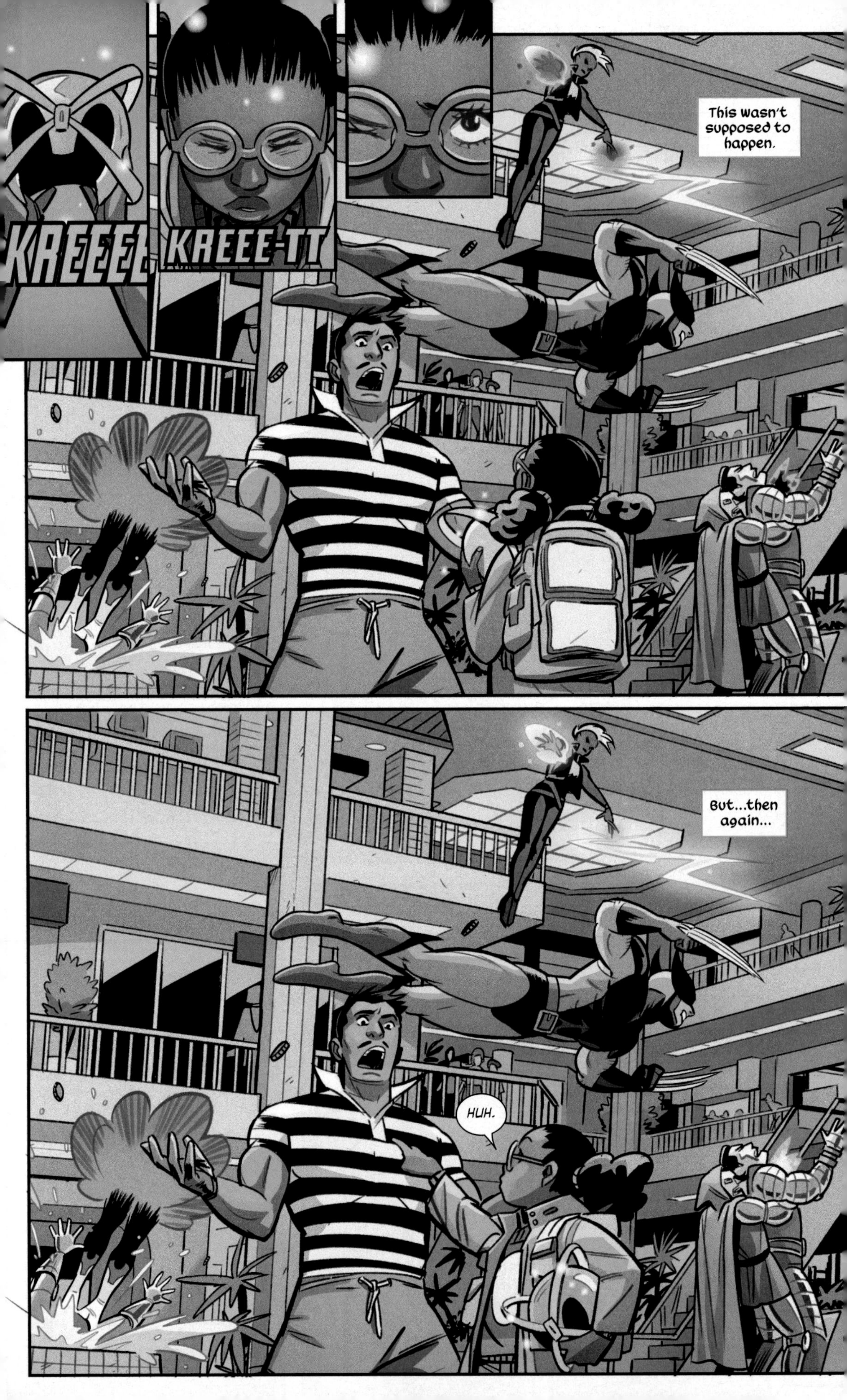

KREEEE
KREEE-TT
This wasn't supposed to happen.
But...then again...
HUH.

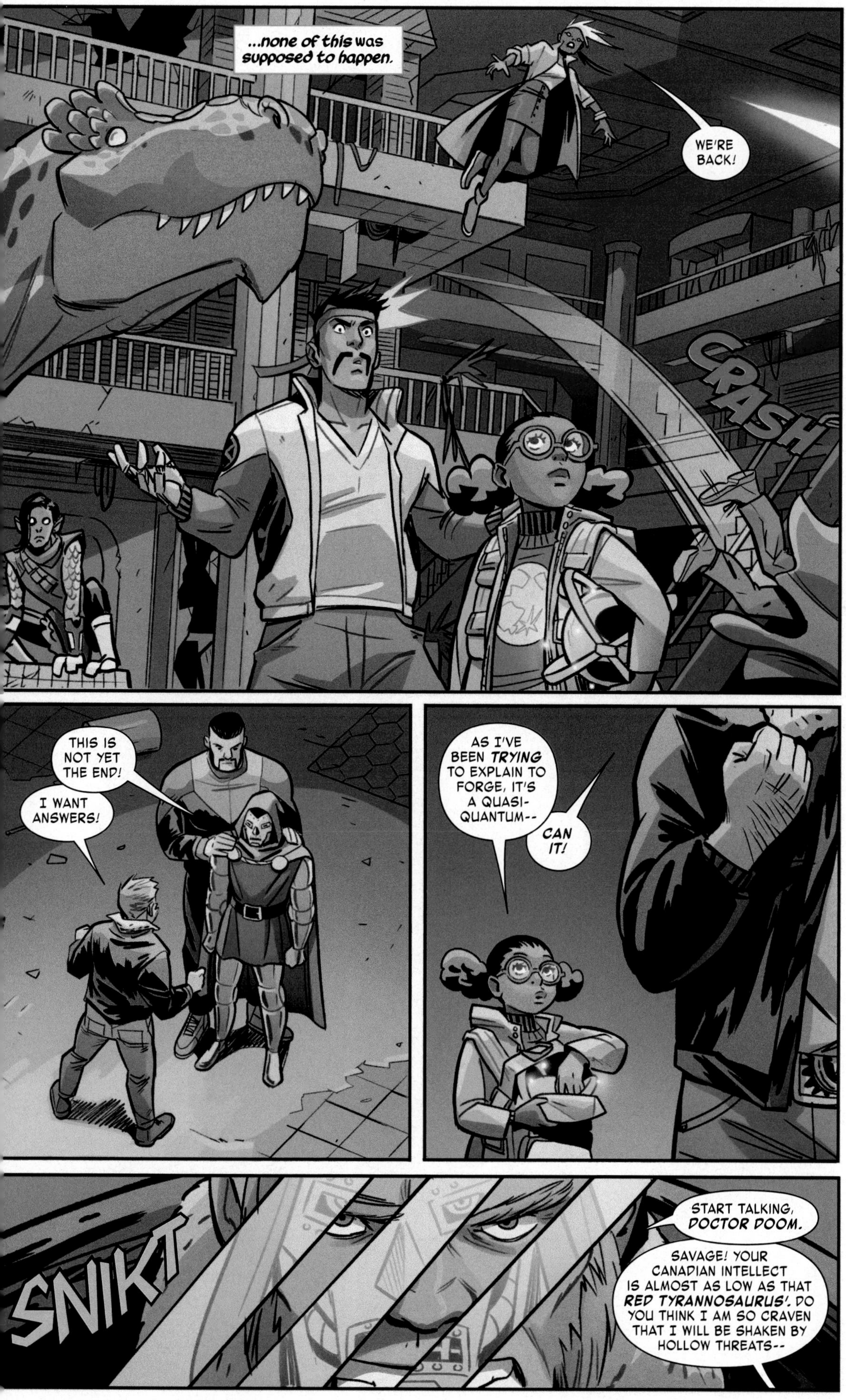
...none of this was supposed to happen.
WE'RE BACK!
CRASH
THIS IS NOT YET THE END!
I WANT ANSWERS!
AS I'VE BEEN TRYING TO EXPLAIN TO FORGE, IT'S A QUASI-QUANTUM--
CAN IT!
SNIKT
START TALKING, DOCTOR DOOM.
SAVAGE! YOUR CANADIAN INTELLECT IS ALMOST AS LOW AS THAT RED TYRANNOSAURUS'. DO YOU THINK I AM SO CRAVEN THAT I WILL BE SHAKEN BY HOLLOW THREATS--

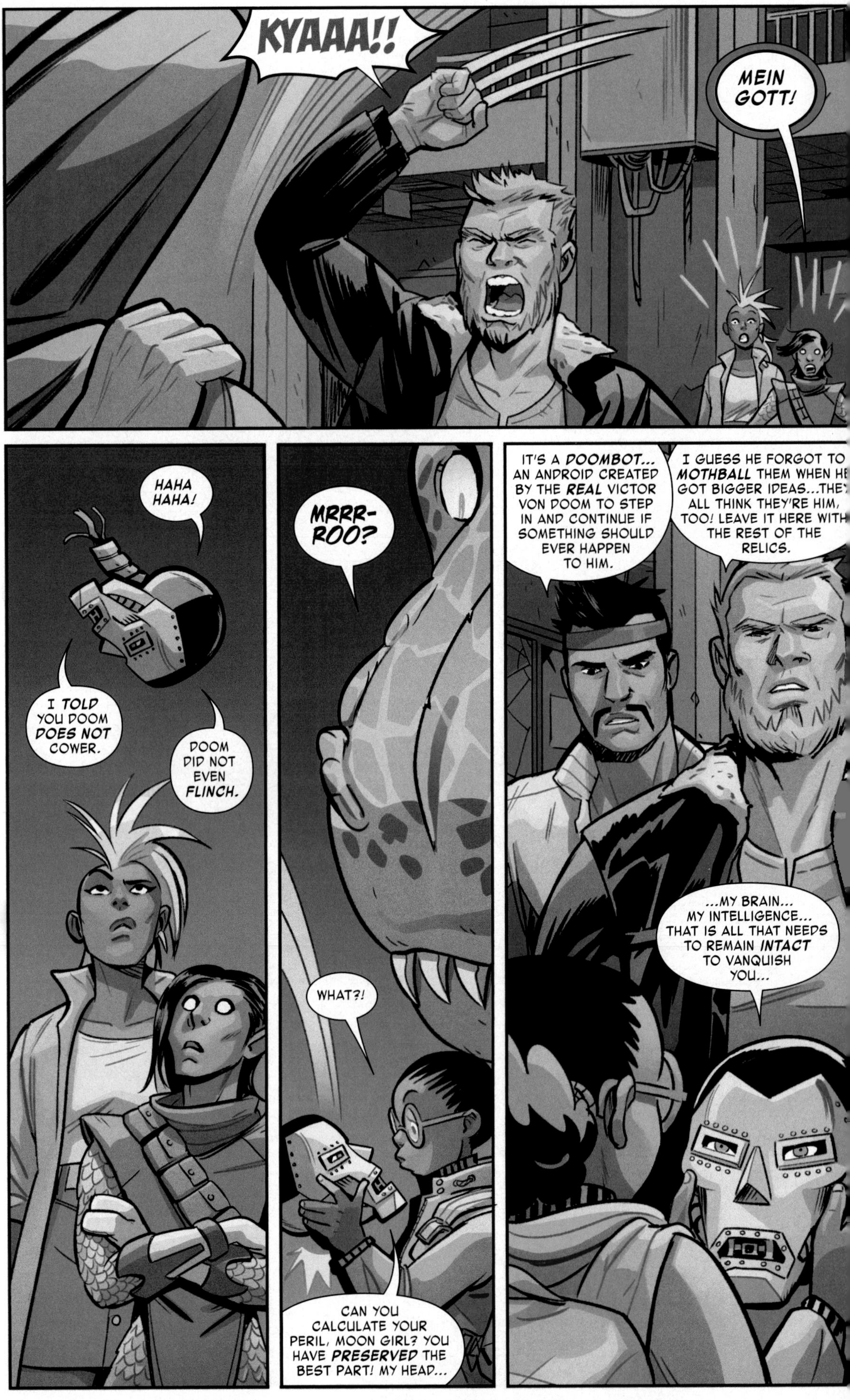

KYAAA!!
MEIN GOTT!
HAHA HAHA!
I TOLD YOU DOOM DOES NOT COWER.
DOOM DID NOT EVEN FLINCH.
MRRR-ROO?
WHAT?!
CAN YOU CALCULATE YOUR PERIL, MOON GIRL? YOU HAVE PRESERVED THE BEST PART! MY HEAD...
IT'S A DOOMBOT... AN ANDROID CREATED BY THE REAL VICTOR VON DOOM TO STEP IN AND CONTINUE IF SOMETHING SHOULD EVER HAPPEN TO HIM.
I GUESS HE FORGOT TO MOTHBALL THEM WHEN HE GOT BIGGER IDEAS...THEY ALL THINK THEY'RE HIM, TOO! LEAVE IT HERE WITH THE REST OF THE RELICS.
...MY BRAIN... MY INTELLIGENCE... THAT IS ALL THAT NEEDS TO REMAIN INTACT TO VANQUISH YOU...

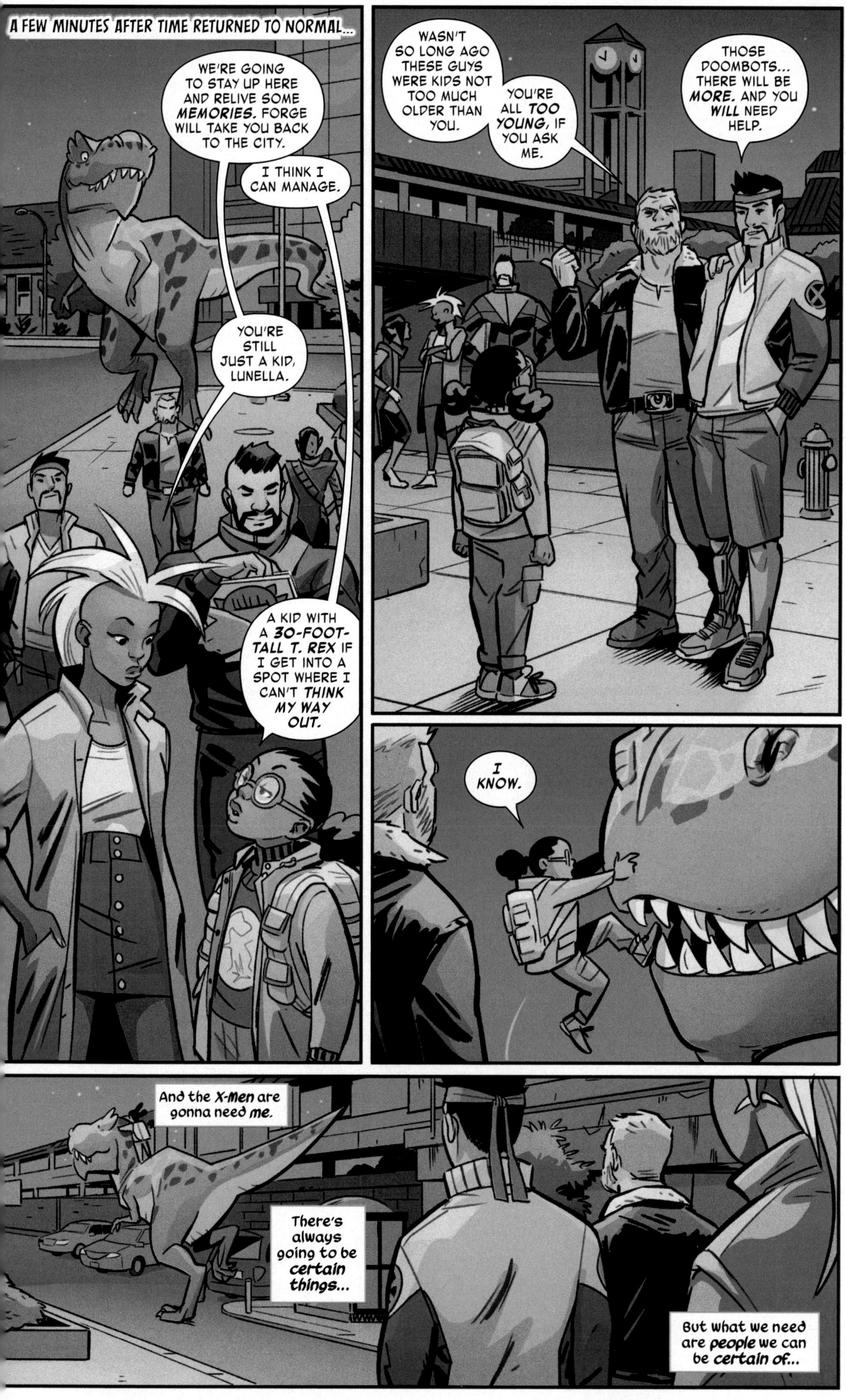
A FEW MINUTES AFTER TIME RETURNED TO NORMAL...
WE'RE GOING TO STAY UP HERE AND RELIVE SOME MEMORIES. FORGE WILL TAKE YOU BACK TO THE CITY.
I THINK I CAN MANAGE.
YOU'RE STILL JUST A KID, LUNELLA.
A KID WITH A 30-FOOT-TALL T. REX IF I GET INTO A SPOT WHERE I CAN'T THINK MY WAY OUT.
WASN'T SO LONG AGO THESE GUYS WERE KIDS NOT TOO MUCH OLDER THAN YOU.
YOU'RE ALL TOO YOUNG, IF YOU ASK ME.
THOSE DOOMBOTS... THERE WILL BE MORE. AND YOU WILL NEED HELP.
I KNOW.
And the X-Men are gonna need me.
There's always going to be certain things...
But what we need are people we can be certain of...

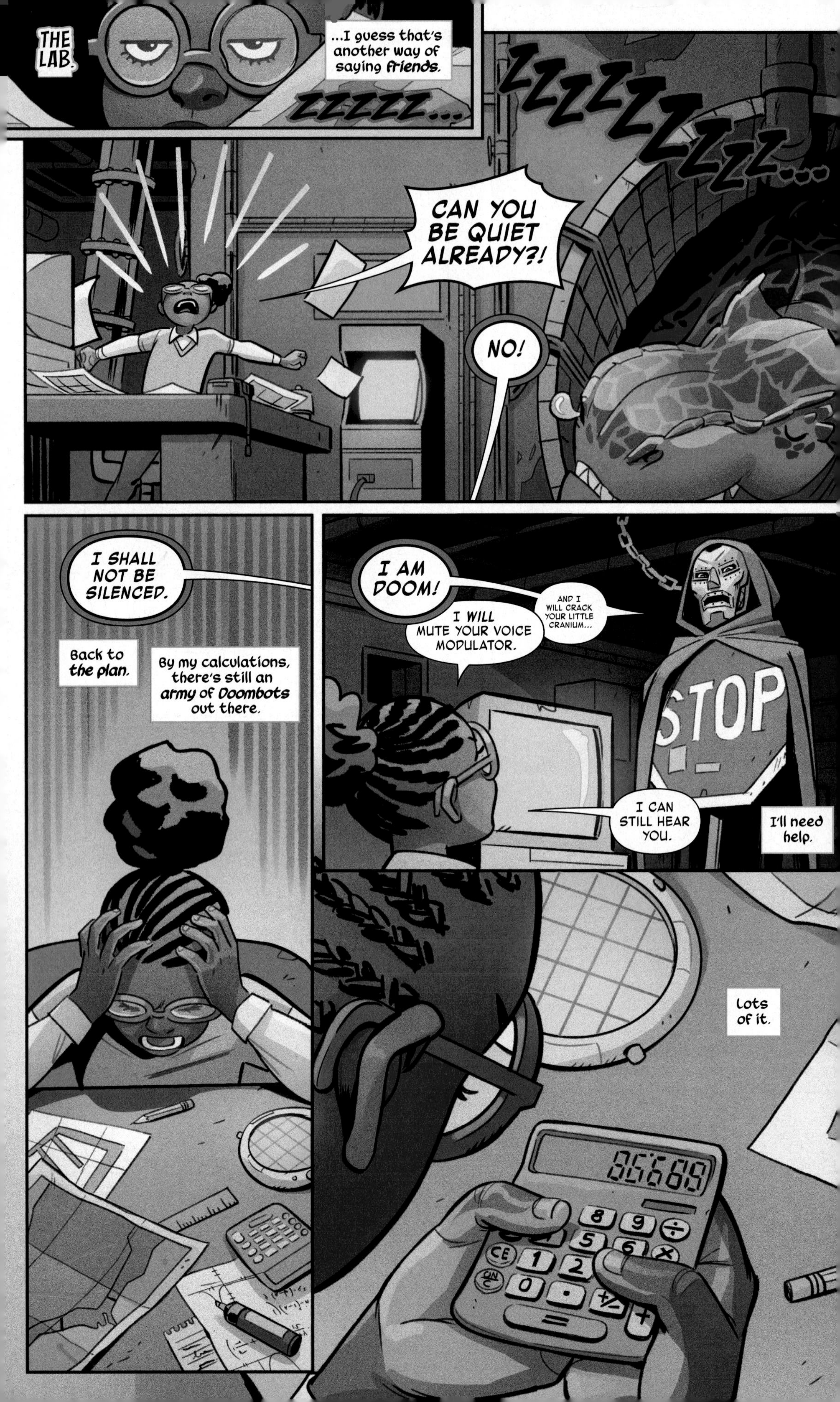
THE LAB.
...I guess that's another way of saying friends.
ZZZZZZ...
ZZZZZZZZZZZZ...
CAN YOU BE QUIET ALREADY?!
NO!
I SHALL NOT BE SILENCED.
Back to the plan.
By my calculations, there's still an army of Doombots out there.
I AM DOOM!
AND I WILL CRACK YOUR LITTLE CRANIUM...
I WILL MUTE YOUR VOICE MODULATOR.
STOP
I CAN STILL HEAR YOU.
I'll need help.
Lots of it.

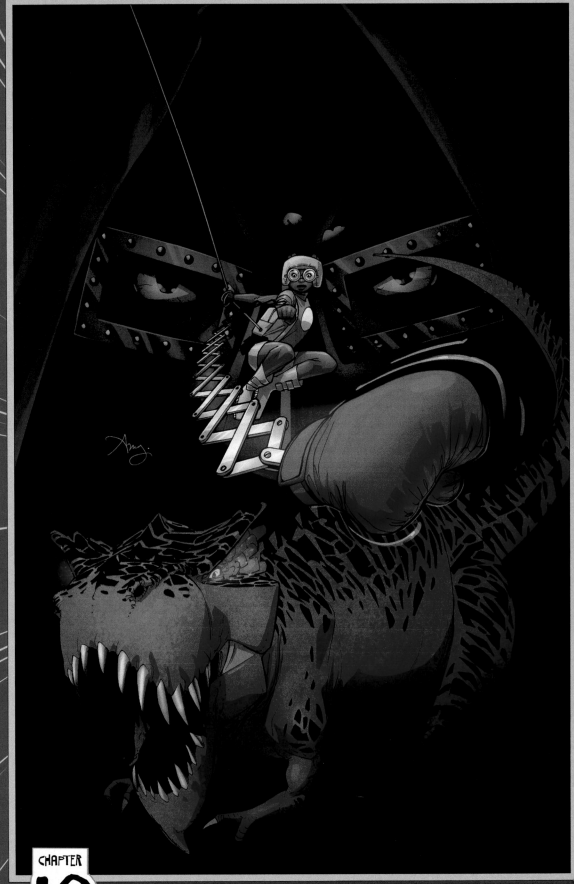

CHAPTER
18 "FULL MOON"

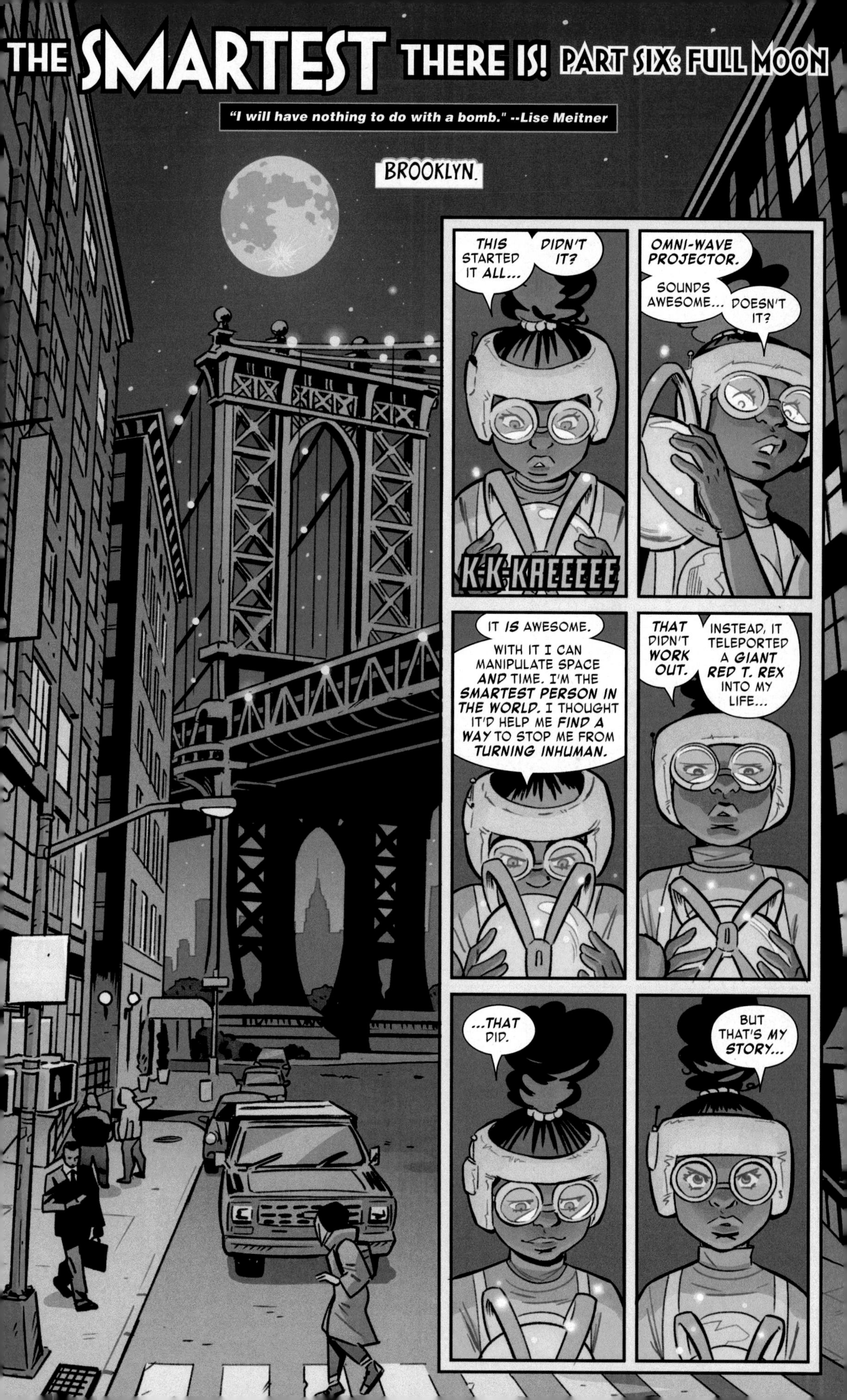
THE SMARTEST THERE IS! PART SIX: FULL MOON
"I will have nothing to do with a bomb." --Lise Meitner
BROOKLYN.
THIS STARTED IT ALL...
DIDN'T IT?
K-K-KREEEEEE
OMNI-WAVE PROJECTOR.
SOUNDS AWESOME...
DOESN'T IT?
IT IS AWESOME.
WITH IT I CAN MANIPULATE SPACE AND TIME. I'M THE SMARTEST PERSON IN THE WORLD. I THOUGHT IT'D HELP ME FIND A WAY TO STOP ME FROM TURNING INHUMAN.
THAT DIDN'T WORK OUT.
INSTEAD, IT TELEPORTED A GIANT RED T. REX INTO MY LIFE...
...THAT DID.
BUT THAT'S MY STORY...

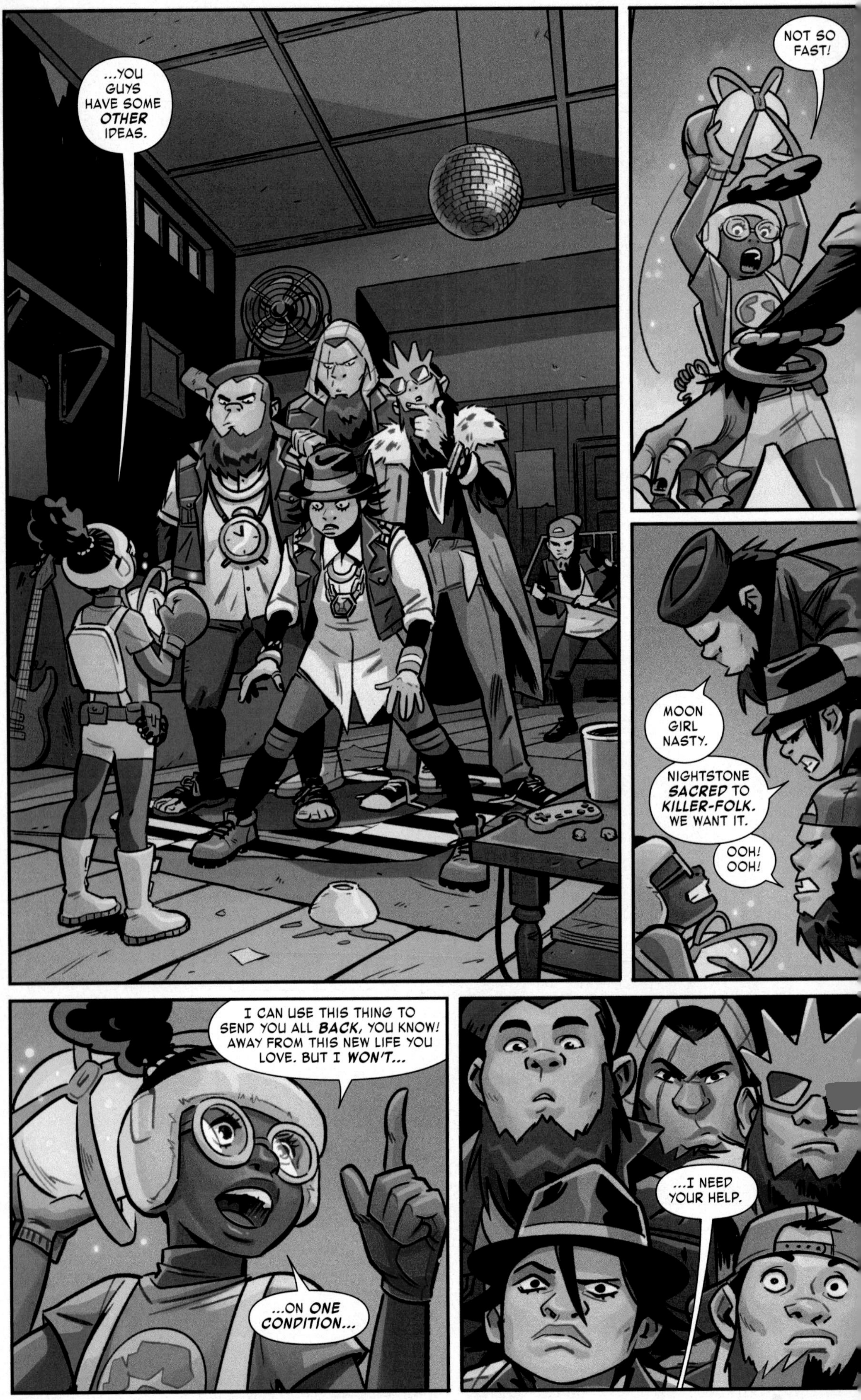
...YOU GUYS HAVE SOME *OTHER* IDEAS.
NOT SO FAST!
MOON GIRL NASTY.
NIGHTSTONE *SACRED* TO *KILLER-FOLK.* WE WANT IT.
OOH! OOH!
I CAN USE THIS THING TO SEND YOU ALL *BACK*, YOU KNOW! AWAY FROM THIS NEW LIFE YOU LOVE. BUT I *WON'T...*
...ON *ONE CONDITION...*
...I NEED YOUR HELP.

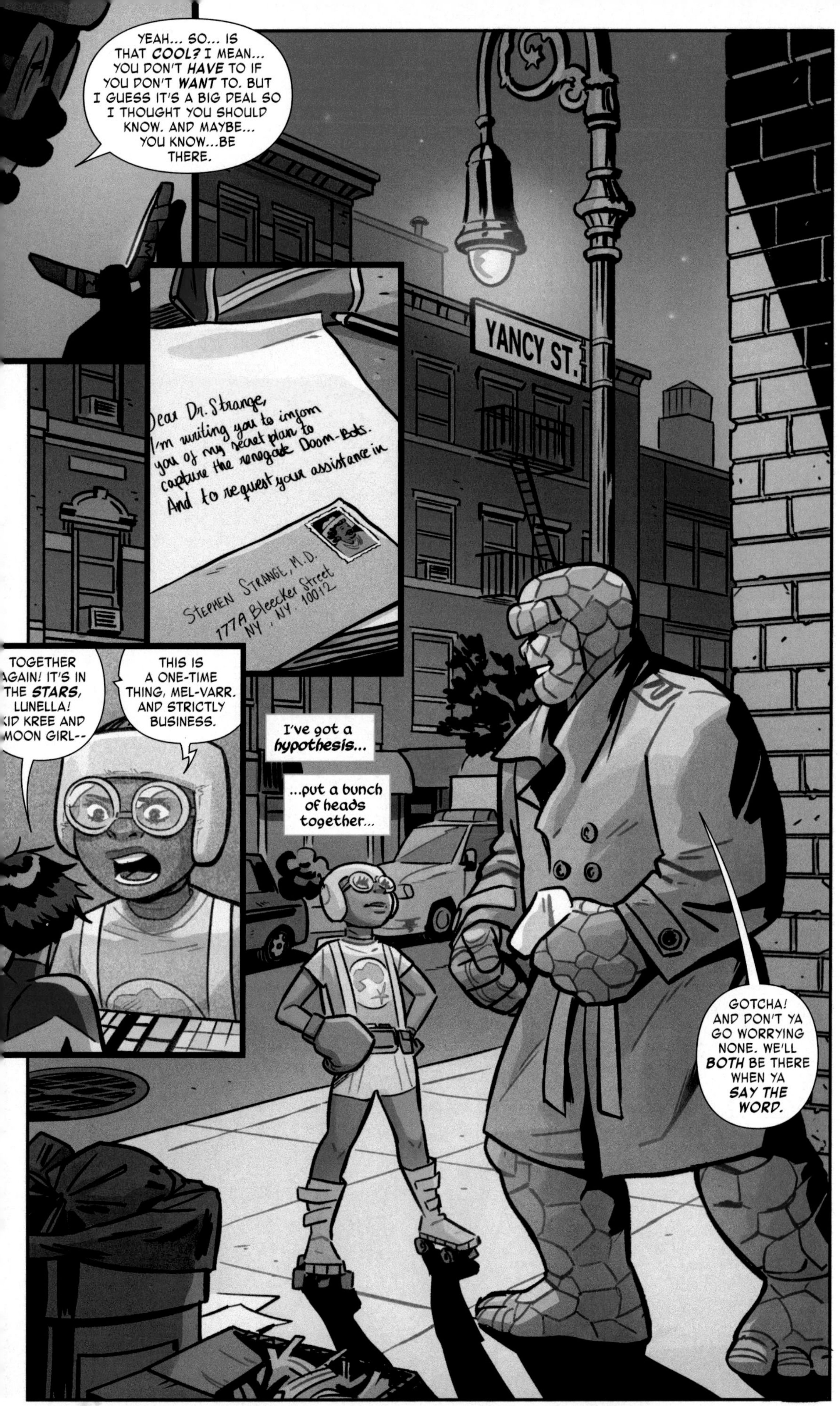
YEAH... SO... IS THAT COOL? I MEAN... YOU DON'T HAVE TO IF YOU DON'T WANT TO. BUT I GUESS IT'S A BIG DEAL SO I THOUGHT YOU SHOULD KNOW. AND MAYBE... YOU KNOW...BE THERE.
Dear Dr. Strange,
I'm writing you to inform you of my secret plan to capture the renegade Doom-Bots. And to request your assistance in
STEPHEN STRANGE, M.D.
177A Bleecker Street
NY, NY. 10012
YANCY ST.
TOGETHER AGAIN! IT'S IN THE STARS, LUNELLA! KID KREE AND MOON GIRL--
THIS IS A ONE-TIME THING, MEL-VARR. AND STRICTLY BUSINESS.
I've got a hypothesis...
...put a bunch of heads together...
GOTCHA! AND DON'T YA GO WORRYING NONE. WE'LL BOTH BE THERE WHEN YA SAY THE WORD.

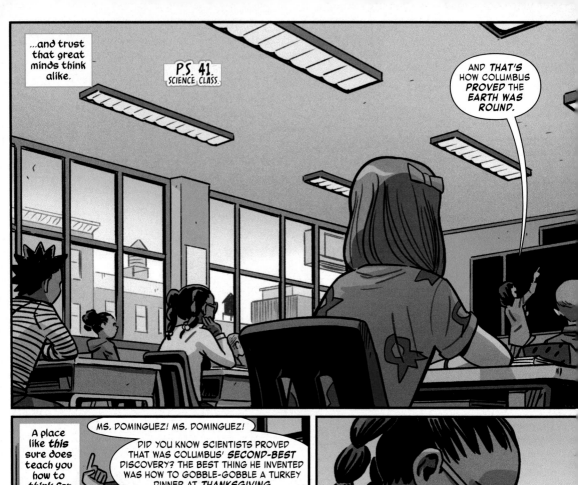

...and trust that great minds think alike.

P.S. 41.
SCIENCE CLASS.

AND *THAT'S* HOW COLUMBUS *PROVED* THE EARTH WAS *ROUND.*

A place like *this* sure does teach you how to *think for yourself...*

MS. DOMINGUEZ! MS. DOMINGUEZ!

DID YOU KNOW SCIENTISTS PROVED THAT WAS COLUMBUS' *SECOND-BEST* DISCOVERY? THE BEST THING HE INVENTED WAS HOW TO GOBBLE-GOBBLE A TURKEY DINNER AT *THANKSGIVING DINNER!*

...because *nobody* here knows what they're talking about!

I used to be all *alone.*

I never could admit that was *hard.*

Nowadays I'm thinking I was *wrong* back then. Being alone was *easier.*

At least for me.

But I know deep down *easier* doesn't mean *better...*

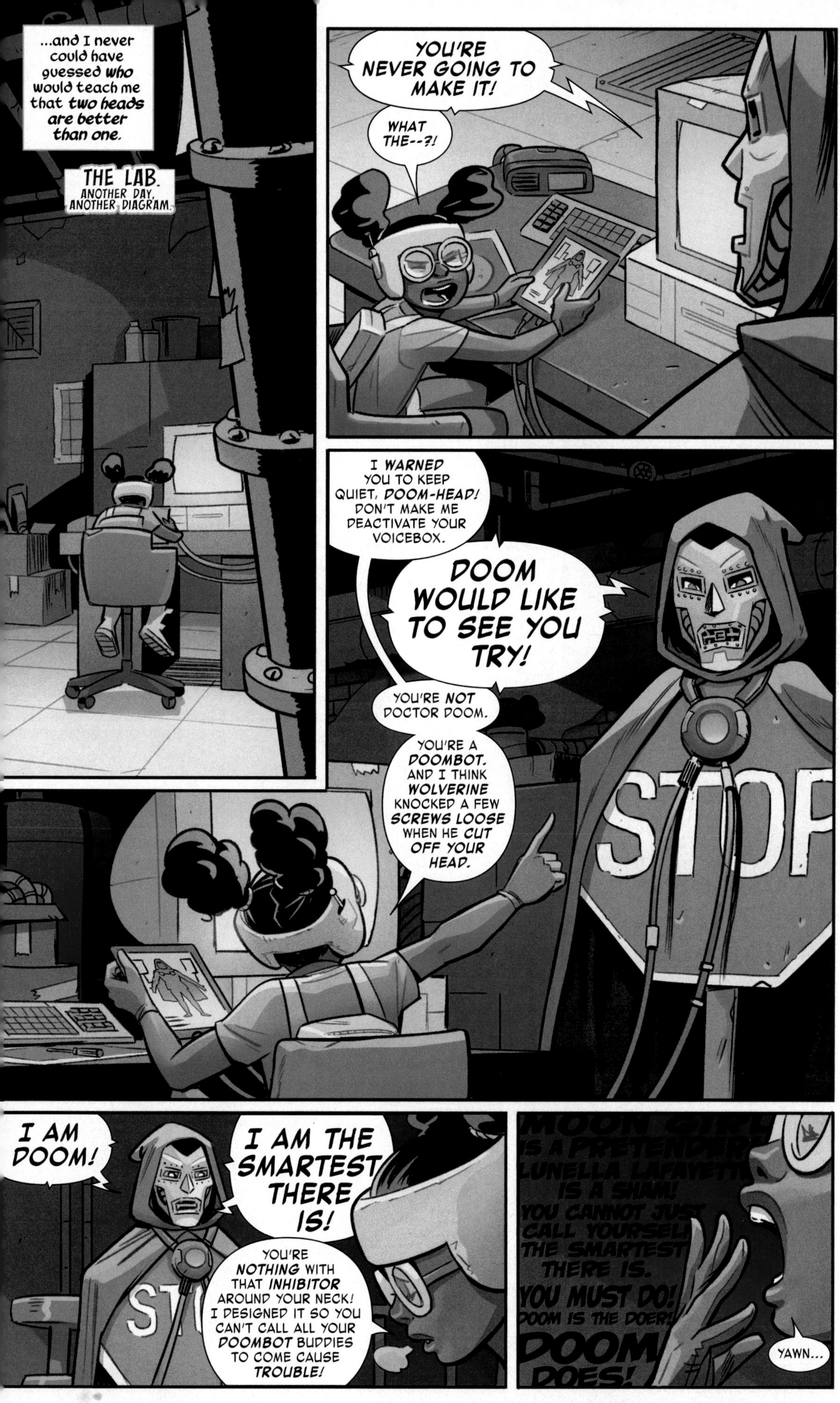
...and I never could have guessed who would teach me that two heads are better than one.
THE LAB. ANOTHER DAY, ANOTHER DIAGRAM.
YOU'RE NEVER GOING TO MAKE IT!
WHAT THE--?!
I WARNED YOU TO KEEP QUIET, DOOM-HEAD! DON'T MAKE ME DEACTIVATE YOUR VOICEBOX.
DOOM WOULD LIKE TO SEE YOU TRY!
YOU'RE NOT DOCTOR DOOM.
YOU'RE A DOOMBOT. AND I THINK WOLVERINE KNOCKED A FEW SCREWS LOOSE WHEN HE CUT OFF YOUR HEAD.
STOP
I AM DOOM!
I AM THE SMARTEST THERE IS!
YOU'RE NOTHING WITH THAT INHIBITOR AROUND YOUR NECK! I DESIGNED IT SO YOU CAN'T CALL ALL YOUR DOOMBOT BUDDIES TO COME CAUSE TROUBLE!
LUNELLA LAFAYETTE
IS A SHAM!
YOU CANNOT JUST
CALL YOURSELF
THE SMARTEST
THERE IS.
YOU MUST DO!
DOOM IS THE DOER!
DOOM
DOES!
YAWN...

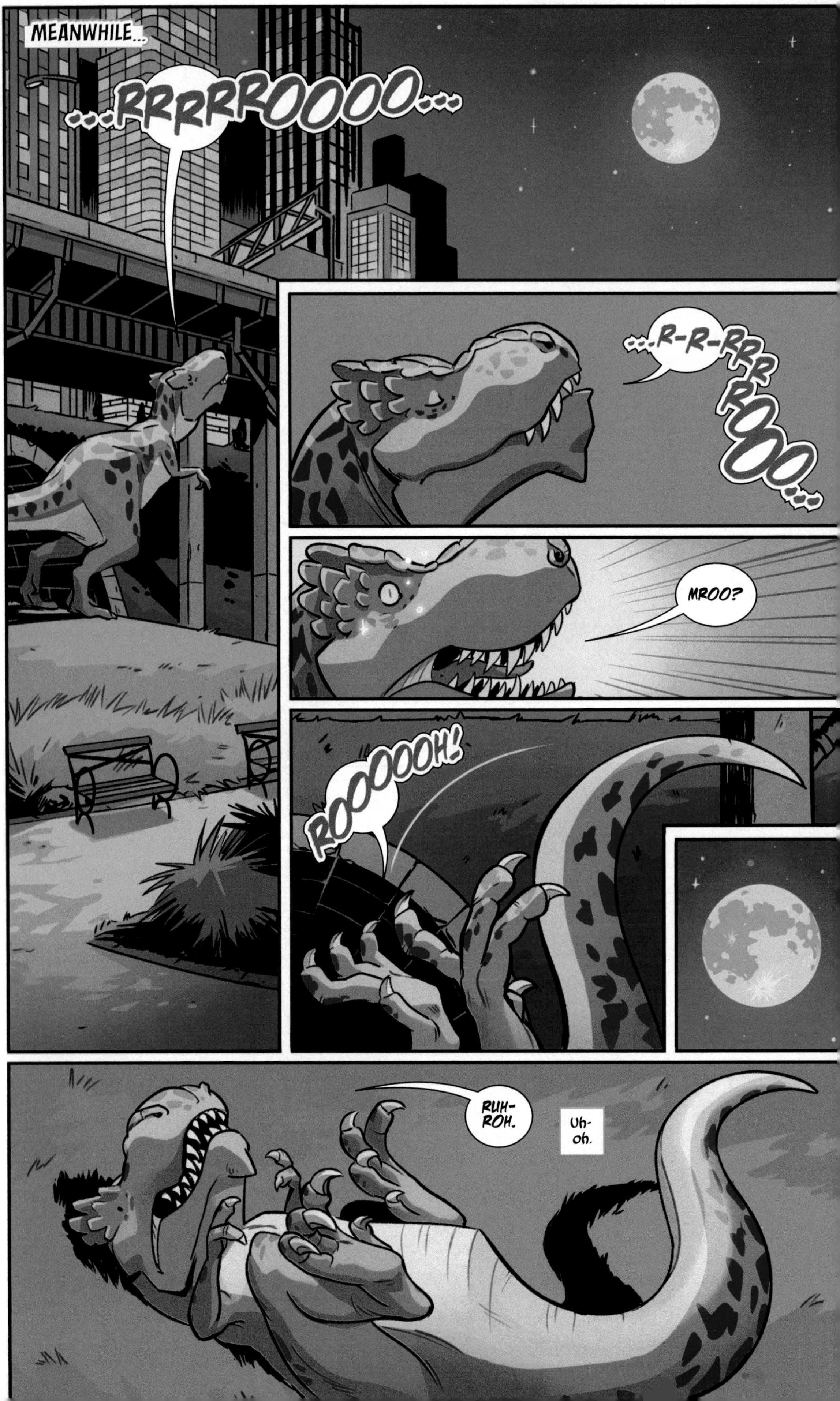

MEANWHILE...
...RRRRROOOO...
...R-R-RRRRROOO...
MROO?
ROOOOOH!
RUH-ROH.
Uh-oh.

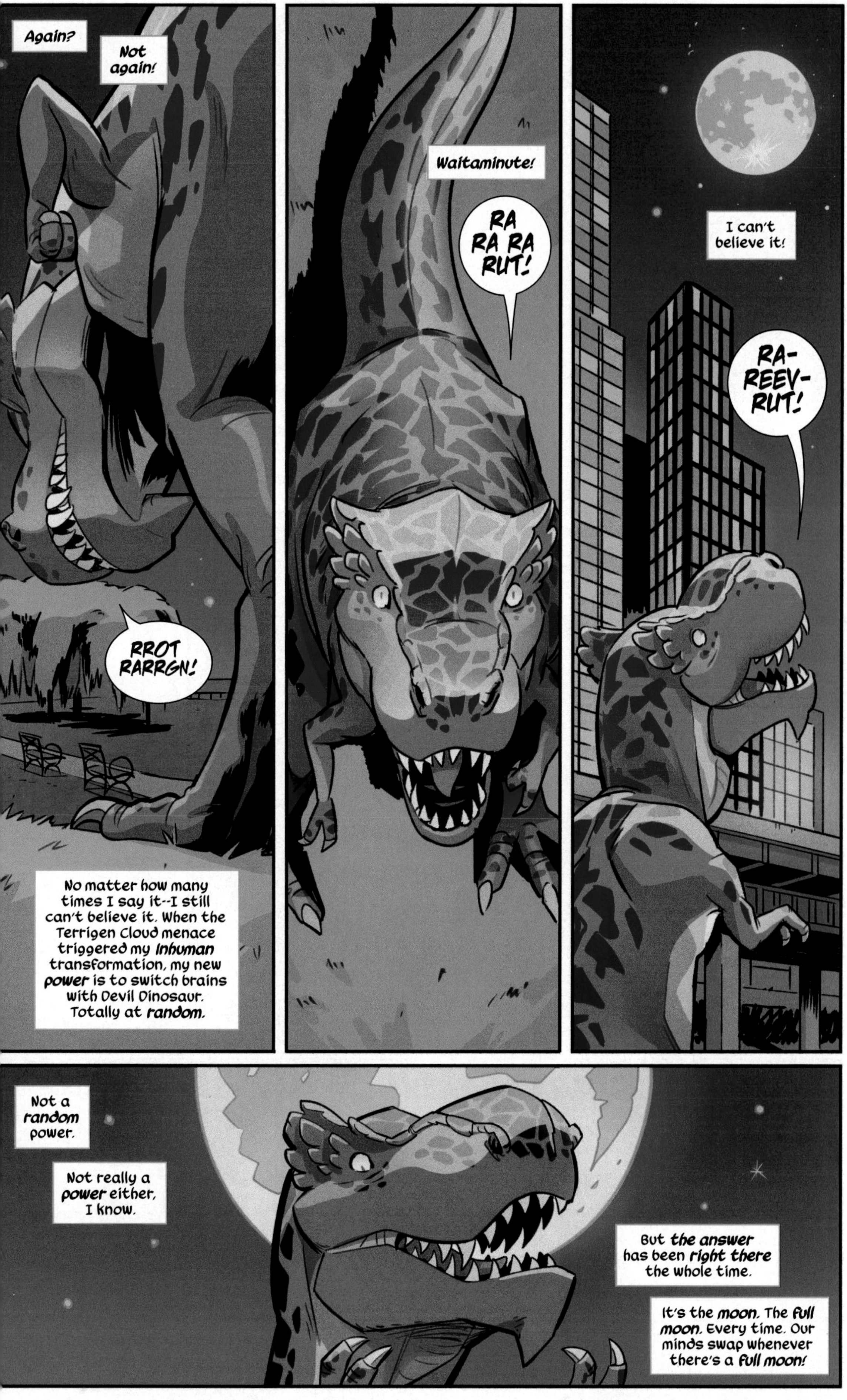
Again?
Not again!
RROT RARRGN!
No matter how many times I say it--I still can't believe it. When the Terrigen Cloud menace triggered my Inhuman transformation, my new power is to switch brains with Devil Dinosaur. Totally at random.
Waitaminute!
RA RA RA RUT!
I can't believe it!
RA-REEV-RUT!
Not a random power.
Not really a power either, I know.
But the answer has been right there the whole time.
It's the moon. The full moon. Every time. Our minds swap whenever there's a full moon!

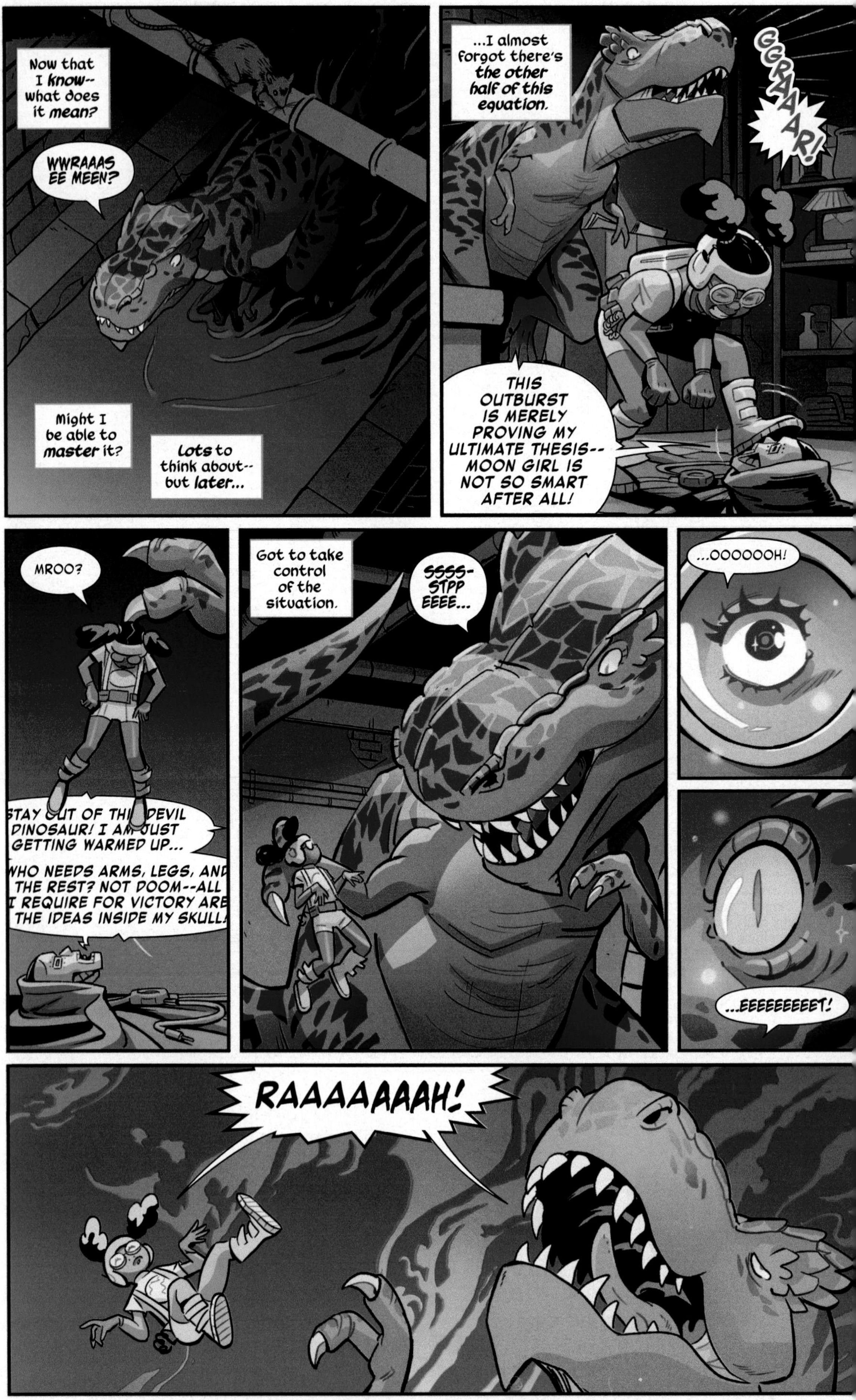
Now that I know-- what does it mean?
WWRAAAS EE MEEN?
Might I be able to master it?
Lots to think about-- but later...
...I almost forgot there's the other half of this equation.
GGRAAAR!
THIS OUTBURST IS MERELY PROVING MY ULTIMATE THESIS-- MOON GIRL IS NOT SO SMART AFTER ALL!
MROO?
STAY OUT OF THIS, DEVIL DINOSAUR! I AM JUST GETTING WARMED UP...
WHO NEEDS ARMS, LEGS, AND THE REST? NOT DOOM--ALL I REQUIRE FOR VICTORY ARE THE IDEAS INSIDE MY SKULL!
Got to take control of the situation.
SSSS-STPP EEEE...
...OOOOOOH!
...EEEEEEEEET!
RAAAAAAAH!

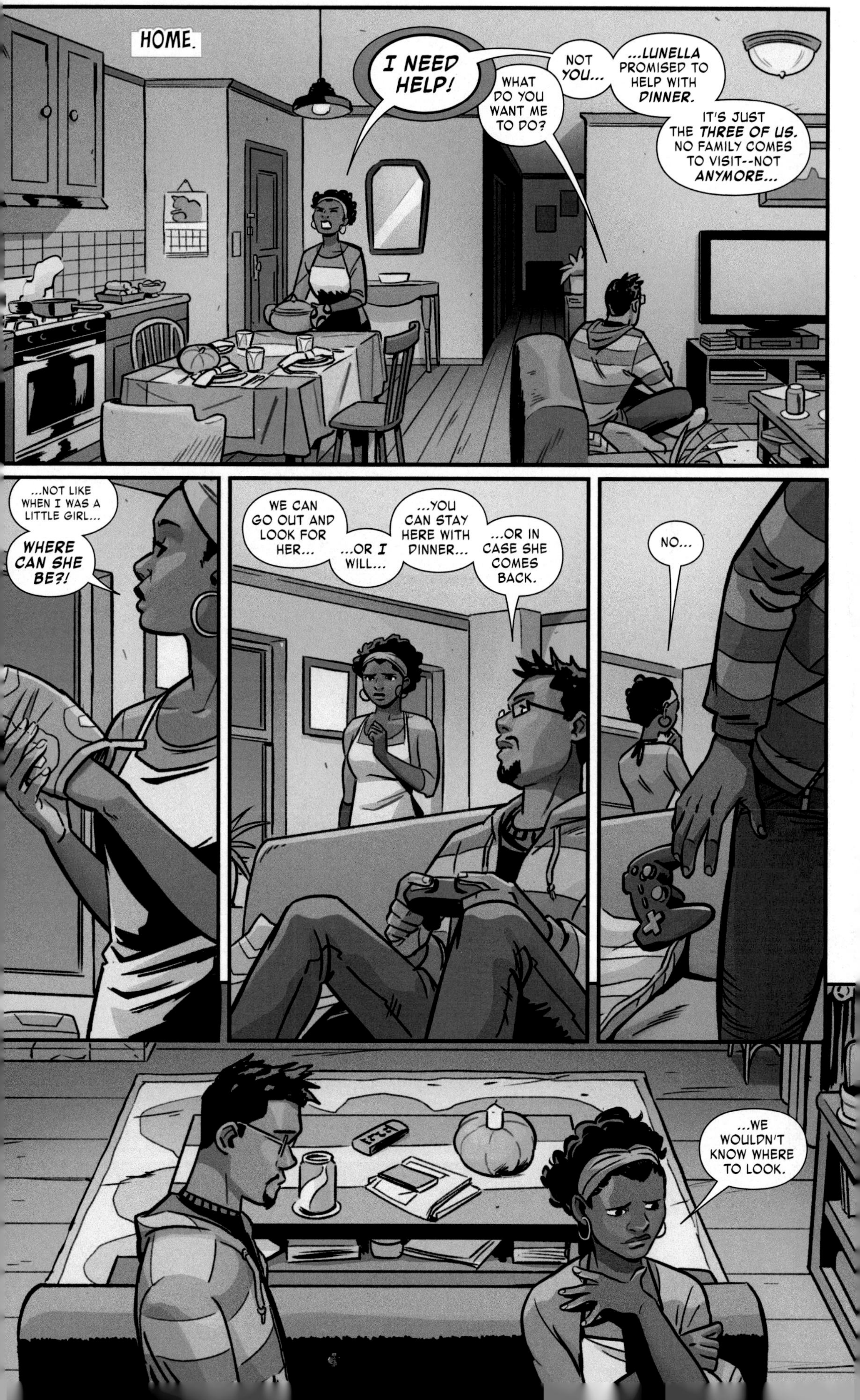
HOME.
I NEED HELP!
WHAT DO YOU WANT ME TO DO?
NOT YOU...
...LUNELLA PROMISED TO HELP WITH DINNER.
IT'S JUST THE THREE OF US. NO FAMILY COMES TO VISIT--NOT ANYMORE...
...NOT LIKE WHEN I WAS A LITTLE GIRL...
WHERE CAN SHE BE?!
WE CAN GO OUT AND LOOK FOR HER...
...OR I WILL...
...YOU CAN STAY HERE WITH DINNER...
...OR IN CASE SHE COMES BACK.
NO...
...WE WOULDN'T KNOW WHERE TO LOOK.

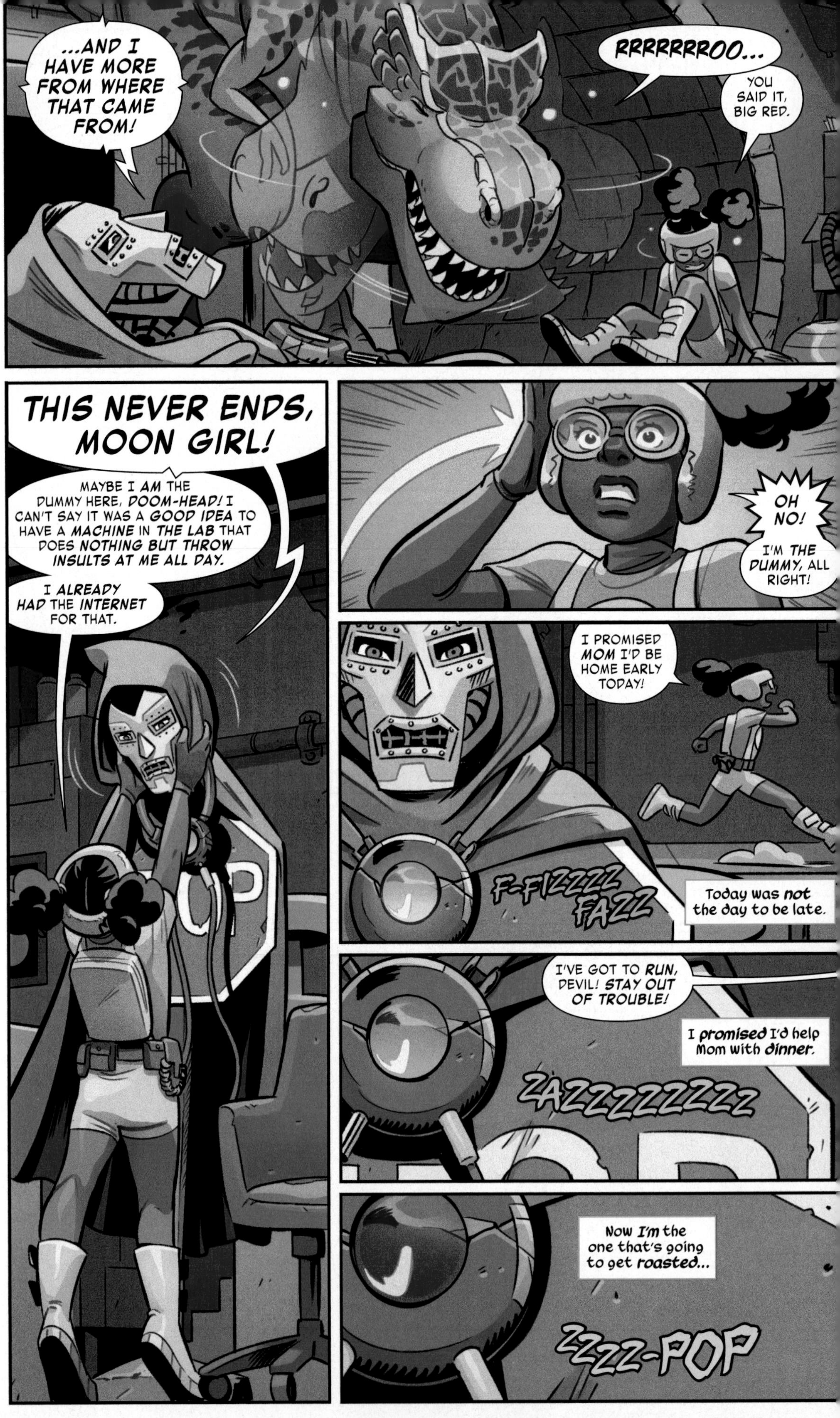
...AND I HAVE MORE FROM WHERE THAT CAME FROM!
RRRRRRROO...
YOU SAID IT, BIG RED.
THIS NEVER ENDS, MOON GIRL!
MAYBE I AM THE DUMMY HERE, DOOM-HEAD! I CAN'T SAY IT WAS A GOOD IDEA TO HAVE A MACHINE IN THE LAB THAT DOES NOTHING BUT THROW INSULTS AT ME ALL DAY.
I ALREADY HAD THE INTERNET FOR THAT.
OH NO!
I'M THE DUMMY, ALL RIGHT!
I PROMISED MOM I'D BE HOME EARLY TODAY!
F-FIZZZZ FAZZ
Today was not the day to be late.
I'VE GOT TO RUN, DEVIL! STAY OUT OF TROUBLE!
I promised I'd help Mom with dinner.
ZAZZZZZZZZZ
Now I'm the one that's going to get roasted...
ZZZZ-POP

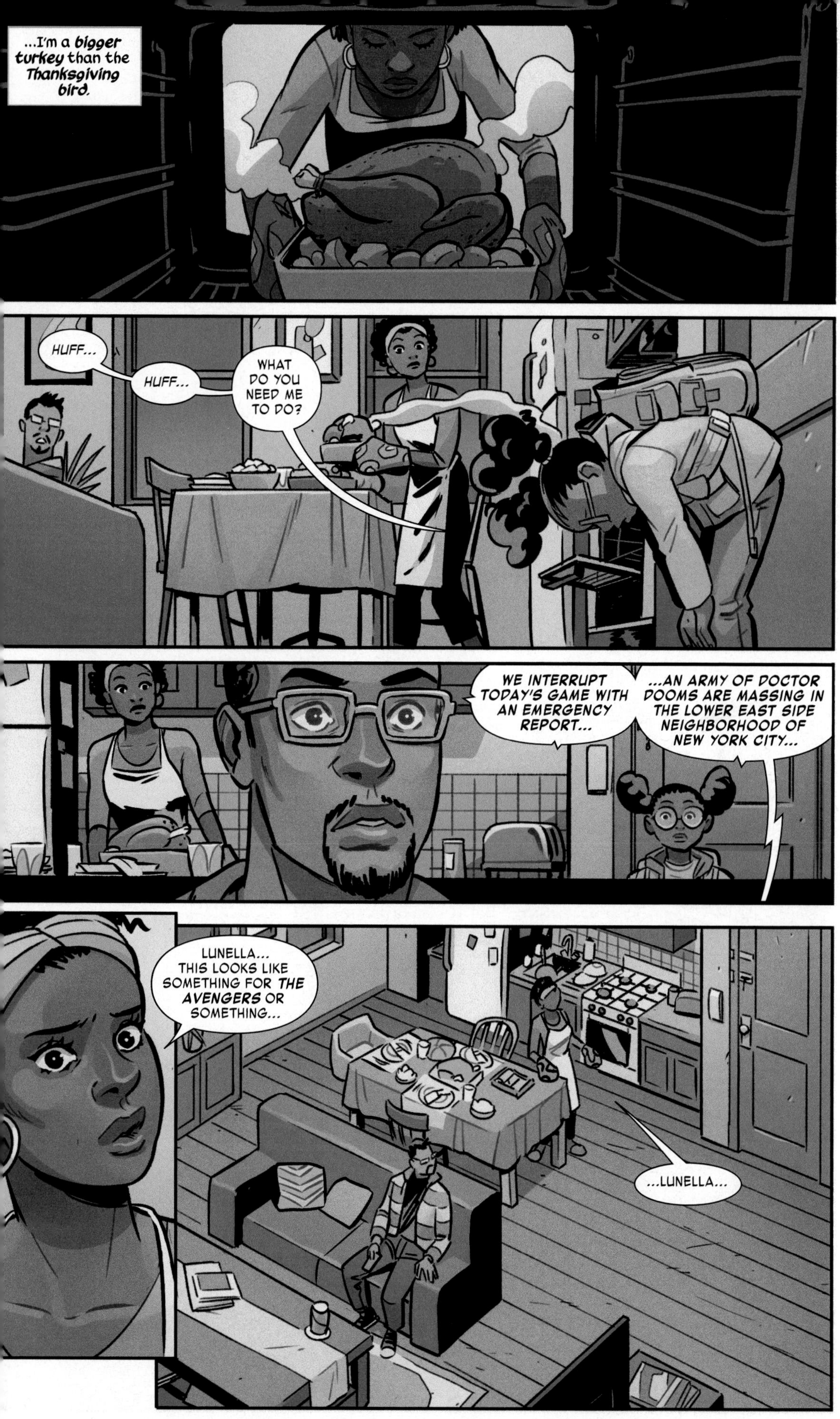
...I'm a bigger turkey than the Thanksgiving bird.
HUFF...
HUFF...
WHAT DO YOU NEED ME TO DO?
WE INTERRUPT TODAY'S GAME WITH AN EMERGENCY REPORT...
...AN ARMY OF DOCTOR DOOMS ARE MASSING IN THE LOWER EAST SIDE NEIGHBORHOOD OF NEW YORK CITY...
LUNELLA... THIS LOOKS LIKE SOMETHING FOR THE AVENGERS OR SOMETHING...
...LUNELLA...

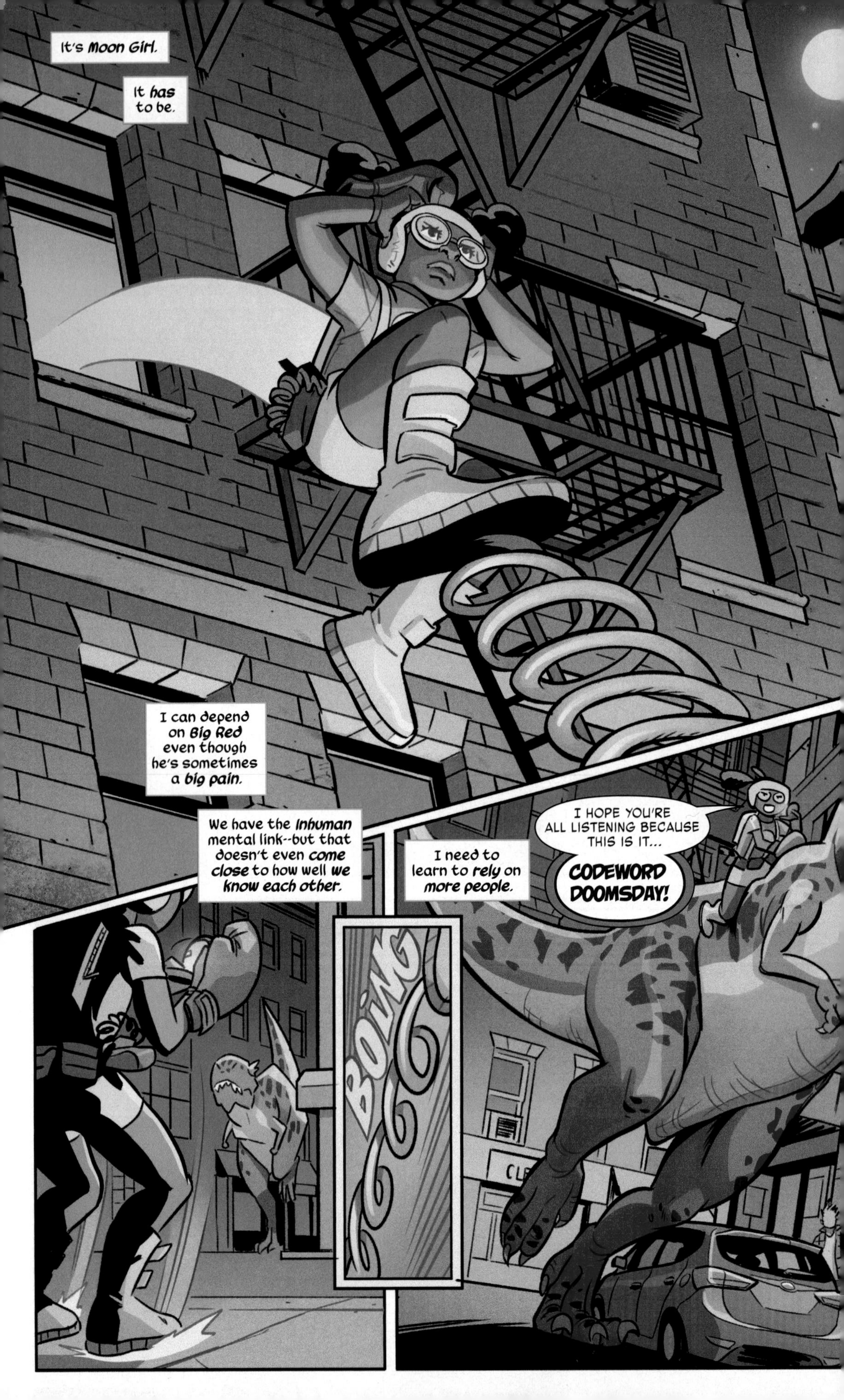

It's Moon Girl.
It has to be.
I can depend on Big Red even though he's sometimes a big pain.
We have the Inhuman mental link--but that doesn't even come close to how well we know each other.
I need to learn to rely on more people.
I HOPE YOU'RE ALL LISTENING BECAUSE THIS IS IT...
CODEWORD DOOMSDAY!
BOING

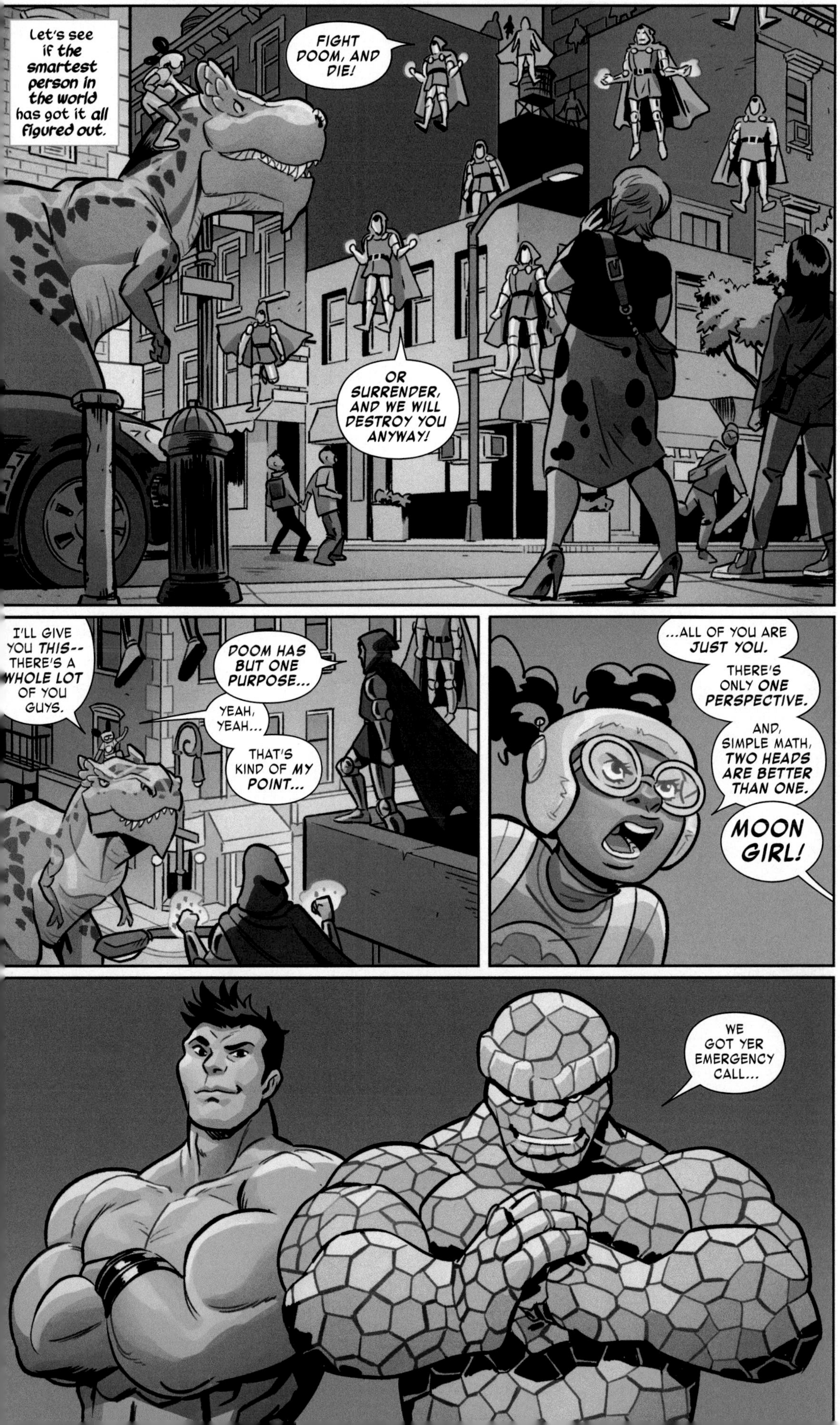
Let's see if the smartest person in the world has got it all figured out.
FIGHT DOOM, AND DIE!
OR SURRENDER, AND WE WILL DESTROY YOU ANYWAY!
I'LL GIVE YOU THIS-- THERE'S A WHOLE LOT OF YOU GUYS.
DOOM HAS BUT ONE PURPOSE...
YEAH, YEAH...
THAT'S KIND OF MY POINT...
...ALL OF YOU ARE JUST YOU.
THERE'S ONLY ONE PERSPECTIVE.
AND, SIMPLE MATH, TWO HEADS ARE BETTER THAN ONE.
MOON GIRL!
WE GOT YER EMERGENCY CALL...

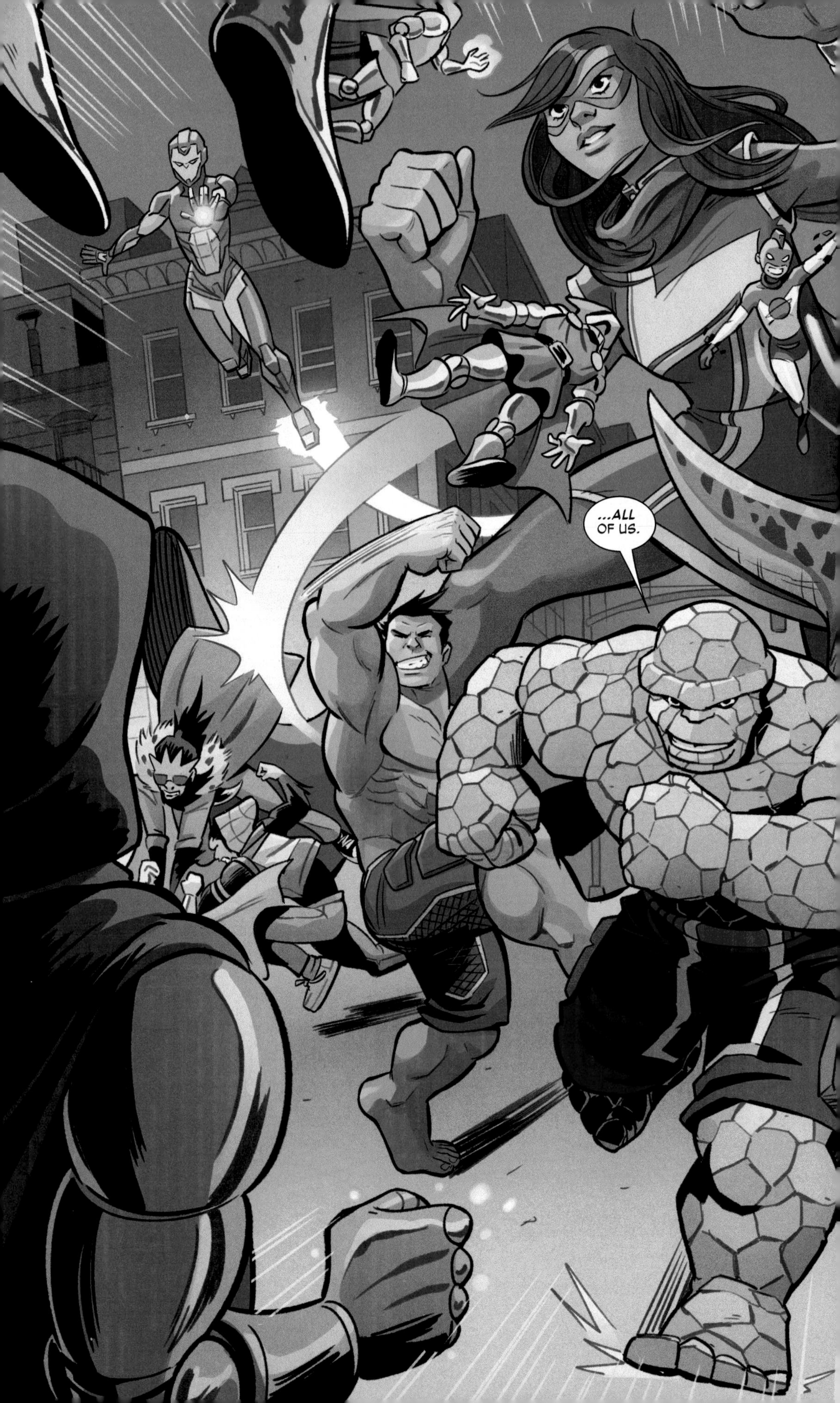
...ALL OF US.

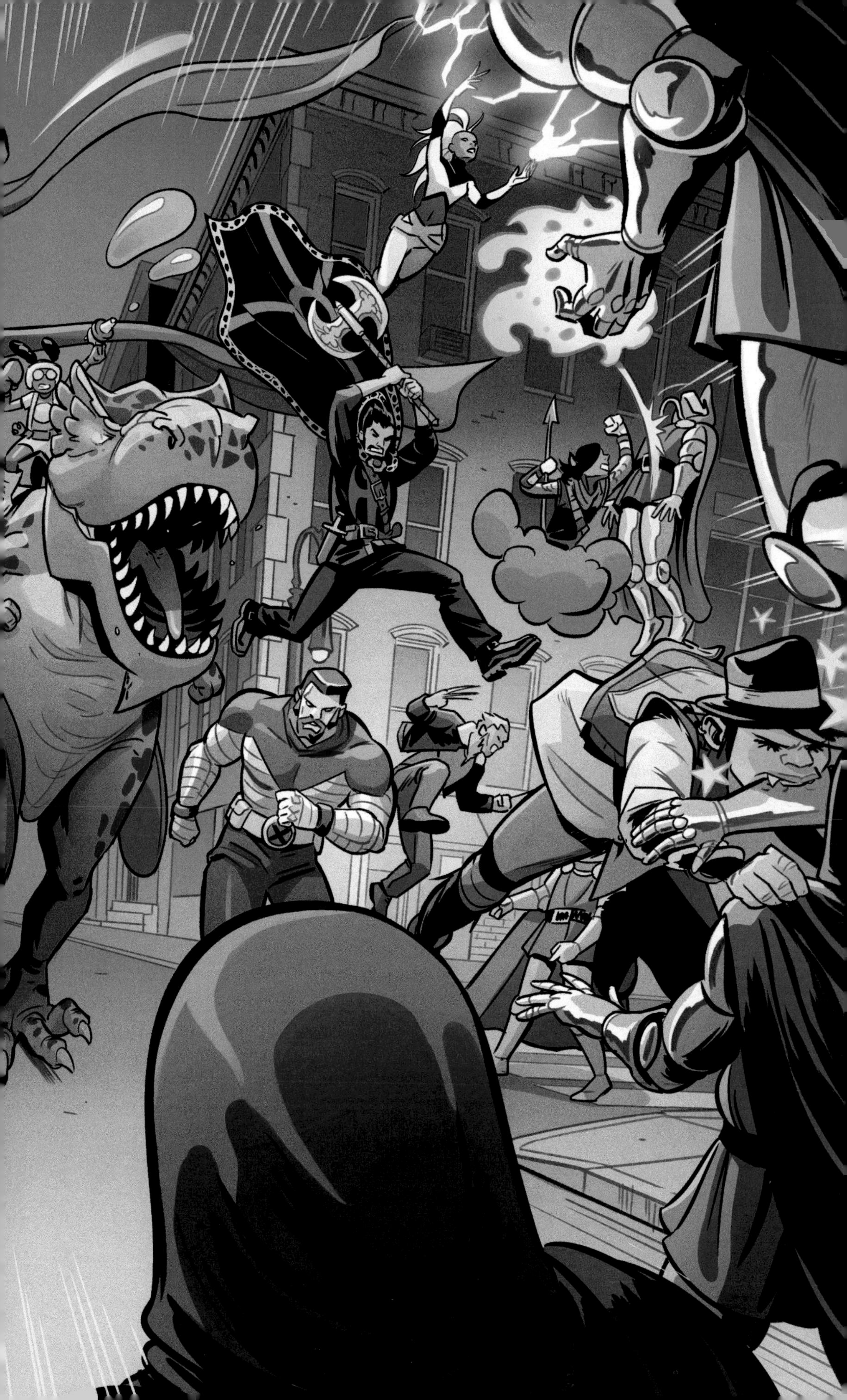

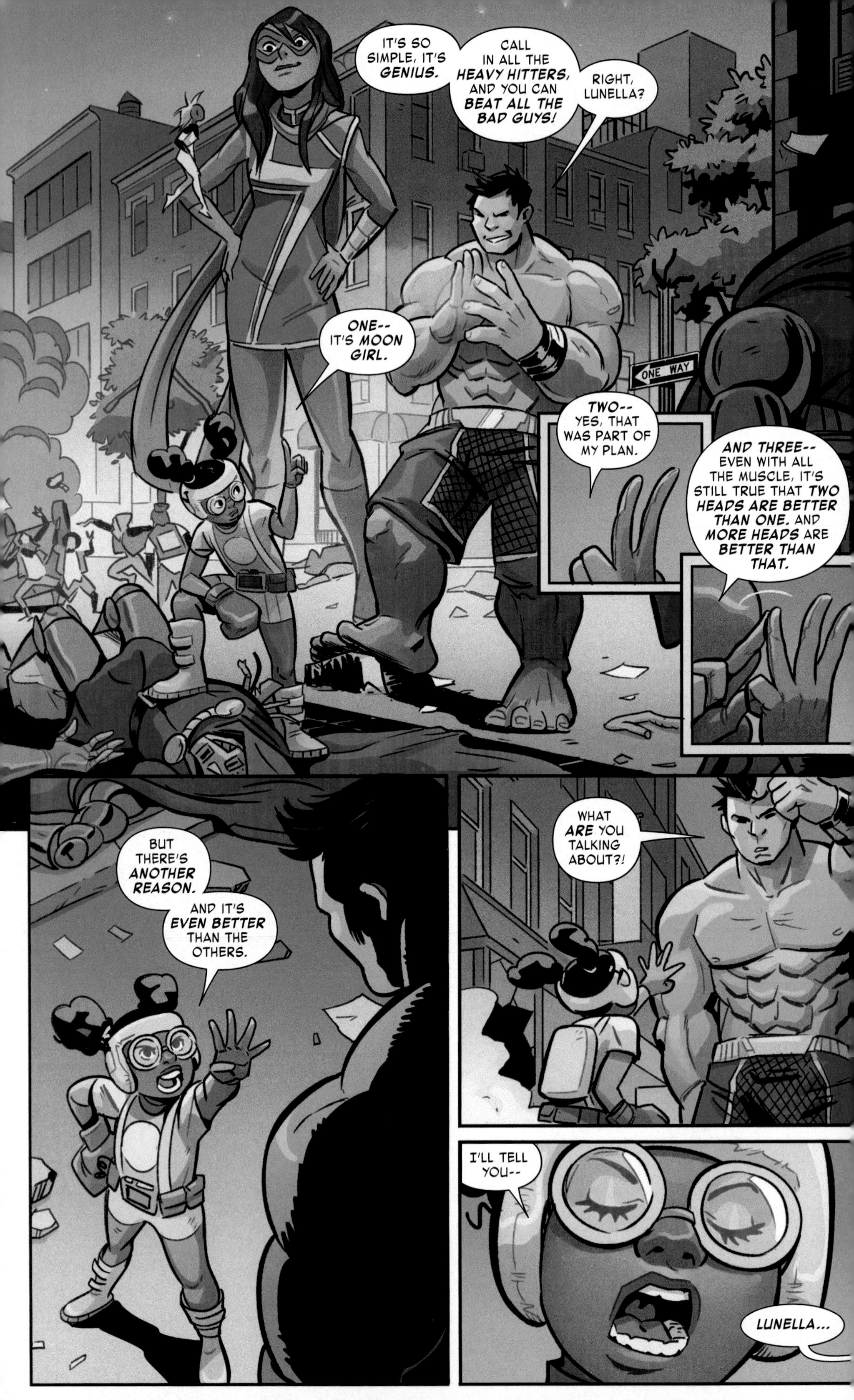
IT'S SO SIMPLE, IT'S GENIUS.
CALL IN ALL THE HEAVY HITTERS, AND YOU CAN BEAT ALL THE BAD GUYS!
RIGHT, LUNELLA?
ONE-- IT'S MOON GIRL.
ONE WAY
TWO-- YES, THAT WAS PART OF MY PLAN.
AND THREE-- EVEN WITH ALL THE MUSCLE, IT'S STILL TRUE THAT TWO HEADS ARE BETTER THAN ONE. AND MORE HEADS ARE BETTER THAN THAT.
BUT THERE'S ANOTHER REASON.
AND IT'S EVEN BETTER THAN THE OTHERS.
WHAT ARE YOU TALKING ABOUT?!
I'LL TELL YOU--
LUNELLA...

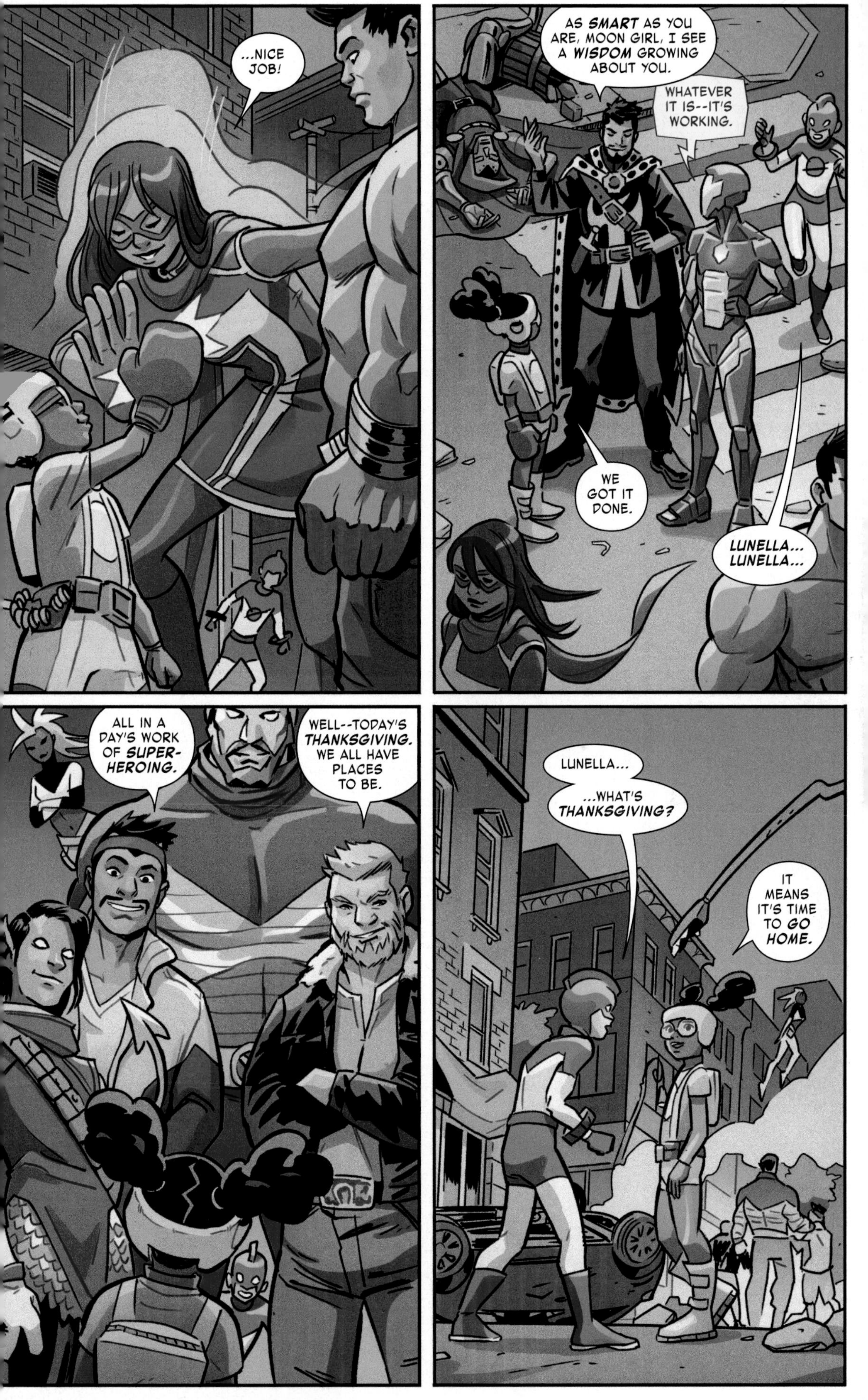

...NICE JOB!
AS SMART AS YOU ARE, MOON GIRL, I SEE A WISDOM GROWING ABOUT YOU.
WHATEVER IT IS--IT'S WORKING.
WE GOT IT DONE.
LUNELLA... LUNELLA...
ALL IN A DAY'S WORK OF SUPER-HEROING.
WELL--TODAY'S THANKSGIVING. WE ALL HAVE PLACES TO BE.
LUNELLA...
...WHAT'S THANKSGIVING?
IT MEANS IT'S TIME TO GO HOME.

YA KNOW I LOVE *YANCY STREET*.

'CUZ IT'S REAL GOOD TO HAVE A PLACE WHERE YA BELONG.

AND YA BELONG, MOON GIRL.

WITH *ALLA* US.

Remember what I said about *two heads are better than one?*

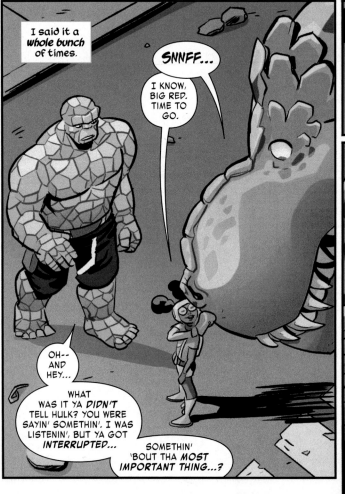

I said it a *whole bunch* of times.

SNNFF...

I KNOW, BIG RED. TIME TO GO.

OH-- AND HEY...

WHAT WAS IT YA *DIDN'T* TELL HULK? YOU WERE SAYIN' SOMETHIN'. I WAS LISTENIN', BUT YA GOT *INTERRUPTED*...

SOMETHIN' 'BOUT THA *MOST IMPORTANT THING*...?

IT'S SOMETHING YOU HAVE TO FIGURE OUT FOR YOURSELF.

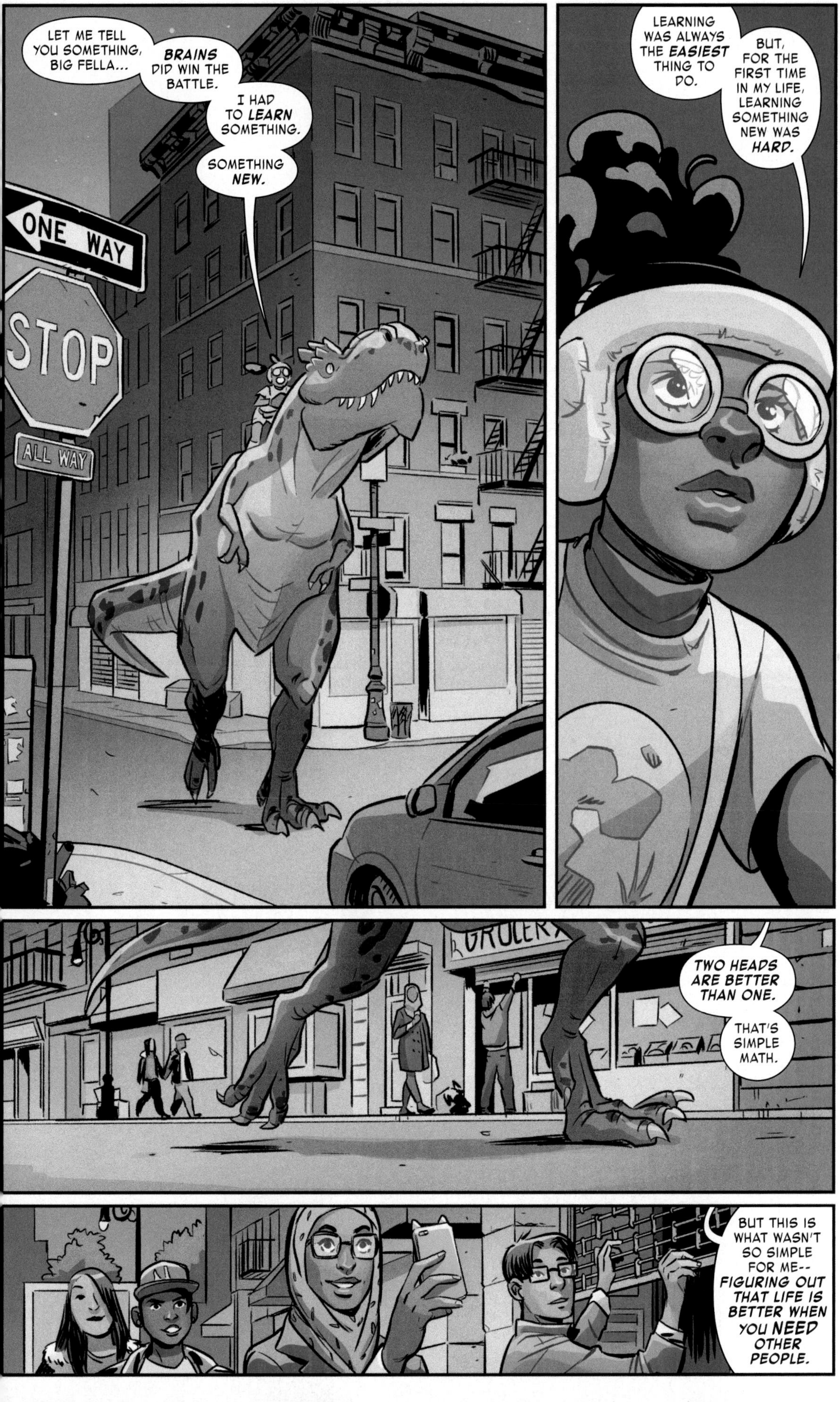
LET ME TELL YOU SOMETHING, BIG FELLA...
BRAINS DID WIN THE BATTLE.
I HAD TO LEARN SOMETHING.
SOMETHING NEW.
ONE WAY
STOP
ALL WAY
LEARNING WAS ALWAYS THE EASIEST THING TO DO.
BUT, FOR THE FIRST TIME IN MY LIFE, LEARNING SOMETHING NEW WAS HARD.
TWO HEADS ARE BETTER THAN ONE.
THAT'S SIMPLE MATH.
BUT THIS IS WHAT WASN'T SO SIMPLE FOR ME-- FIGURING OUT THAT LIFE IS BETTER WHEN YOU NEED OTHER PEOPLE.

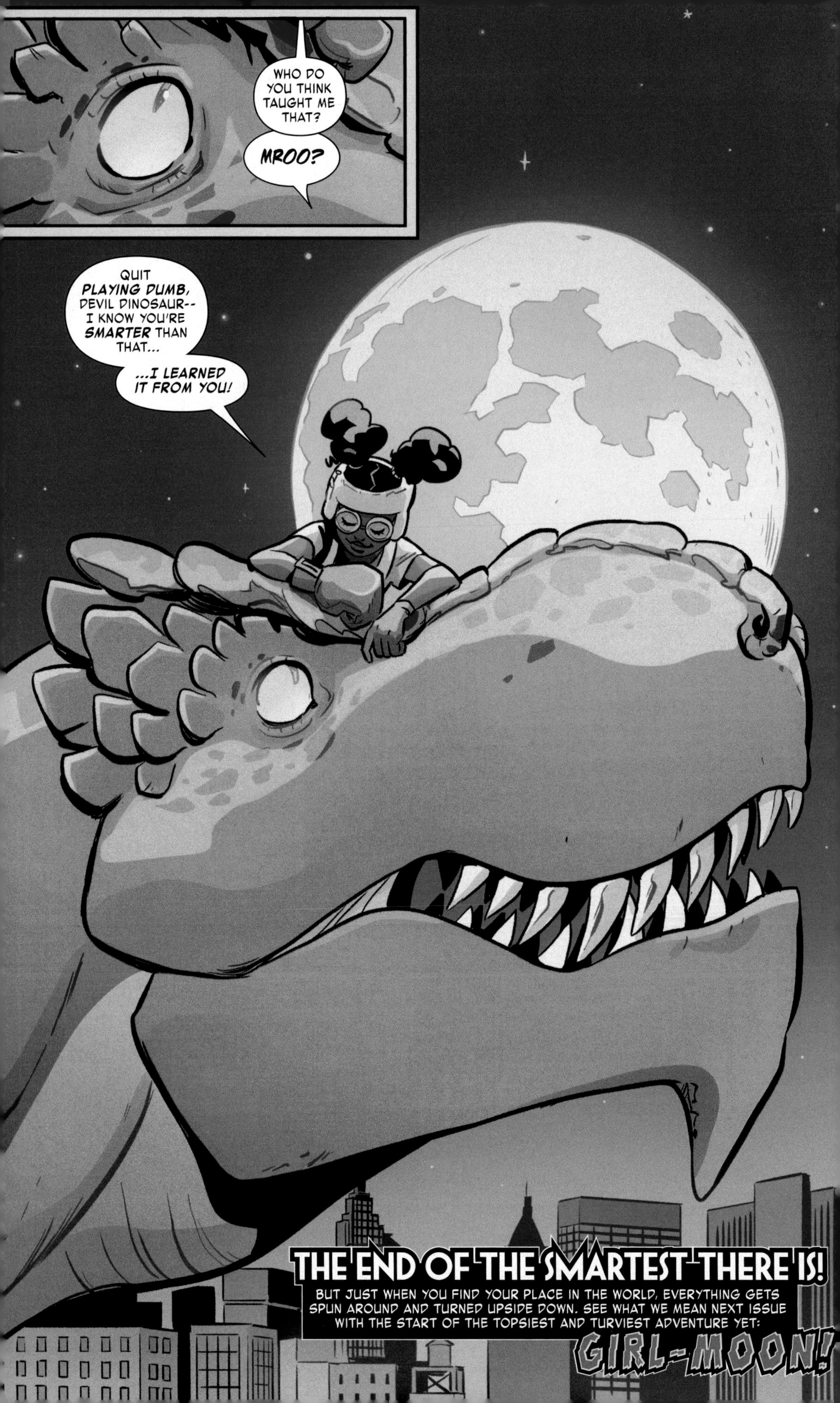
WHO DO YOU THINK TAUGHT ME THAT?
MROO?
QUIT PLAYING DUMB, DEVIL DINOSAUR-- I KNOW YOU'RE SMARTER THAN THAT...
...I LEARNED IT FROM YOU!
THE END OF THE SMARTEST THERE IS!
BUT JUST WHEN YOU FIND YOUR PLACE IN THE WORLD, EVERYTHING GETS SPUN AROUND AND TURNED UPSIDE DOWN. SEE WHAT WE MEAN NEXT ISSUE WITH THE START OF THE TOPSIEST AND TURVIEST ADVENTURE YET:
GIRL-MOON!

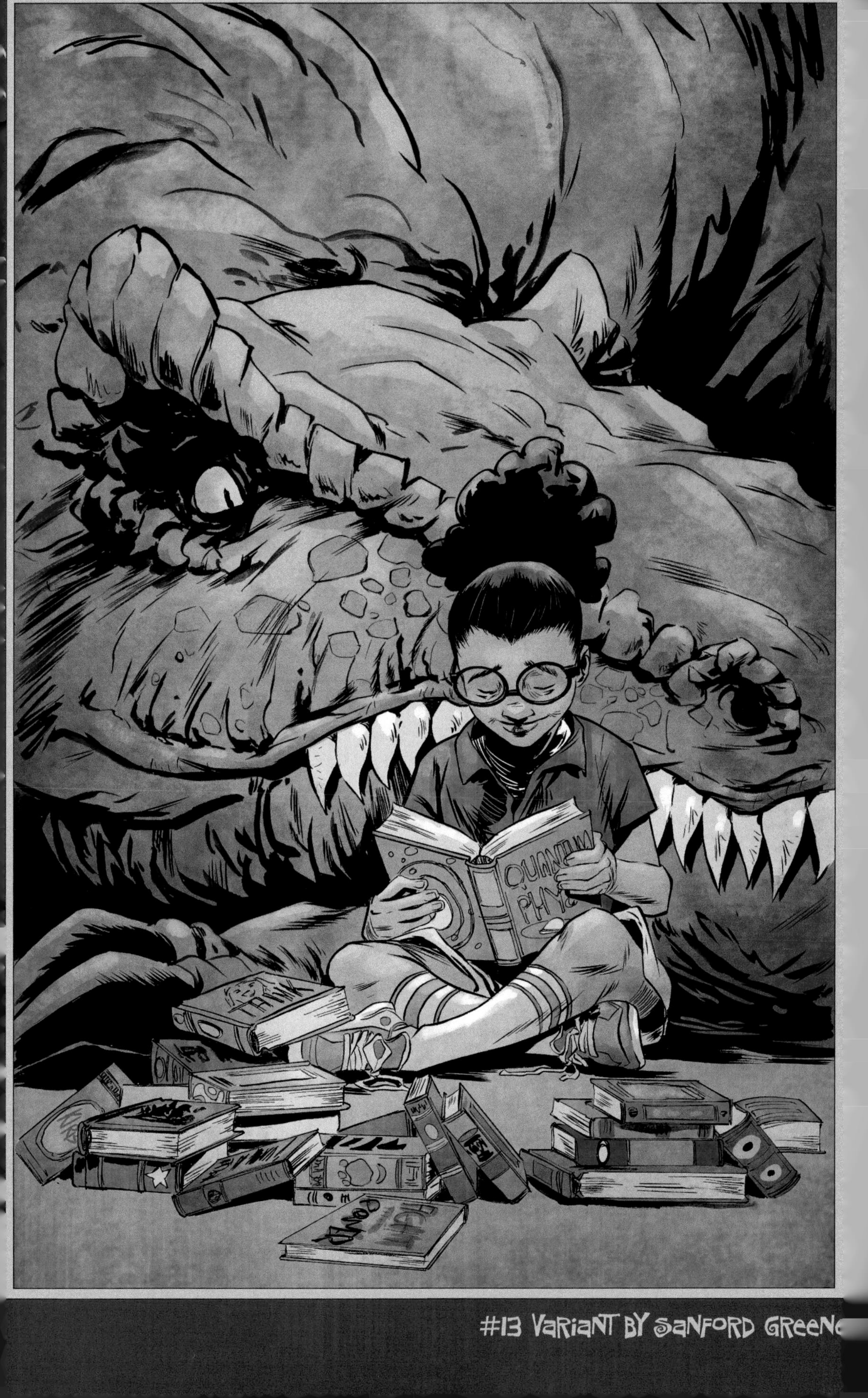

#13 VARIANT BY SANFORD GREEN

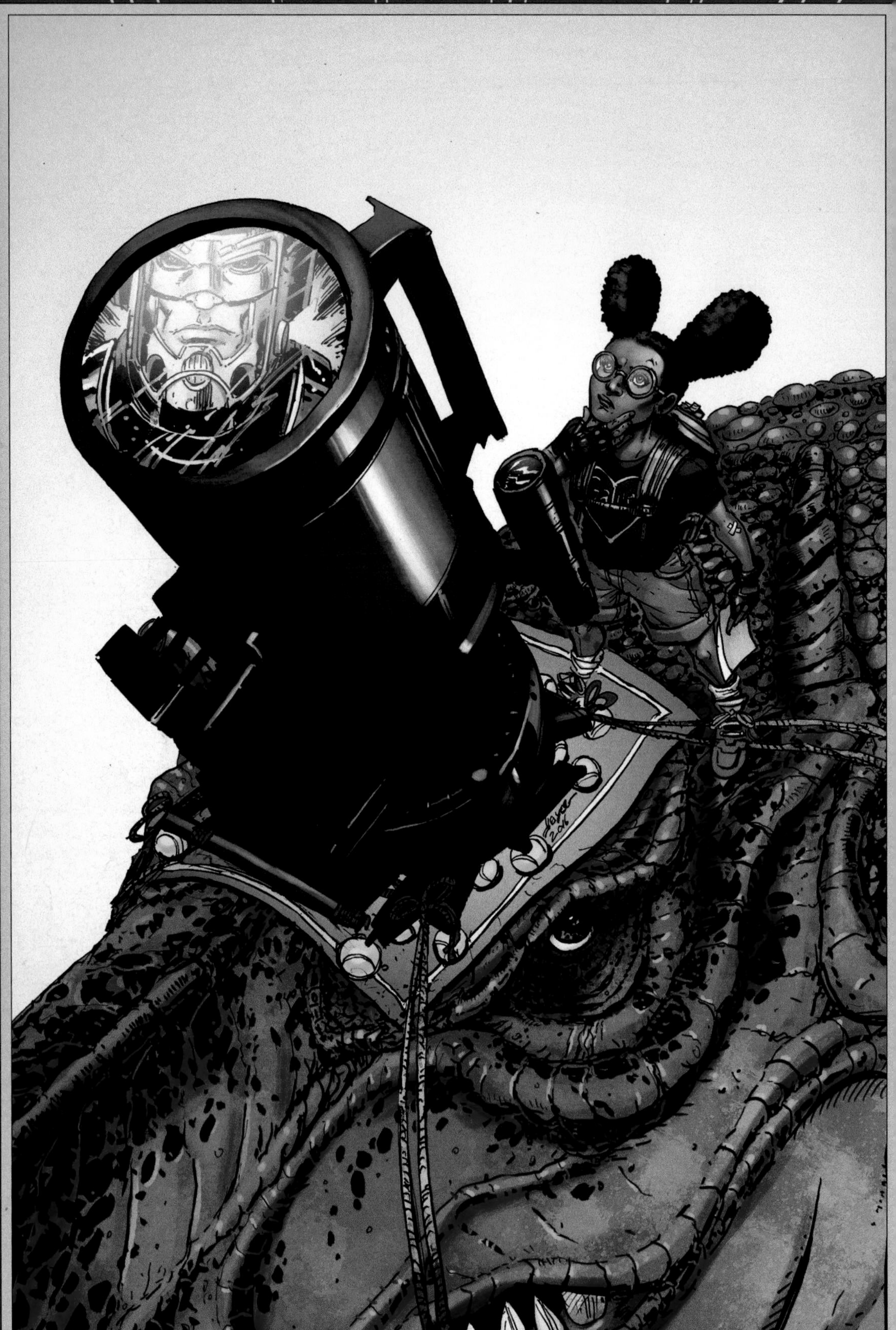

#13 S.T.E.A.M. VARIANT BY JOYCE CHIN & CHRIS SOTOMAYOR

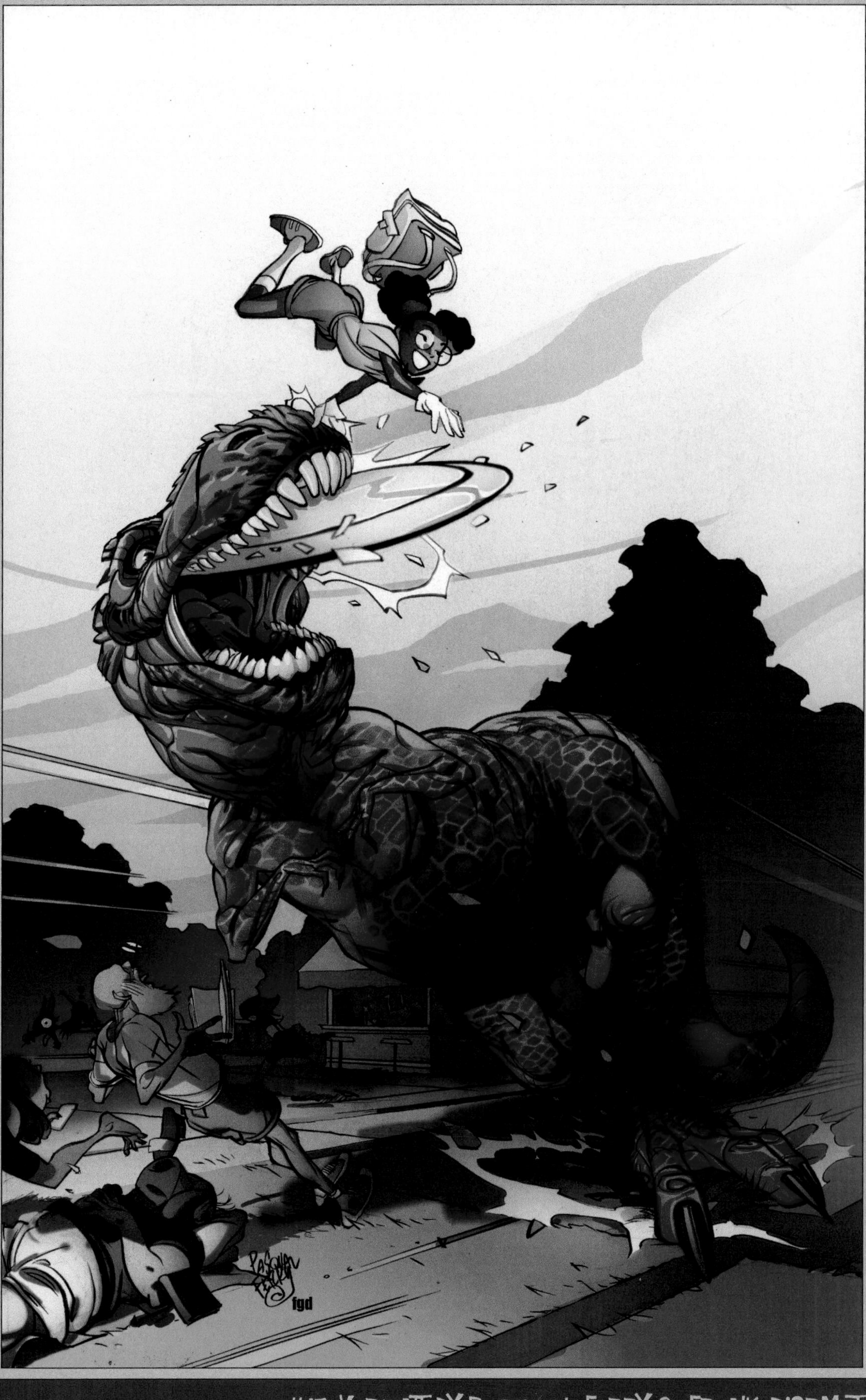
fgd

#13 VARIANT BY PASQUAL FERRY & FRANK D'ARMATA

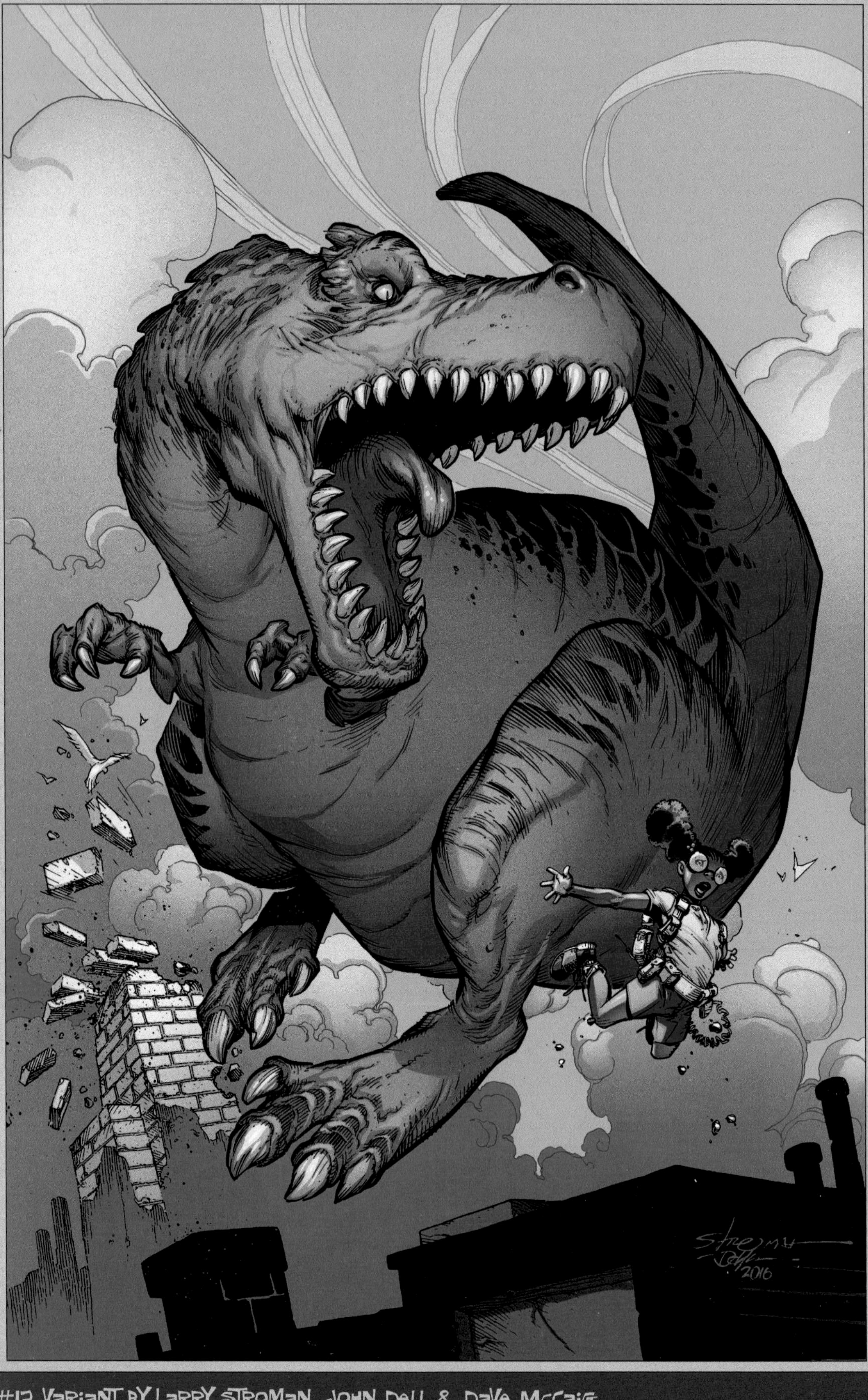
Stroman
Dell
2016

#13 VARIANT BY LARRY STROMAN, JOHN DELL & DAVE McCAIG